THE PATH OF LOVE

Extemporaneous talks given by Osho in
OSHO International Meditation Resort, Pune, India

the path of **love**

Understanding that Nothing Is Perfect in Life

ON THE SONGS OF KABIR

OSHO

This book is a series of original talks by Osho, given to a live audience. All of
Osho's talks have been published in full as books, and are also available as
original audio recordings. Audio recordings and the complete text archive can
be found via the online OSHO Library at www.osho.com/library

Osho comments in this work on selected excerpts from *One Hundred Poems of
Kabir*, translated by Rabindranath Tagore, assisted by Evelyn Underhill. First
edition: 1915 The Macmillan Company of India Ltd.

OSHO MEDIA INTERNATIONAL
New York Zurich Mumbai
an imprint of
OSHO INTERNATIONAL
www.osho.com/oshointernational

Distributed by Publishers Group Worldwide
www.pgw.com

Library of Congress Catalog-In-Publication Data is available

Printed in India by Manipal Technologies Limited, Karnataka

ISBN: 978-0-9836400-7-3
This title is also available in eBook format ISBN: 978-0-88050-228-3

contents

preface

The really spiritual person is one who is absolutely ordinary. Kabir is very normal; you would not have been able to find him in a crowd. His specialty is not outward. You cannot find him by just looking at his face. It is difficult... Buddha was special, a very beautiful man, a charismatic personality. Jesus is very special, throbbing with revolution, rebellion. But Kabir? Kabir is absolutely ordinary, a normal person.

Remember, when I say normal I don't mean average. The average is not the normal. The average is only normally abnormal; he is as mad as all others are. In fact, normal people don't exist.

I have heard...

A famous psychiatrist, conducting a university course in psychopathology, was asked by a student, "Doctor, you have told us about the abnormal person and his behavior, but what about the normal person?"

The doctor was a little puzzled, and then he answered, "In my whole life I have never come across a normal person. But if we ever find him, we will cure him!"

Kabir is really that normal person that you never come across in life, with no desire to be special. When he became enlightened, he remained in his ordinary life. He was a weaver; he continued to weave. His disciples started growing in numbers: hundreds, and then thousands, and then many more thousands were coming to him. They

would always ask him to stop weaving: "There is no need. We will take care of you."
But he would laugh and say, "It is better to continue as existence has willed me. I have no desire to be anything else. Let me be whatsoever I am, whatsoever existence wants me to be. I am a weaver because it wants me to be a weaver. I was born a weaver and I will die as a weaver."
He continued in his ordinary way. He would go to the marketplace to sell his goods. He would carry water from the well. He lived very, very ordinarily. That is one of the most significant things to be understood. He never claimed that he was a man of knowledge; no man of knowledge ever claims that. To know is to know that to know is not to know, and that not to know is to know. A real man of understanding knows that he does not know at all. His ignorance is profound, and out of this ignorance arises innocence. When you know, you become cunning. When you know, you become clever. When you know, you lose that innocence of childhood.
Kabir says that he is ignorant; he does not know anything. This has to be understood because it will form the background in your mind for his poetry. From where does this poetry come? It comes out of his innocence, flowers out of his innocence.

Osho
Ecstasy: The Forgotten Language

CHAPTER 1

love is the master key

He is dear to me indeed who can call back the wanderer to his home. In the home is the true union; in the home is enjoyment of life. Why should I forsake my home and wander in the forest? If Brahma helps me to realize truth, verily I will find both bondage and deliverance in the home.
He is dear to me indeed who has power to dive deep into God, whose mind loses itself with ease in his contemplation.
He is dear to me who knows God, and can dwell on his supreme truth in meditation; and who can play the melody of the infinite by uniting love and renunciation in life.
Kabir says: The home is the abiding place; in the home is reality, the home helps to attain him who is real. So stay where you are, and all things shall come to you in time.

O Sadhu! The simple union is the best. Since the day when I met with my Lord, there has been no end to the sport of our love. I shut not my eyes, I close not my ears, I do not mortify my body; I see with eyes open and smile, and behold his beauty everywhere. I utter his name, and whatever I see, it reminds me of him; whatever I do, it becomes his worship.

The rising and setting are one to me; all contradictions are solved.
Wherever I go I move round him. All I achieve is his service: When I
lie down, I lie prostrate at his feet. He is the only adorable one to
me; I have none other.
My tongue has left off impure words, it sings his glory day and
night: whether I rise or sit down, I can never forget him, for the
rhythm of his music beats in my ears.
Kabir says: My heart is frenzied, and I disclose in my soul what is
hidden. I am immersed in that one great bliss which transcends all
pleasure and pain.

Religion has very rarely existed in a healthy way – only when a Buddha walks on the earth, or a Christ or a Krishna or a Kabir. Otherwise, religion has existed as pathology, as illness, as neurosis. One who has realized religion through his own being has a totally different understanding of it; the understanding of one who has been imitating others is not understanding at all. Truth cannot be imitated. You cannot become true by becoming a carbon copy. Truth is original, and to attain to it you have to be original too.

Truth is not attained by following somebody; truth is attained by understanding your life. Truth is not in any creed, in any argument; truth is hidden as love in the deepest core of your being. Truth is not logic; it is not a syllogism, it is an explosion of love. And whenever truth explodes in you, you attain to a totally different vision of life, of godliness, of religion. Your eyes have a different quality, a different transparency, clarity. When your mind is clouded with thoughts borrowed from others, whatsoever you call religion is not religion, it is just dreaming.

And the basic difference makes an imitative person pathological. A Christian is pathological, a Hindu too. Krishna is healthy, superbly healthy, so is Christ. When Christ says something, he has known it. He is not repeating somebody else, he is not a parrot. It is his own realization, and that makes the whole difference.

When you become a Christian you repeat Christ. By and by, you become more like a shadow. You lose your being. You lose yourself. You are no longer true, real, authentic. A Christian is already dead, and religion is concerned with rebirth. Yes, it is a crucifixion too: the old has to die for the new to be born.

But following a dead creed, a dogma, a church, you never allow the old to die – and you never allow the new to be born. You never take the risk. You never move in danger. When Christ goes to face his own being, he is moving dangerously, he is taking a great risk; he is going into the unknown.

Just the other night I initiated a young man into sannyas and I told him to seek the unknown. He asked, "But why? And how? How can I seek the unknown? That which I don't know, how can I seek it?"

We only seek the known. But if you only seek the known you will never know God – because you don't know God. If you seek the known you will move in a circle, in a rut. You will become mechanical. Seek the unknown, because through seeking the unknown you move out of the rut, out of the repetitive, mechanical way of life. He is right; he asks, "How to seek the unknown?"

Drop the known, don't cling to the known, and wait for the unknown. If you don't cling to the known, if you put the known aside, the unknown comes on its own accord. The unknown is just waiting at the door, but you are so full of the known that there is no space left for the unknown to come in. The unknown would like to become a guest, but the host is interested only in the known. The host is much too occupied with the known; the host is not free even to look at the unknown.

Yes, I can understand his question: How to seek the unknown? Whatsoever *you* seek will be the known. Mind cannot seek the unknown, so mind is the barrier for the unknown. Mind can only seek the known again and again and again. Mind is repetitive.

That's what meditation is all about: the way, the art of dropping the mind – at least for a few moments – so you can look at the unknown, not knowing where you are going. But those are the most beautiful moments when you don't know where you are going, when you don't know who you are, when you don't know the direction, the goal; when knowledge exists not.

When knowledge exists not, there is love. Knowledge is against love. Knowledgeable people cannot love, and people who can love are never knowledgeable. Love makes you wise, but never knowledgeable. Knowledge makes you cunning and clever, but never loving.

The known is the mind, the unknown is God. And Jesus says, "God is love." Love comes through the unknown, with the unknown, as part of the unknown. To move into the unknown, one needs

courage, tremendous courage. To cling to the known there is no
need to have any courage – any coward can do it, cowards *only*
do that.

When you become a Christian you are a coward; when you
become a Mohammedan you are a coward; when you become a
Hindu you are a coward. When you become religious you are tremendously courageous – you are going for an adventure, you are seeking
the unknown, you are moving into the uncharted, the unmeasured
and the immeasurable. There is every danger you may be lost, there
is every danger you may not be able to come back; there is every
danger that you will lose all control: you may go mad. That's the price
one has to pay for real religion.

People are afraid, so they cling to false substitutes: Christianity,
Hinduism, Islam. These are false substitutes, cheap, very easily
available. You don't have to do anything; you are born into a certain
family and you become a Christian, you are born into another family
and you become a Hindu. You have not done anything, you have not
chosen anything consciously; you have not moved an inch. There
has been no pilgrimage, you have not searched.

Of course religion can then be just a label, and these labels
become pathological. Why do they become pathological? – because
your inner reality remains the same, but the labels are totally different.
Peek deeply into a Hindu and a Mohammedan and a Christian and a
Jaina and a Buddhist, and you will find that only labels differ – deep
inside, the same human being. And these labels create trouble.

The Bible goes on saying to love your enemy – and you cannot
even love your friend. You cannot even love yourself, and Jesus says,
"Love your neighbor as you love yourself." You cannot even love yourself; how can you love your neighbor? Jesus says, "Love your enemy,"
and you have not yet known even how to love your friend, how to love
your beloved. You don't know the ways of love. Then what will you do?
You will pretend, you will become a hypocrite; you will become a false
entity. This is the pathology: you become dual. Deep inside you will be
one thing, and on the surface you will go on pretending something
else. Deep inside tears, and on your face you will go on smiling. This
will tear you apart; this is what schizophrenia is, this is what split personality is. This is the root cause of all neuroses.

Hence, religion becomes pathological. Imitated, religion creates
pathology, a neurotic world. Realized by oneself, religion gives you

tremendous health, well-being, celebration of life, joy, benediction. These two different types of religion have to be understood well. If your religion is just borrowed it will create trouble in your life because it will be against life. Every moment you feel it is against life, it will be life-negative; it will make you a masochist. You will start torturing yourself because you will always find yourself in conflict with your religion. What to do? You will feel guilty. Each moment of your life will become a moment of guilt, whatsoever you do. Even if you are innocently sipping a cup of tea, there are religions which will make you feel guilty.

In Mahatma Gandhi's ashram, tea was prohibited. If somebody was caught sipping tea he was punished; he had to fast for one or two days as a punishment. Now, just an innocent thing like tea can create guilt – what to say about other things? Anything... You find anything, and you will find some religion or other condemning it.

These condemnations don't allow you to live a full life. And when you cannot live a full life, at the optimum, you will never know what God is, because God can be contacted only at the optimum: when your flame is burning bright, when your torch is burning from both ends, when you are a fire of living energy – only then. At the optimum, at the maximum, at the peak, you will have your first glimpse of God. When you are at your peak, it is the first step toward God.

Abraham Maslow is right when he says that peak experiences make a man healthy, and only a healthy man can have peak experiences. Yes, that is right. Whenever you have a peak, whenever you get totally absorbed in any moment, the door opens. You touch the feet of the divine at the peak of your experience when you are at a crescendo.

That's why Tantra says that when making love, when your orgasm is total, when your whole being is involved in it, every fiber of your being is throbbing and pulsating, and every cell of your body is alive, totally alive; when you have become just an ocean and you are completely lost and you don't know where you are, all boundaries have merged; in that moment of orgasm you have your first glimpse of God, your first glimpse of satori, *samadhi*, nirvana. And, in *any* situation, if you can come to the peak, you will attain a glimpse of God.

But your so-called religions don't allow you any peaks. They cripple you, they paralyze you; they cut you short. They only allow you a minimum of life. That's what renunciation means: live at the minimum. Only the basic needs have to be fulfilled. Your so-called religions don't teach you how to overflow, they only teach you how to become more and more narrow. They make you into tunnels, narrow tunnels. Real religion will make you open, open as the sky.

A real religion is bound to be affirmative. Jesus is affirmative, tremendously in love with life; Christians are not life-affirmative. Krishna is life-affirmative, dancing, singing, loving; Hindus are not life-affirmative. Their so-called mahatmas, their so-called saints, are all life-negative, poisoning life.

If religion happens as your own experience, you will always find this distinction: your religion will be life-affirmative. You will say yes to life and you will say yes totally. You will become a yea-sayer, and through that yes God enters you.

If your religion is just a conditioning – borrowed, cheap, a substitute, imitative – then it will be life-negative. You will be afraid of living, you will feel guilty, you will always be confused about what to do and what not to do: "Is it right, is it wrong, is it good, is it bad?" Borrowed religion never goes beyond morality. Authentic religion is amoral, it is always beyond morality: good and bad, it knows no distinctions. If you understand this, you will be able to understand these beautiful sutras of Kabir. He is not a Hindu, he is not a Mohammedan, he is not a Christian. He is simply an authentic man, and his sayings are some of the purest sayings in the world. And he is not worried about anything – whatsoever he has felt he has said, without any compromise.

Before we enter into the sutras, two or three more things. One: down through the centuries, religion has existed as a renunciation of life. "Escape from life, life is wrong. Become a monk, an ascetic, drop out of life" – as if to be alive is a sin, as if to be alive is a punishment. That's how so-called religious people have always thought: you are sent into life because you have sinned in your past lives. You have been thrown here to be punished – that is the Hindu concept. The Christian concept makes you an even greater sinner because Adam disobeyed God – so every man, from the very beginning, is a sinner. You are born in sin.

Buddhists go on saying that life is a bondage, so get out of it, the sooner the better. Escape from it! And down the centuries only one prayer has continued all over the earth, and the prayer has been: "Don't send us again into the world."

Kabir says: I am not for renunciation. If God creates the world, the world is beautiful. If it comes out of God, it is beautiful; it cannot be a punishment, it is a reward. It is a very revolutionary statement that the world is not a punishment; the world is a reward. God has not thrown you into a dark and dismal cell; it is a celebration. God has loved you so much that he has created this world for you to play with, to dance with. It is a celebration.

Kabir is not for renunciation; he's all for celebration – that's one thing. The second thing Kabir says: life is in community. Life is a communion, so don't try to escape from the world, and don't try to remain in a solitary life because the richness is in the community. You are enriched by the community, by your relationships. The more you are related to people the richer you are. A solitary person living in a Himalayan cave is very poor, impoverished. Because rivers of relationships don't flow in him he becomes a desert.

Each time somebody looks into you, a river flows in. Each time somebody shakes hands with you, energy moves into you. Each time there is a contact you gain something. When you drop out of all contacts, out of all relationship, and you become a solitary monk in a Himalayan cave, you have almost committed suicide – you are only one percent alive. Just because you breathe, you are alive. This is a sort of death: you are living at the minimum, you are not living at all; you are living very grudgingly, you are living very reluctantly, you are living with a deep complaint that you don't want to live and you have been forced to. You don't want this world at all: the rainbows and the trees and the stars and the people... No, you don't want to relate to anybody.

When you don't want to relate to anybody, your contact with the divine is diminished, terribly diminished. When you come into relationship with a man, or with a tree, or with an animal, you are coming in contact with God in different forms.

Kabir says: to be in the community is the only way to be really alive. Relationship is life, and relationship is beautiful.

The third thing Kabir says: don't make religion a ritual. Ritual is a way of avoiding religion. Religion should be spontaneous, non-ritualistic. You should do it because you love doing it – not that it is a duty – and you should do it only spontaneously, when your heart feels like it. There is no need to go to the mosque or to the temple every day. There is no need to pray every day in the same way again and again – because if you repeat the same prayer every day you will not repeat it consciously, it will become mechanical.

I have heard...

It happened: a German scholar came to India to see a certain old sage. His name was very famous, because he knew the Rig Veda just by memory. He had memorized the whole Rig Veda; that was his fame. I don't think he was a sage; he was just a great scholar, with a very good memory. You can call him a good computer, but not a sage.

And this German scholar came to discuss something and he told him a few sutras from the Rig Veda: "I would like you to discuss these with me."

The old man said, "Never heard of it before" – because the German scholar had not said that these were from the Rig Veda.

The old man said, "Never heard it before."

The German was surprised. He said, "I have heard that you know the whole Rig Veda, and you say you have never heard this before?"

He said, "I cannot remember pieces. I remember the whole text, from the beginning to the end. I can repeat it whole, but if you bring two sentences, then I don't know them."

It happens many times: you can repeat the whole thing more easily because no consciousness is involved in it; it is just a mechanical repetition, just replaying a tape-recording. It is just like a gramophone. If something is asked, you cannot even remember that you know about it because it is out of context. You remember only in the context of the whole. You can do a ritual, you can go every day to the mosque and do *namaj,* the yoga of Islam, or you can do a Hindu ritual, or any other ritual, or you can invent your own ritual and you can do it every day and you can do it religiously, and it will become part of your habit. It is not going to enhance your being at all.

Kabir says be spontaneous. If you are sitting silently and a prayer arises, say it. There is no need to repeat any formal prayer. Say whatsoever you feel like saying.

Jesus introduced a tremendously new insight into prayer. He used to call God *abba.* Christians translate *abba* as father. That is absolutely wrong: *abba* is not father. *Abba* can be translated only as papa, or dad, daddy, but not father. And it was Jesus who introduced *abba*; before him no Jew had ever prayed that way. God was father. To call God *abba*, daddy, must have looked like sacrilege – but it was more spontaneous, more intimate, more personal. To call God "father" is not right. *Father* is a very clinical term, untouched with love, not intimate, not close. Love is not flowing. *Father* is an institutional word. *Papa* has a totally different quality. Jews were very angry when they heard that Jesus called God *abba*: "Who is this man? And who does he think he is?" They could never forgive him. Jesus' prayer is very spontaneous; it had no ritual around it. Sometimes, suddenly he would say to his disciples, "Now I would like to go and pray. The feeling is coming." Sometimes he was talking amidst a crowd, teaching, and then suddenly he would say to his disciples, "Now let us go to some lonely spot. I would like to pray."

It is not a ritual, it is a feeling; it is not being done through the head. When the heart feels it, then let it overflow. Sometimes you may be silent, nothing will come out – then silence comes out. Silence is as prayerful as anything else, even more prayerful than words. Sometimes some words will come, but don't force them; it is not a performance. Just say that which comes, don't improve upon it. Don't rehearse any prayer, let the prayer be absolutely spontaneous. That's what Kabir calls *sahaj*, spontaneous. And he says if you remain spontaneous, by and by you will come to *samadhi*; by and by you will come to those inner spaces where everything disappears, those tremendously beautiful blanks, emptinesses, when nothing is left. Only in that vacuum the ultimate descends and you are fulfilled.

This he calls *sahaj samadhi*, spontaneous ecstasy. And he says that your whole life should be infused with prayerfulness. Religion should not be a part; it should be your whole life: not that in the morning you do the prayer and you are finished with your religion; or on Sunday you go to church, then for six days you are free from religion.

Religion, if it is going to be at all significant, has to have continuity in you. Eating, you should be prayerful; walking, you should be prayerful; talking, you should be prayerful; listening, you should be prayerful. Let prayerfulness spread in each of your activities and non-activities. Sleeping, you should be prayerful. Only then does the natural ecstasy arise.

And Kabir is tremendously in love with natural ecstasy. He says there are two types of ecstasy. One: practiced, forced, the yogis do that – the posture, the breathing. They train themselves for it. It is a trained thing, with great effort. And Kabir says something trained is bound to be false. It is a performance.

He says: *Santo, sahaj samadhi bhali.* Oh monks, oh disciples, the spontaneous ecstasy is the best. You should not practice it. By practicing you poison it. You should not make any dramatic effort for it. You should remain relaxed, and by and by slowly, slowly disappear into it.

Now the sutras:

He is dear to me indeed who can call back the wanderer to his home. In the home is the true union; in the home is enjoyment of life. Why should I forsake my home and wander in the forest? If Brahma helps me to realize truth, verily I will find both bondage and deliverance in the home.

He is a tremendous lover of home. He says: don't go from your home, and don't become a wanderer, don't become a renunciate. Remain with your family. Don't change the given situation, accept it. Whatsoever God has given is good; accept it in deep gratitude, don't reject it. Rejecting it, you are rejecting God himself.

The mother, the father, the brother, the wife, the children – whatsoever has naturally happened, allow it to be there. Don't try to create an artificial situation, because through the artificial you will never reach to the natural. Nobody is born as a renunciate; nobody is born as a monk. Everybody is born in a family, in a community; everybody is born out of a mother and a father; everybody is born in a milieu of love. The monk is a human invention, the family is divine.

He is dear to me indeed who can call back the wanderer to his home...

And Kabir says: whoever helps the wanderer to come back home is dear to me.

If he was here, he would have loved me tremendously. I have called many wanderers, and I have stopped many potential wanderers from becoming wanderers. I have helped them to be *there,* wherever they are – not to change the outward circumstance, but to change themselves. Changing the circumstance is a deception of the mind; it is not going to help. Change your consciousness!

He is dear to me indeed who can call back the wanderer to his home: back to the world, back to the family, back to love, back to relationship. *In the home is the true union; in the home is enjoyment of life. Why should I forsake my home and wander in the forest? If God helps me to realize truth, verily I will find both bondage and deliverance in the home.*

Yes, home is a bondage, and home is a deliverance too. It depends on you. If you are against the home, it will appear like bondage; if you are not against it, it becomes your deliverance. It is basically your attitude that determines. Even chains can become deliverance; it depends on you. And you can make chains out of your freedom too.

He is dear to me indeed who has power to dive deep into God; whose mind loses itself with ease in his contemplation.

...who easily, without any tense effort, dissolves into God.

He is dear to me indeed who has power to dive deep into God; whose mind loses itself with ease...
He is dear to me who knows God, and can dwell on his supreme truth in meditation; and who can play the melody of the infinite by uniting love and renunciation in life.

That is the highest harmony: uniting love and renunciation. People come to me and they say, "You are creating a new type of sannyasin who lives in the house; then what type of sannyasin are they?" Because the old concept is that the sannyasin is one who leaves the world, leaves the family, goes into the forest, becomes a wanderer. "Then why do you call your sannyasins, 'sannyasins' if they don't leave the house, if they live with their wives and with their children, and if they live in love – then why do you call them sannyasins?"

I call them *real* sannyasins, more real than the old type – because the old type was not in harmony. He was divided. He was not total, he was partial.

My neo-sannyasins are total: they have renounced, and yet they have not escaped. They will live in love and they will not cling to love – that is their renunciation. They will live in the world and they will not be possessive – that is their renunciation. They will live in love but they will not be jealous – that is their renunciation. They will use things but they will not be used by things – that is their renunciation. They will find the creator in the creation, and they will not divide the creator and the creation; they will not tolerate any division. They will try to find the harmony in the opposites.

He is dear to me who knows God...and who can play the melody of the infinite by uniting love and renunciation in life.
Kabir says: The home is the abiding place...

You are born in a home; there is no possibility of being born without a home, the home is your natural element. Be in the home. And remember the difference between a house and a home: a house is a place where you live without love; a home is a house where you live with love. When the house is infused with love, it becomes a home. Not all houses are homes. Many people live in houses and they think they live in a home. Don't be deceived; not all houses are homes, although all homes are houses. A home has something more than a house – a house is just the structure, it has no soul in it. When love, warmth, closeness, intimacy, openness, friendship thrives there, when there is love, then the house becomes a home, the house becomes luminous.

And you can see the difference. When you enter a house you can immediately feel whether it is a home or a house. If it is a home you will feel welcome, you will feel warmth. You will feel a different vibe, a different milieu. If it is only a house you will feel a cold structure: cement and concrete, but no soul. It may be coldly beautiful too, good architecture, but you don't feel any warmth, you don't feel any vibration that the people who live there live in love, that the people who live there live in celebration, that the people who live there live in delight, that the people who live there are grateful to existence. Cold, uninviting, then it is a house; warm, welcoming, you will suddenly feel warmth surrounds you. Maybe there is nobody in the house, but if love exists there, then the house goes on vibrating with love.

Once I used to live with a very beautiful man: a poet, a mystic, and we used to travel together. He had a very curious habit: whenever we would go into any house he would go to this corner and that, and sniff. I asked, "What are you doing?"

He said, "I try to see whether it is a house or a home." And he had exact clarity about it, he was absolutely certain. I had never found him to be wrong. Immediately he would sniff, he would say, "This seems to be a home; we can stay." And he was always right. Or sometimes he would say, "Escape from here. This is a house, it will kill!"

On the surface you may not see the difference, but a home is also an alive thing. If there is love then it is alive. The difference is the same... You may see a body lying there – how do you decide whether it is a corpse or an alive body? You go and touch, you feel the warmth, you put your hand close to the nose, you feel the breathing; you can see the heaving heart, you can listen to the beat, then you say it is not a corpse. In exactly the same way, a home has a beat, has a song, breathes, pulsates. A house is dead, it is a corpse.

Now, in the world there are many, many houses, but homes have disappeared.

Kabir says: The home is the abiding place; in the home is reality...

You are born in a home; you are rooted in the home. You should live in the home and you should die in the home – and there is no need to go anywhere else. God has destined it this way. Just as a tree is rooted in the earth, you are rooted in home, in love, in community.

...the home helps to attain him who is real. So stay where you are, and all things shall come to you in time.

Don't be in a hurry, and don't hanker, and don't desire for things to happen instantly. Wait! There is no need to go to the forest or to the Himalayas, no need to move to any Catholic monastery. There is no need to become a Jaina monk. Be wherever you are – be in love, be in deep relationship, and wait. When the time is ripe he comes, he reveals himself. Waiting is one of the greatest religious qualities, waiting is more important than effort. Effort is a shadow of the ego. When you make an effort, you say, "I am *going* to have it; I will possess even the divine. I cannot allow reality to escape from me. I have to know. I am going to hold God in my hand. I am going to declare to the world one day: 'Yes, I have arrived.'"

Effort is of the ego, waiting is egolessness. Waiting is passive: one waits... That's why all the great mystics have said that to know the divine, one has to become feminine. The male is aggressive. The male is effort, attack, will; the feminine is passive, receptive, welcoming. The feminine is a womb. When the divine comes, the passive mind, the waiting mind, becomes a womb, receives the divine, becomes pregnant with the divine.

O Sadhu! The simple union is the best.

Sahaj samadhi – the spontaneous ecstasy is the best. Don't create complex structures around it. So many disciplines, postures, breathing exercises – don't create too many structures around it. Kabir is all for the simple. Don't make it complex, let it be natural. And what does he preach?

Since the day when I met with my Lord, there has been no end to the sport of our love.

God is continuously playing with you. You may not see him; he is continuously sending gifts and gifts, he is constantly pouring his being into your being. You may have completely forgotten, but his play continues. The only thing that is needed is *surati*, remembrance. What Gurdjieff used to call self-remembering, Kabir calls *surati*, remembrance.

Nothing is needed. We *are* in the play, God is the other partner, and this old love affair has continued forever and ever. We have just forgotten; we have forgotten the obvious. Remember:

I shut not my eyes...

Listen. Kabir says: *I shut not my eyes* – even that much effort I don't do.

I shut not my eyes, I close not my ears, I do not mortify my body; I see with eyes open and smile.

...because I see him everywhere: how beautifully he is hiding!

I see with open eyes and smile, and behold his beauty everywhere.

I utter his name, and whatever I see, it reminds me of him;
whatever I do, it becomes his worship.
The rising and setting are one to me: all contradictions are solved.

Kabir's religion is very aesthetic, artistic. He's a great poet, uneducated though – but what does poetry have to do with education? A great poet, one of the greatest: his poetry is simply sublime, not of this world. He says that one has to look for the beauty. It is all over, the whole of nature is full of beauty. And beauty is nothing but God, hidden. All beauty is that. When you see a beautiful human face, a man's, a woman's, it is the face of God. When you look into two beautiful eyes, you are entering the temple of God. When you see a flower opening, it is an invitation from God.

I have heard…

Thirty-eight years ago, the philosopher George Santayana came into a sizeable legacy and was able to relinquish his post on the Harvard faculty.

The classroom was packed for his final appearance, and Santayana did himself proud. He was about to conclude his remarks when he caught sight of a forsythia uncurling in a patch of muddy snow outside the window. He stopped abruptly, picked up his hat, gloves and walking stick, and made for the door.

There, he turned, "Gentlemen," he said softly, "I shall not be able to finish that sentence. I have just discovered that I have an appointment with April."

Each flower is an invitation, an appointment with God. Each song of the bird, and each cloud floating in the sky, is something like a message, a code message. You have to decode it, you have to look deep into it; you have to be silent and listen to the message. Kabir says: *I see with eyes open and smile, and behold his beauty everywhere.* There is no need even to close your eyes. Eyes closed or eyes open, you see him, because he is within and without. *I utter his name, and whatever I see, it reminds me of him; whatever I do, it becomes his worship.*

The rising and setting are one to me; all contradictions are solved. All contradictions are solved only when you have achieved God, never before – because mind creates contradictions. When you

have attained to God, mind is no more, and with no mind, all contradictions are gone. Then day and night, both are one. And life and
death too, both are one. Then whether you are or you disappear,
makes no difference. Then breathing in and breathing out are not
two things, but one process.

> *Wherever I go I move round him. All I achieve is his service: When I*
> *lie down, I lie prostrate at his feet. He is the only adorable one to*
> *me; I have none other.*
> *My tongue has left off impure words, it sings his glory day and*
> *night: whether I rise or sit down, I can never forget him; for the*
> *rhythm of his music beats in my ears.*
> *Kabir says; My heart is frenzied, and I disclose in my soul what is*
> *hidden. I am immersed in that one great bliss which transcends all*
> *pleasure and pain.*

Contradictions are our creations – remember it – because we
cannot see the total, because we can only see the partial, hence the
contradiction. We can see only the aspect, never the whole, hence
the contradiction. Have you observed: even if you are looking at a
small pebble in your palm you cannot see the whole of it at one
time? You see one part, the other part is hidden; when you see the
other part, the first part goes into hiding. You can never see even a
small pebble in its totality; not even a grain of sand can you see in
its totality. When you are looking at my face, my back is just an
inference – maybe it is there, maybe it is not there. When you look
at my back, my face is just an inference – it may be there, it may
not be there. We never see anything in totality because the mind
cannot see totality in anything. The mind has a partial outlook.

When the mind is dropped and meditation has arisen, then you
see the total. Then you see the whole as it is, all the aspects together.
Then summer and winter are not separate; then spring and fall are
not separate. Then you will see that birth and death are two aspects
of the same process. Then happiness and unhappiness are not opposites, they are joined together: like a valley and a mountain, they are
together. And when you see this togetherness of life, choice stops.
Then there is nothing to choose.

Have you not seen it? Whenever you choose happiness, you
become the victim of unhappiness; whenever you want success,

failure comes in; whenever you hope, frustration is waiting for you; whenever you cling to life, death comes and destroys. Have you not seen it happen every day, every moment? These are not opposites, they are together. When one sees them together, then what is there to choose? There is nothing to choose, one becomes choiceless.

That's what Krishnamurti goes on saying: be choiceless, be in a state of choiceless awareness. But it cannot happen unless you have seen the togetherness of things. Once you have realized that all things are together, choice then becomes impossible. Then there is nothing to choose, because whatsoever you choose comes with the opposite. Then what is the point? You choose love and hate comes; you choose friendship and the enemy comes; you choose anything, and immediately the opposite comes as a shadow. One stops choosing. One remains choiceless. And when one is choiceless, one has transcended all contradictions.

To transcend contradictions is to transcend mind, and to transcend mind is to know what love is.

Whatsoever you have known up to now as love has nothing to do with love. It is a misuse of the word. *Love* has been very much misused. There are only a few words which have been misused like *love* – *God* is another, *peace* is another, but *love* is at the top of the list. Everybody talks about love and nobody knows what it is. People sing about it, people write poetry about it, and they don't know what it is.

My own observation is this: whenever a person writes a poem about love, know well he has missed. He has not known what love is. Otherwise, who bothers to write poetry about love? If you can love, you will love, rather than write poetry about it.

I have looked into poets and I have never seen a poet who knows what love is. Only mystics know. Love has nothing to do with all those things that have become associated with love. And how you misuse the word! You can go into the cafeteria and you can see people talking, and somebody says, "I love ice cream!" Somebody loves a Cadillac car, and somebody loves his dog, and somebody loves his cat, and somebody loves his woman... People go on using the word *love* for anything.

Love knows no object, love is not addressed. Love is only of God. When you love your woman, if you really love her, you will see the woman has disappeared and God is standing there. If you love the tree, you will suddenly see the tree has disappeared and God is the very green in it, blooming. Love is only of God. Love is never of the part; love is only of the whole. Love is almost synonymous with prayer. But we have not known love.

And from the very childhood, we have been distorted. The mother says to the child, "Love me, I am your mother" – as if just by being a mother you can force love. The father says, "Love me, I'm your father" – as if love is logical: "Because I am your father, you have to love me." And the child does not know what to do. How to love just by the declaration that somebody is your father? And the child starts feeling guilty if he does not love, so he pretends, he shows love. Not knowing what it is, he smiles. He says, "I love you Mommy, I love you Daddy," and daddy is very happy. People are very happy with empty words. And the mommy is very happy because the child is smiling, and she feels very good that somebody at least finally loves her; at least her own child loves her. Nobody has loved her...

And the child is simply becoming a politician; he is learning the ways of deception. Sooner or later he will become so efficient in it that he will go on pretending his whole life, and talking about love. He will say a hundred times in the day to his wife, "I love you, I love you," and these are content-less words. There is nothing behind them, they are empty. But they help, because people live only with words. People don't know the reality; they have lost all contact.

Dale Carnegie says to his followers that even if you don't love your wife, at least three, four times in the day, say, "I love you," and it helps. There is no need to mean anything, but just say it, even saying it helps. People know only words, they don't know reality.

Once a child has learned how to pretend love, he will never know love – because love is not something that you can do. It happens, it is not a doing on your part. Love is something bigger than you, vaster than you. You cannot manage and manipulate it. Remember this, and remain open. Don't pretend. When it comes, feel grateful; when it disappears, wait again – but don't pretend.

If you don't pretend, one day you will see love has arisen, the flower has opened. And whenever love opens in your heart, the fragrance goes to the feet of God. It may take any route – it may go through your child, through your wife, through your husband, through your friend, through a tree, through a rock. It may go through anything, via anything – but it always reaches the divine.

Love is something addressed to the whole. Wait for it. And love is the secret key to open all the locks and all the blocks. A block is nothing but a lock in your being.

Love is the secret key. It opens all the locks: the master key.

Enough for today.

CHAPTER 2

so far, so good

The first question:

Osho,
Many people in the West are engaged in the creation of a science or technology of enlightenment. The need is certainly there, but how do you see the possibility? Is it irresponsible to engage in its creation without having reached the state of enlightenment? Is the Arica method a valid approach?

The first and most fundamental thing to be remembered is that enlightenment can never have a technology. By its very nature, it is impossible. But the West is obsessed with technology, so whatsoever comes into the hands of the West, it starts reducing into a technology. Technology is an obsession. For the outside world science is a valid approach, but partial, not total – not the only approach, but only one of the approaches. Poetry is as valid as science.

Science is knowledge without love, and that is the danger in it: because it is knowledge without love, it is always in the service of death and never in the service of life. Hence, the whole progress of science is leading man toward a global suicide. One day when man has committed suicide, the Third World War, cockroaches will think, "We are the most fit to survive." Some Darwin, some cockroach-Darwin, will prove, "We are the fittest because we have survived – the survival of the fittest."

Man has committed suicide, he has destroyed himself. Knowledge without love is dangerous, because poison is in its very root. Love keeps balance, never allows knowledge to go too far, so it never becomes destructive. Science is knowledge without love – that is its danger. But it is one of the valid approaches – the object, the material, can be known without love; there is no need for love.

But life is not only matter; life is suffused with something tremendously transcendental. That transcendental is missed. And then science, by and by, automatically turns into a technology, it becomes mechanical. More and more it becomes a means to exploit nature, to manipulate nature. From the very beginning, science has had the idea of how to conquer nature. That's a foolish idea.

We are not separate from nature, how can we conquer it? We *are* nature, so who is going to conquer whom? It is absurd. With that absurdity, science has destroyed much: the whole of nature is destroyed, the climate is poisoned, the air, the water, the seas, everything polluted. The whole harmony is dying, the ecology is being continuously destroyed. Please remember, *this* is enough, more than enough.

Don't turn science inward. If the application of scientific methodology has been so devastating for the outer nature, it is going to be more devastating to the inner nature – because you are moving toward the more subtle. Even for the outside nature a different kind of knowledge is needed, which is rooted in love; but for the innermost core of your being, the subtlest, the transcendental, knowledge is not needed at all. Innocence is needed, innocence with love – then you will know the inside, then you will know the interior of your being, the subjectivity.

But the West is obsessed with technology. It seems technology has succeeded over nature; we have become more powerful. We have *not* become more powerful, the whole idea is just fallacious; we have not become more powerful. We are becoming weaker every day because the natural resources are being exhausted. Sooner or later the earth will be empty, it will not grow anything. We are not becoming powerful, we are becoming weaker and weaker and

weaker every day. We are on the deathbed. Humanity cannot survive for more than fifty years, the way it has been behaving with
nature – sixty years, or, at the most, one hundred years, which is
nothing. If the Third World War does not happen, then we will be
committing a slow suicide. Within a hundred years we will be gone,
not even a trace will be left.

And man will not be the first to disappear; many other animals,
very strong animals, have disappeared from the earth. They used to
roam the earth, they were the kings of the earth, bigger than the ele-
phant. They are no longer anywhere. They thought they had become
very powerful – they were huge, with tremendous energy – then they
began to become bigger and bigger and bigger, a moment came
when the earth could not supply food for them, they had to die.

The same is happening with man: man thinks he is becoming
more and more powerful. He can reach the moon, but he is destroying the earth. He is destroying the whole possibility of future life.
Slowly, humanity is disappearing. Please, don't turn your technology
toward the inner; you have done enough harm. Enlightenment cannot
be reduced to a technology.

So the first thing: the inner journey is of innocence, not of knowledge; certainly not of science, *absolutely* not of technology. It is
more of love, innocence, silence. Meditation is not really a technique,
but because you cannot understand anything other than technique, I
have to talk in terms of technique; otherwise, meditation is not a
technique at all. Meditation is nothing that you do. Meditation is
something that you fall in, just like love. Meditation is something in
which you can be, but you cannot do it, doing ceases.

How can there be a technology for non-doing? Technology is
relevant to doing: you have to do something. Meditation is not
something that you do. It is only when your doer has gone and you
are totally relaxed, not doing anything, in a deep let-go, rest, that
there is meditation. Then meditation flowers, it is the flowering of
your being. It has nothing to do with becoming. It is not an achievement, it is not an improvement; it is just being that which you
already are. What technique is needed?

People are foolish; that's why techniques have to be talked
about. If you understand, nothing is needed. Just being silent and just
being yourself, not moving in any direction, not moving at all, and
you will see the benediction, the meditation. When this meditation

has become such a spontaneous flow that you need not even sit in a certain posture for it, that you need not find a small corner in the house where nobody disturbs you; when it is also there in the marketplace: talking, walking, doing, eating, it is there; when it is always there, even when you are asleep – you go on feeling it, it goes on like breathing, or the beating of the heart – that's what Kabir calls *sahaj samadhi,* spontaneous ecstasy. It needs no technique; it needs only spontaneity, it needs only naturalness, it needs only simplicity.

So I say to you, blessed are the ignorant, for theirs is the kingdom of God. Become innocent and become ignorant. Don't remain knowledgeable.

But in the West it is happening. Now, they are trying to manipulate the mind, they are trying to create mechanisms to manipulate the mind. This is going to be far more dangerous than science. This is going to be far more dangerous, because once you know how to manipulate the mind of man, you will reduce him also to automata, that's what's going to happen. Once you know that man and his mind can be manipulated, totally manipulated, then all freedom will be gone, all individuality will be gone.

Then electrodes can be put into your head without your ever knowing, and you can be manipulated from Delhi, from Moscow, from Washington...from the capital. You can be manipulated just by radio waves. The whole country can be ordered, and nobody will see the order coming from anywhere – it will come from within you. An electrode is there; you can be ordered just by radio waves and you will follow it automatically. All freedom will be gone. You can be hypnotized at any moment. You can be put into any hallucination and you will believe in it, it will be so real – and it will be coming from within you. Then from Delhi, from Moscow, from Washington, from London, from the capital places...

There is no need to keep police and no need to keep a magistrate; that is too costly and uneconomical. These are like bullock carts – no need. Better technology will be available; no need to keep all these people to enforce, no need even for the priest to go on teaching morality and religion. Just from the capital the orders can be given: that you are all happy – and you will all feel happy; that you are all content – and you will all feel content. You may be dying, starving, but you will feel content. You may be on your deathbed, suffering, but if the order comes that you are happy and that there is no death, you will believe you are happy and that there is no death. And this will be coming from within you. That's what Delgado proposes to do someday, and he says, "Then man will be happy, nobody will be unhappy." But this happiness will not be true happiness. Then there are mechanisms by which alpha waves can be created in your mind, just by electrical stimulation. That is dangerous, because that will not allow you to know the reality. And those alpha waves will be created from the outside; they will not be true, they will not be real. And God will disappear, then there is no need for God. You are not unhappy, so why seek happiness? And you will believe in the dogma – whatsoever dogma happens to be there, followed by your politicians and your priests – you will believe in the dogma, you will *absolutely* believe in the dogma, and there will be no doubt. Skepticism will disappear. This is a dangerous step.

Meditation should not be reduced to technology, and enlightenment *cannot* be reduced. Enlightenment means awareness, witnessing. Enlightenment is neither of the body nor of the mind, it is of the beyond. The body can be manipulated by mechanisms, the mind can be manipulated by mechanisms, but your soul is beyond and cannot be manipulated by any mechanism whatsoever.

You ask, "Many people in the West are engaged in the creation of a science or technology of enlightenment." Those people are criminals. They are dangerous people; avoid them. These same people were engaged in creating technology two hundred years ago. They have destroyed nature; now they are turning toward consciousness. They will destroy that too.

Now there is a movement all over the world to protect the ecology of nature, the naturalness of nature. But it is too late really. Now nothing can be done, nothing much can be done. And these people who propagate in favor of ecology appear to be eco-nuts, another species of Jehovah's Witnesses – fanatics, desperately fighting something which seems impossible. Before the plague of technology turns on human consciousness, stop it. Stop it in the seed.

And you say, "The need is certainly there..." It is not, certainly not. There is no need. "...but how do you see the possibility?" There is no possibility either.

But man is dangerous: the more impossible a thing, the more he becomes attracted and challenged. That's what Edmund Hillary said when he reached the top of Everest. Somebody asked him, "Why did you try it at all? What is the point? Why?" Edmund Hillary said, "I had to – because Everest is there. Because it is there, I had to. It stands like a challenge."

Anything unconquerable is a challenge to man's ego. There is no possibility; naturally, it will never happen. But that very impossibility can become a challenge to these mad, obsessed people who want to reduce everything into technique. They cannot create a technology of enlightenment. That is not possible at all – in the very reality. But they can create a technology which can manipulate the mind, and even deceive people and create an illusion of enlightenment.

That's what is happening with drugs. Drugs have become a technology of enlightenment. And the guru of drugs, Ginsberg, goes on talking as if all the mystics of the world were saying the same things, were trying to give you the same vision as LSD can give, or psilocybin or marijuana. It is nonsense! No drug can lead you to enlightenment, but drugs can create an illusion of enlightenment.

"Is it irresponsible to engage in its creation without having reached the state of enlightenment?" Only people who have not known enlightenment can try it. Those who have known cannot even think of the possibility. And it is irresponsible.

"Is the Arica method a valid approach?" The Arica method is technology, techniques, knowledge without love – and hence the danger is there. It will turn people into robots.

Remember always, freedom is the goal, *moksha*, absolute freedom, is the goal. You can turn human beings into robots; they will be less miserable. In fact, if you become a perfect robot, how can you be miserable? A machine is never miserable – of course, never happy too, but never miserable.

Arica methods, or any methods which exist without love, are dangerous. And in this again it is very difficult to make a distinction, because the same method can be used with love, and then it is meaningful; and the same method can be used without love, and it becomes dangerous. And it is very difficult to see from the outside whether the method is being used with love or without love.

The Arica methods have been chosen from different schools: Sufi, Gurdjieff, Tibetan, Indian, Japanese. It is eclectic. They have chosen techniques from all over the world. In the first place, they are chosen from different schools; there is no harmony in them, there is no center in them. It is just like a piled-up thing – a crowd of people, a mob, not a family – because the techniques come from different schools.

A Sufi technique is bound to be different from a Zen technique. Both function, both work, but they work in their own system; they cannot work outside the system. It is as if you take one part of one car, and try to fix that part into another car of a different make. And it doesn't work, and you are puzzled: "Why doesn't it work?" It used to work in the first car, there was harmony, it was meant for that car.

A Zen method works in Zen philosophy; a Sufi method words in Sufi philosophy; a Tibetan method works with Tibetan occult esoteric Buddhism; a yoga method works with Patanjali's system. You cannot just choose those methods from anywhere, otherwise you can make a car with a few parts from a Rolls Royce, a few from a Lincoln, a few from a Cadillac, and a few from a Fiat – and you go on jumbling parts from everywhere. Your car is dangerous. In the first place it is not going anywhere – and you are fortunate if it doesn't move. It moves? – then you are more unfortunate.

Arica has chosen from different schools. Arica is very greedy, eclectic, but there exists no center. It is not an orchestra; it is a market-noise.

First thing: if you follow the Arica method too much, you will not arrive at your center. You will come to many experiences on the periphery, but you will never arrive at your center. And all your experiences will not be of a family, but fragmentary. And it is dangerous, you can fall into pieces.

The second thing: there is no love because there is no center – and love arises only from the center. This collection of so many methods is soul-less, there is no soul in it. So you can become very, very efficient in the methods, and yet you will see that your heart is not flowering. You will become efficient, but you will not become blissful. You may become less miserable, you may be less tense, you may become more capable of controlling yourself, you may have a stronger ego, but you will not have a soul.

The methods are all valid taken in their own context. But Arica does not yet have any philosophy, it has no harmony. And this is not the way to create a harmony; the way is just the opposite. In fact, Buddhism was born when Buddha became enlightened. The center came first, and then he started creating a few methods to help those people who were not yet enlightened, to help them come to the center that he had already achieved. The center came first, then the periphery.

So it is with Jalaluddin Rumi: he became enlightened first. And when he became enlightened he was dancing, he was whirling – but not to become enlightened; he had never known about it. He just liked whirling very much, and he felt very peaceful. It was a coincidence. While he was whirling he became enlightened. When he became enlightened he started thinking how to help people – the center came first. Then he started the Sufi methods. The same was the case with Patanjali.

With Arica it is totally different. There is no enlightened being at the center; of course, a very clever person, who has collected many methods from many sources and many directions and many traditions – but there is no center. It is only a periphery. So people who go into Arica will, sooner or later, feel stuck. It will take you so far, and then suddenly you will see there is going to be no more growth. You will become dry, like a desert – because unless love flows, flowers never come up, trees don't grow, rivers don't flow.

The ultimate blooming is always that of love.

The second question:

Osho,
One day you said that you were an egoist. On another day, that an egoist could not be happy – and you say you are happy.
Can you comment please?

Never listen to what I say! Only look at *me*, listen to me; don't be too bothered by the words. Look directly… Can you see any ego in this person sitting here talking to you? Don't be too concerned with what I say. In fact, only an absolutely egoless person can say, "I am the biggest egoist in the world."

Ordinarily, the ego tries to hide itself. You tell somebody, "You are an egoist"; he will feel offended. He may be, but he will feel offended. The more he is, the more he will feel offended. The ego wants to function from the unconscious, from the dark corner. It never comes into the light. I can say to you that I am the greatest egoist in the world because there is no problem.

And I told you that my ego includes all. How can an ego include all? The ego has to exclude, otherwise definition is lost. The ego has to say: you are you and I am I, and I am higher than you and greater than you. The ego has to depend on definition, demarcation. When I said that I include you all, my ego is so vast that it includes all – it does not exclude anything, not even the Devil – then the "you" disappears, and when the you disappears how can the "I" exist?

But the question is from an Englishman. That's natural: Englishmen don't have a sense of humor. He took it seriously. They are serious people. He must have started thinking, "This man is contradicting."

I am a nonserious person – I am allowed to contradict.

It is said that when a joke is told to an Englishman, he laughs three times: first, when he listens to the joke, and of course, he never understands it. He laughs just to be polite, so the other person does not feel offended that, "You have not understood," or his joke was missed. Not to make him embarrassed, he laughs loudly.

Then he laughs a second time in the night, in the middle of the night, when he catches hold of the joke. "Right!" he says, then he laughs. And then he laughs a third time at his own ridiculousness: laughing in the middle of the night. How foolish, and how un-English!

The third question:

Osho,
Curiosity and a strong thirst to have the eternal goal have brought me to your camp. Can curious, suspicious persons not become good followers? Your advice to me, to leave your camp immediately, seems rather harsh.

First: curiosity and strong thirst never exist together. Curiosity is never thirst. Curiosity is childish; one simply wants to know. It is like an itching, nothing serious is involved, you are not ready to pay anything for it, you are simply curious. You are not serious about it, it is not a deep thirst in you. It is not that through knowing it you are going to change your life, your style, your way, your being. Just by the way you want to know, you are not much concerned.

Many people come to me, they ask one question. Somebody comes and says, "What do you think, does God exist or not?" Now, even to ask such a question takes a very stupid man. The question is so vast, so unutterable, that if you are really thirsty you will not be able to verbalize it. You may cry, you may weep, but you will not be able to utter it. The question is so vast, so tremendous – how can you say it? Even to say it is to make it profane; it is a sacrilege. The question is so sacred, so holy, that you throb with it, but you cannot formulate it.

I know those people also. They come and they start trembling, and they say, "We don't know what we have to ask." Sometimes a person comes to me and says, "Osho, what should I ask?" Now this is a man of a totally different quality. He cannot even formulate his question – because life is so vast and big, how to put it into a question? The moment you put it into a question it looks childish. Questions and answers exist only in schools, not in life.

Somebody comes and asks, "Does God exist?" And he's expecting an answer, yes or no. You have been trained in your schools, colleges, universities, to answer. You have been trained to answer everything and anything. You have never been trained to question, remember – you have been trained to answer. Your examination papers simply give you a few questions; you have to answer. An answer is expected; the question is not important, but the answer is.

"Does God exist?" – and you wait there. And of course there can only be two answers, yes or no. But will it be meaningful to say, "Yes, God exists"? Will it solve anything at all? You must have heard that answer before. Or, if it is answered, "No, God does not exist," is it going to help you at all? You have heard that answer before too, both answers are known. What are you asking? It is better to be silent, it is better to throb, it is better to cry and weep, it is better to open your heart. Your intensity, your thirst, will not be curiosity. Curiosity never exists with a strong thirst.

And you say, "Curiosity and a strong thirst to have the eternal goal have brought me to your camp." I don't think so. Curiosity may have brought you. And this person has been asking foolish questions; he must have asked at least a hundred questions within ten days.

Intense thirst will make one question out of all questions. If your thirst is intense, then all questions are reduced to one question, and that question is, "Who am I?" Now all else is irrelevant.

A thirsty person is not worried about God, he is not worried about whether there is a hell or heaven, he is not worried about past lives, he is not worried about the theory of karma and reincarnation. His whole problem is: "I don't know who I am" – this is the first and the last question – "I have to know this. If I know this, then every-thing else is secondary and can be known; but if I don't know myself, what is the point of knowing anything else?"

When there is passion for truth, then you have only one question: "Who am I?" And in the hundred questions the man has asked, there has not been a single question about "Who am I?" He has not asked that question. The man is curious, and he says, "...to have the eternal goal." He is greedy too.

You don't know yourself and you are hankering for the eternal goal. The greed, the ego – they desire the world, they desire the other world too. They desire money, a bigger bank balance, bigger houses, bigger cars, and then they start desiring heaven and para-dise and God. Everything has to be in their fists – greedy people.

You have to know who you are, and by knowing it, the eternal is revealed. Not by grabbing the eternal do you know yourself, no. You cannot grab the eternal. You are so tiny.

Just think: a man, a very accidental man, thinking to grab the eternal! A small fever will kill you. Ninety-eight point six degrees and you are okay; four or five degrees below ninety-eight, and you are gone; four, five degrees above ninety-eight, and you are gone. You cannot exist beyond one hundred and ten degrees, and you want to grab the eternal? You cannot exist without breath for more than a few minutes – for more than eight minutes – and you want to grab the eternal?

A body that is already dying... From the very moment you were born your body is dying. Seventy years is nothing in this timeless procession, in this eternity. A man who is going to live seventy years wants to grab eternity? Such a small head – where will you put eternity in it? It is as if somebody is trying to put the whole sea in a spoon.

I have heard about a great philosopher – it must have been Aristotle. I don't know exactly, but I suspect... He was taking a walk on the beach in the morning sun, and he saw a madman. The man looked mad, and he was carrying water in a teaspoon from the sea and was pouring it... He had dug a hole, and he would run again to the sea and would come again and again. Aristotle saw him and he said to himself, "What is he doing?" He came close and asked, "What are you doing?"

The man said, "I have decided to empty the whole ocean into this hole."

Aristotle said, "Have you gone mad – with that teaspoon, and in this small hole, and that vast ocean?"

The madman started laughing, and he said, "I was thinking that *you* are mad. I have heard that you want to understand the eternal truth. In this small head? Who is mad?"

The man must have been a great seer. He shocked Aristotle very much, but he was true. Truth always shocks. Don't be greedy about truth, because truth comes only when you are not greedy. And when you are not greedy, you are not small. Greed makes you small. When all greed disappears, your boundaries disappear. Then you are not a small hole by the side of the ocean; then the ocean is a small hole by the side of you – when the greed is not there. Truth is not something that you have to possess; it is something that has to possess you. You have to allow it.

But this man is very knowledgeable, and knowledge never allows truth entry. In all his hundred questions he has been showing his knowledge: all the scriptures that he knows, and all that he has heard, and all that has been conditioned into his head.

"Can curious, suspicious persons not become good followers?" A curious person, a suspicious person, cannot even become a follower. "A good follower" is far away, because to follow, you need to be in trust. To go with somebody into the unknown, at least you will have to have a little trust. And this man knows no trust; he is suspicious, but he knows no trust.

Doubt cannot lead you into the inner journey. Doubt is good in science, science depends on doubt. Doubt is a method in the world of science. If you trust, you will not move into science at all; you have to distrust. Science is an inimical method; it depends on antagonism. Religion, mysticism is totally different, diametrically opposite. Trust is the method there, not doubt. If you trust me, you can come with me. There is no other way.

And the questioner says, "Your advice to me, to leave your camp immediately, seems rather harsh." Harsh? You say harsh? Then you don't know anything about masters. It is not harsh, it is very polite. Have you heard about Zen masters? If you had asked the same question to a Zen master, he would have jumped on you. He would have pounded you then and there. He would have thrown you out of the ashram. Some day I will do it. Wait... Otherwise, why do I have Sant and Kamal and Gurudayal? They will do the pounding. You wait a little longer, you trust me a little more, and you will see.

Harsh, you say? It is not harsh; it is simple compassion for you. You need it, you deserve it because a knowledgeable person needs shocks, electroshocks. I'm not here to make you more knowledgeable, I am here to help you drop all your knowledge. The work is almost as if someone is fast asleep and you have to wake him, of course it is harsh. Have you not seen it yourself? – when the alarm goes off early in the morning and you are getting ready for Dynamic Meditation, and you want to say, "To hell with it," and you want to throw the clock. It is harsh.

A master is an alarm. A master has to be very shocking: he has to shake you to your very roots, because he has to uproot your mind and transplant you in a totally different world. He has to change your level of being. It is not easy, it is arduous; it is painful too. It needs sacrifice. If you are ready to sacrifice, only then be here. Otherwise, leave me – because you will be wasting your time and mine too. If you are ready to go through all this suffering that is a must, this sacrifice...

This word *sacrifice* is beautiful. It means to make something holy, to make something sacred. If you are ready to take my shocks in deep trust, in love, they will become sacred. Then my harshness will not look like harshness, it will look like compassion. You will feel that I said so because I loved so much. Otherwise, why should I bother?

The fourth question:

Osho,
You, Buddha, Jesus, etc. are all men. You say women are closer to no-mind.
Why did you choose a man's body? Why are there no women masters?

It is from Chandan – of course, a woman who belongs to the Lib Movement. It is significant. The question has to be understood.

It has never been so in the past that a woman was ever a great master, and it will never be so in the future either. The reason is that the feminine mind, by its very nature, is not aggressive, and to be a master one has to be aggressive. It has nothing to do with the male chauvinists, it has nothing to do with the male-oriented society. Your question is almost like this: Why is the man always the father and never the mother? Nothing can be done about it, it is natural. Only once has it happened: let me tell you the anecdote...

A priest was in hospital for an exploratory operation to determine the cause of abdominal pains from which he had been suffering. In the hospital, at the same time, a young unwed girl came and gave birth to a baby boy which, she explained to the doctor, she did not wish to keep.

The quick-thinking physician approached the priest's bed as he awoke after the operation and explained to him that a miracle had occurred: God had given him a son. The priest, at first shocked, took the baby boy in his arms and bowed his head in prayer, thanking God for the miracle. What else to do?

Many years passed. The priest and boy were living together as father and son. The time came for the boy to leave home to go to college. The night before his departure, the priest approached the boy and chokingly said, "My son, I have a terrible confession to make to you." The puzzled boy looked up as the priest continued to speak. "I have always led you to believe that I am your father. Well, my son, it is not true. I am your mother. The bishop is your father."

Only the male mind can be a master. To be a master means to be aggressive. A woman cannot be aggressive. Woman, by her very nature, is receptive. A woman is a womb, so the woman can become the best disciple possible. It is very difficult for a man to become a disciple; it is very simple for a woman to become a disciple.

The master-disciple relationship is a man-woman relationship. You may not have looked at it that way, but try to look at it that way. The disciple is receptive, the disciple is a womb. That's why it is very difficult for males to become disciples – some reluctance, some resistance, some fight, some ego continues. It is very difficult for a man to become a disciple.

The greatest disciples have always been women: Mary Magdalene was the greatest disciple Jesus had, but she could not become an

apostle, she could not become a master. Yes, Buddha was also surrounded by beautiful, tremendously capable women. Mahavira was
surrounded, he had forty thousand sannyasins – thirty thousand
women, ten thousand men. The proportion has always been so. Four
disciples come: three are women; one is a man. And that one man is
not very reliable. He may have come for the women; he may not have
come for the master. That danger always exists.

But the greatest masters have always been men. Now this is a
paradox, but this is how it is – because a master has to go out in
a thousand and one ways, to work on you. A master has to move
out – to help you, to hold your hand, to protect you, to shock you, to
drag you into the unknown, to push you. He has to do a thousand
and one things which are aggressive, that's why. It has nothing to do
with the male-oriented society. Even in the future, when all equality
has been established absolutely, man will be the father, and woman
will be the mother. And miracles don't happen.

The fifth question:

Osho,
Everything is perfect, but also the Third World War is coming.
You say: do not try to change the world – but just outside the
ashram gate, a beggar's child looks like he is nearly starving. What
to do?

"Everything is perfect, but also the Third World War is coming" –
that is going to be perfect too. It will kill utterly. It will be a total war
– the perfect, the most perfect ever.

Now, the problem arises: the world war is coming, and what are
you doing here, meditating? You should go into the world and prevent the world war. Can you do that? Is it possible to prevent it? Is it
possible to do anything about it? You will be wasting your life. You
have a very short life. These few moments are very valuable – and
they were never so valuable before because the Third World War is
coming. Before, there was always time. Now, it seems, any moment,
time will be finished. It can happen tomorrow morning. Anybody can
go berserk.

Richard Nixon, when he was in a turmoil after Watergate, had
ideas in his mind to create a Third World War. He had the key to trigger

the phenomenon, and of course he was in great anxiety and anguish. And I must say this one thing in favor of this man: he resisted the temptation. It would have been very easy to trigger the war, and he would have become the last president of America...dearly lost, and he would have ended the whole of history. He would have been the most historical person of all. Of course, there would have been nobody to write the history; that is another thing. And it would have been better, at least for him, not to be in such disgrace. He could have saved his own ego. This much must be said about the man: that he resisted the temptation, which was not very easy. He could have simply started dropping atom bombs on Moscow. Within fifteen minutes, just within fifteen minutes, every single soul on the earth would have been dead.

We have the capacity to kill the whole earth seven times. We have the capacity to super-kill. Each person on this earth can be killed seven times; that many atom and hydrogen bombs are ready, piled up waiting. Any day, any politician can go berserk – and politicians are mad people, they are not very sane; otherwise why should they be in politics in the first place? You are sitting on a volcano. Never before has it been so dangerous. And you think, "What am I doing here meditating?" What else can you do? While the time is still there, meditate. If the volcano erupts and you die meditating, you will know the taste of the deathless.

And if many people in the world decide to meditate, the Third World War may never happen, because it has been observed again and again down the centuries, that if in a village of a hundred people only one person starts meditating, the whole quality of the consciousness of the village changes – one percent only – because the one person comes in contact with the ninety-nine persons of the village, a small village. He is related to everybody: somebody is an uncle and somebody is something else; somebody is a brother, somebody is related through the wife. He is related, interconnected. He starts vibrating a different energy, meditative energy. The whole quality of the village consciousness changes with a single person's meditation. If only one percent of humanity started meditating, there is a possibility that the Third World War can be avoided. There is no other possibility.

Why, in the first place, are people so violent that they have to fight again and again? In three thousand years, there have been fifteen thousand wars, five wars to each year. The whole of humanity seems to be insane, we have just been fighting and doing nothing else. Now, out of these three thousand years' violence, there is a crescendo coming: the final war, the total war.

You would like to go into the world and convince the politicians, or arrange a protest march toward Washington and Moscow. That is not going to help because, have you seen, the people who join in the protest marches are very violent people, have you not seen it? Their shouting, their slogans – they are all violent, aggressive people. Maybe they are for peace, but they are ready to fight for it. And fighting is the problem. What will you do? You will start shouting, you will create slogans, and you will get heated up by it; you will start fighting.

That's what politicians have always been doing. Moscow is not for war, neither is Washington. The communist says they have to arrange for war because they want peace in the world; and the capitalist says the same. The capitalist and the communist and the fascist are not different; they all prepare for war, and they all say they are preparing for peace. Now you go on a protest march, and you are a violent person.

The only protest march can be: meditate. Sit silently, and create a meditative energy.

Once in this ashram there was a competition, an essay competition to describe the meditative person. And of course, as can be expected, Mulla Nasruddin came first. His description is really beautiful. Mulla Nasruddin explained the difference between a person who is meditative and one who is not, in this way: "A non-meditative person is one who, if he jumps off a skyscraper, goes whoosh, splat! – finished. A meditative person is still clicking his fingers halfway down, saying, "So far, so good."

If it is going to happen, it is going to happen; you click your fingers and say, "So far, so good." You are still alive. The Third World War has not yet happened; don't miss this chance to dance. And by your dancing, I am saying you will create a ripple. Meditate – by your meditation, you will release a different quality of energy into the world.

If you can convert one percent of the whole world into mad orange people, dancing, singing, meditating, not at all political...

Those protest marchers *are* political; politics is the root cause. We need nonpolitical persons. I have never voted in my life, and people would come to me and say, "But you can vote for the person you would like."

I said, "For whomsoever I vote, it goes to a politician. I cannot vote. I am a nonparticipant. They are all the same, only their names differ."

Now this pacifist is also a political person. I would like you to create a few people who are nonpolitical. *Nonpolitical* is what I mean by religious: a person who says, "Okay, if it is going to happen, it is going to happen. Why should I waste my time? I should meditate, I should enjoy, I should delight. Meanwhile, I am going to dance. If it is going to happen, it will happen, but why should I miss the dance? The time is short."

If you start dancing, if you start loving, if you become friendly, if you enjoy life, you will create energy which will be for peace – without thinking of peace at all. So I don't talk about peace, I talk about love. Peace follows love energy like a shadow.

I know there is poverty; there are beggars, but what to do? Whatsoever you do is not going to help. Down through the centuries, people have been serving people, donating, giving money, clothes, food; there has been much philanthropy, but nothing has happened.

Then there have been communist countries, where they saw that religion had failed. In fact, religion has never been tried, but it looks as if religion has failed because these people are thought to be religious people – those who donate, give charity, and do things like that. These are not religious people, these are guilty people. They feel guilt. When a person accumulates too much money he starts feeling guilty. Now he has to do something to unburden his guilt so he gives to charities. This is just to console his conscience.

It happened...

Andrew Carnegie had donated to many libraries, to many colleges, to many universities, medical colleges, and a thousand and one institutions. When he was dying – he was one of those robberbarons – he inquired of his secretary, "How much have I donated in my whole life?" He had donated millions of dollars. The secretary rushed to the treasurer and inquired. It was a big list. He listened; the total was millions and millions of dollars. He was surprised. He opened his eyes, he suddenly became very much alive, and he said, "But from where, I wonder, could I get that much money, from where? Have I donated that much? But from where could I get that much money?"

You have got it from the same people to whom you donate. From one pocket you take, with the other hand you give to them. And of course you never give the whole, total amount, you just give a part of it. It is a trick. And this has not helped.

If you need a world without poverty, greed has to disappear. Charity is not going to help; it has not helped. Greed has to disappear, hoarding has to disappear. That's what I am trying to teach you. If you love life, you never become a hoarder. Life is so beautiful, who bothers about tomorrow? That's why I go on repeating again and again: live in the moment, then there will be no beggars. But you live in the future – then there are going to be beggars. You accumulate for the future; then certainly it cannot be available to all who are alive right now.

The earth is enough for the people who are alive. If nobody gathers for the future, hoards for the future, thinks of the future, everybody will be happy, and everybody will have enough. But you think about the future. You are not happy right now, you think, "Tomorrow I will be happy." So you sacrifice your present, and you sacrifice somebody else's present too, to hoard for the future.

The beggar on the street is not the problem; the beggar on the street is simply a symptom. Your greed is the problem. You can give something to the beggar, I am not saying don't give; it will give you a consolation that you have done something. You give to the beggar, and the beggar is in the same boat: he is also hoarding. He may not be as beggarly as he looks – because I know about beggars who have bank balances – it may just be his profession, so he has to be beggarly. He has to show that he is dying because you have become so hard: unless somebody is dying, you will not melt. He has to sit there, shivering in the cold. He can afford a blanket, he has enough money; but he cannot afford to, because if he has the blanket you will not feel sorry, you will not feel guilty. His shivering gives you a shivering. He has to pretend.

I used to know a student; he was my student in the university.

I inquired of him, "Where do you live?"

He said, "Don't ask, sir." I insisted, so he said, "I have never told anyone, because my father has told me not to say it to anyone. But I can say it to you. Please don't tell anybody."

I said, "What is the matter?"

He said, "My father is a beggar. You must have seen him; he begs at the railway station."

I said, "He is your father?"

"He's my father. And he has enough money... But I cannot say it to anybody, otherwise his prestige as a beggar will be at stake."

And this boy used to always live like a rich man. And I knew that beggar, because I was continually traveling, every day I was coming and going from the station. And I was one of the persons whom he was cheating; he would always take something from me. Coming or going, I had to give something to him, he would not leave me. I said, "Okay, next time I will see."

So next time I went, he came running: "I am dying, and my wife is very ill and in the hospital."

I said, "And what about your son?"

He said, "What son?"

I said, "He is my student."

He said, "Sir, please don't say it to anybody, and I will never bug you again!"

If you want to help, help. But remember, that is not my cup of tea. It is your trip, and please, don't try to lay your trips on me. If you want to help beggars, help them. Help to the very extent that you become a beggar; then others will help you. This is how things have been going on.

Because charity has not helped, communism came in, and communism has not helped either. It has not made anybody rich; it has simply made the rich poor. The poor remain the poor; only the rich have disappeared. But now there is no comparison. That's why the Soviet Russians don't allow their citizens to go and see America – that is dangerous, because the American poor are far richer than the Russian rich. It is dangerous. In Russia, the rich man has disappeared; all are poor. Equality has been established because all are poor. Nobody is rich, true, but the poverty has not changed and the greed has not changed – now the state has become greedy. Now the state plans for the future. Seventy percent of their budget goes to war preparation. The country remains hungry: people don't have shoes, people don't have clothes, but seventy percent of the budget goes to war preparations for the future, for some Third World War. This is communism.

Communism has failed. It has failed more than the old ways of charity because it has created a new class. The rich man is not there, but the bureaucrat is. The bourgeoisie has disappeared, but the bureaucracy has come in. Now the rich man is not there; the Communist Party member is the elite now. And the same oppression continues in a far stronger way. Never before on the earth has there been such slavery as exists in Russia and China.

"So what to do?" you ask. My suggestion is: don't think that you can prevent the Third World War, don't think you can change poverty. You can change only yourself. Drop your greed, drop your future, drop your mind; become more loving, become more heartful and live from the heart. And if many people start living that way, that is the only way to change the world. The world cannot be changed directly because there is no soul to the world. The soul exists in the individual; only individuals can be changed.

If you remain a hoarder – greedy, violent, repressed – this society will continue. You can give money to the beggar and he will remain a beggar, because money never changes anything. I have seen millionaires, and they are still beggars, so miserly that whatsoever they have makes no difference.

I have heard...

Two Jewish refugees passed the home of John D. Rockefeller. "If I only had that man's millions," sighed one of them, "I would be richer than he is."

"That does not make sense," the other reminded him. "If you had Mr. Rockefeller's millions, you would be just as rich as he, not richer."

"You are wrong," the first assured him. "Don't forget that I could give Hebrew lessons on the side."

Now a beggar remains a beggar, he will give Hebrew lessons on the side, even if he has all the money of a John D. Rockefeller. People don't change. Money never changes anything. If *you* change, that is an altogether different thing. I am not saying don't have compassion; I am saying have compassion, but don't think that by your compassion the world is going to change. Don't hope for that.

Give whatsoever you can give, share whatsoever you can share, but share only out of love. Don't think in terms of politics, of changing the world, otherwise you will be frustrated. Forget all about it. Do whatsoever you feel like doing. If you meet a beggar and you have a feeling arising in you, do something, whatsoever you feel like doing. I am not saying don't do anything; I am simply saying don't hope that you are changing the world. Nothing is being changed.

The only way to change the world is to change the level of consciousness, and that you can do only in yourself. It cannot be done to anybody else from the outside. Yes, if you change your level of consciousness, you create vibes which change people, which change people without their knowledge.

A different milieu is needed in the world – not a different society but a different milieu. A different spiritual vibe is needed. That's why I am not directly interested. I don't want to make you social servants, missionaries and things like that. I want you to be absolutely selfish.

First try to know who you are: this is the first principle of selfishness. First try to love: this is the second principle of selfishness. Love yourself, so that you can love others. And the third principle of selfishness: live the moment delightfully, celebrating – and then something will start happening through you. You will become a triggering-point; a world process starts.

Whenever a buddha happens, a world process starts. Become a buddha, awakened; that's all that you can do.

The last question – it is from Swami Yoga Chinmaya.

Osho,
As Kabir is singing the path of love, excuse me asking a personal question. I could not resist the temptation, so when did you have your last girlfriend, and the last love relationship?

And he has disappeared; I cannot see him here. Whenever he asks a question, he hides. Just the other day he was sitting in the first row, now he has disappeared.

You are all my girlfriends, boys included. But this will not satisfy him; he needs something esoteric. So for him especially – please, nobody else should listen to it, close your ears. It is especially for Swami Yoga Chinmaya only, because an esoteric thing has to be very secret.

I had a girlfriend when I was young. Then she died. But on her deathbed she promised me she would come back and I was afraid... And she has come back. The name of the girlfriend was Shashi. She died in '47. She was the daughter of a certain doctor, Dr. Sharma, of my village. He is also dead now. And now she has come as Vivek, to take care of me. Vivek cannot remember it. I used to call Shashi "Gudiya," and I have started calling Vivek "Gudiya" also, just to give continuity.

Life is a great drama, a great play; it goes on from one life to another to another.

This is especially for Chinmaya – I hope nobody else has heard it.

And the really, really last one:

Osho,
I have heard that when you walk your feet don't touch the ground.
Have you something to say about it?

That's true. When I walk, my feet don't touch the ground – but there is nothing miraculous about it. They don't touch the ground because I always wear shoes.

If it does not satisfy you – because you would like your master to be a great miracle maker – then just to satisfy you, I would like to say that those shoes are of awareness, and if you also wear the shoes of awareness, your feet will not touch the ground. It is simple, it is not miraculous.

And you have asked, "Have you something to say about it?" That is dangerous. The time is over. I have nothing to say about it, but if I have to say, it takes ninety minutes; and the time is over, and my bladder is full, and I would like to go to the bathroom. Excuse me.

Enough for today.

CHAPTER 3

home is not far away

There is nothing but water at the holy bathing places; and I know that they are useless, for I have bathed in them.
The images are all lifeless, they cannot speak; I know, for I have cried aloud to them.
The Purana and the Koran are mere words; lifting up the curtain, I have seen.
Kabir gives utterance to the words of experience; and he knows very well that all other things are untrue.

I laugh when I hear that the fish in the water is thirsty: you do not see that the real is in your home, and you wander from forest to forest listlessly!
Here is the truth! Go where you will, to Banaras or to Mathura; if you do not find your soul, the world is unreal to you.

Man's quest for the truth is eternal. It is a long pilgrimage without any beginning. Though it comes to an end, it has no beginning. We have been searching and searching and searching; our search has continued through the centuries, sometimes in one form, sometimes in another form. Even those who don't seem to be consciously searching for truth, they too are searching. Man's very being is a search for the truth.

That is the agony of man – and the glory too. No other animal is in search, all other animals are contented as they are. The dog is a dog, and he is not trying to become anything else, there is no becoming. The dog is perfectly satisfied; he's at ease. There is no pilgrimage, he is not going anywhere, there is no future. And so it is the case with every other animal.

Man is a strange animal, very odd, and the strangeness is that he is never satisfied; discontent is his very soul. He is moving; he is dynamic, he is not static. He is a flow, a river searching for the ocean – sometimes knowingly, sometimes not so knowingly, but the search continues. It is in the very being of man to be a seeker, to be a searcher; man cannot be otherwise.

Friedrich Nietzsche has said that man is a rope stretched between two eternities, the eternity of nature and the eternity of God. Man is a bridge. You cannot rest while you are a man, you have to go on. For a while you may rest, but rest cannot become your life; you have to go on – because man is not a being, man is a process.

The dog has a being, and the rock also has a being, but man has no being yet; the being has to come, the being has to flower, the being has to be achieved. Man is very paradoxical: he is, and yet he is not. That is the tension, the anguish, the anxiety: how to be?

A constant abyss surrounds humanity. Man is always facing the bottomless abyss and always afraid of not being, because he is not yet. Man is a promise: he can be, but he is not yet – so there is hope and there is fear, there is possibility and there is apprehension. It may happen, it may not happen, so man is never in certainty.

This whole search for truth can be divided into four stages. And I would like you to ponder over these four stages, because you will be somewhere in these four stages: either in some stage, or passing from one stage to another.

The first stage I call the jungle; the second I call the forest; the third I call the garden; the fourth I call the home.

The jungle: it is the state of deep sleep – man is not consciously searching. The majority live in this state: the search is there but very unconscious, not deliberate yet, groping in the dark but not exactly aware what for, or not even aware that one is groping, very accidental. Sometimes one may come across a window and have a vision, but again that misses. Because one is not consciously searching, one cannot hold these visions. Sometimes in your dream something dawns on you. Sometimes in your love a door opens and closes, but you don't know how it opened and how it closed again. Sometimes, looking at a beautiful sunset, something tremendously beautiful surrounds you: the other world has penetrated you – or at least has touched you, and then it has gone. And you cannot even trust that it was there, you cannot even believe that it happened because you were not consciously searching.

Many times you come across God, mind you. Many times you come across God, you meet him in many points of your life, but you cannot recognize him because in the first place you are not looking for him. And remember, unless you look for a thing you cannot see it. You can see it only when you are looking for it. It may pass by your side, but if you are not looking for it you will not see it. To see something one has to look for it.

The first state is like a jungle: deep, dark, dense, primitive, primordial. No path exists, not even a footpath, and man is not going anywhere: goes on stumbling from one dark corner to another. The majority of humanity lives in the jungle, in the unconscious state of the mind. People are asleep, they are sleepwalkers, they are somnambulists.

That is the teaching of Buddha, Christ, Gurdjieff, Kabir: the majority lives not – only exists, vegetates. You seem as if you are alert; you are not. You live in a dense fog, clouded. Your life is mechanical. Yes, things happen, but they happen just as things happen to a mechanism: you push the button and the light goes on, just like that; you push the button and the mechanism starts functioning, just like that. Somebody pushes a button in you and anger comes; somebody pushes another button in you and you are very happy; somebody else pushes some other button and some other mood surrounds you – and there is not even a single moment's gap between the pushing of the button and the mood arising. It is mecha-nical. You are not a master, you are a slave.

Gurdjieff used to say that man is like a chariot: the driver is drunk, the master is fast asleep inside the chariot, the horses are unruly and wherever they want, they go. All four horses are going in four directions. Any passerby can just jump on the chariot, take hold of it, lead it; the driver is drunk and the master is fast asleep.

And this is the state of your life: your innermost core is fast asleep and your awareness is drunk. Your body is a chariot, and any whim, any desire that enters you, drives you for the time being, takes you somewhere, leaves you there, and then another whim, another desire... And in this zigzag way you go on, stumbling into this rock, stumbling into that tree. In darkness, you go on hurting yourself, wounding yourself. Your whole life is nothing but a deep nightmare.

Try to understand other characteristics of this state. First, it corresponds to what Carl Gustav Jung calls the collective unconscious, and also to what Sigmund Freud calls the unconscious. It is the lowest state of consciousness. In this state no search is possible because you never take hold of your life in your hands, you remain at the mercy of accidents.

There are a few people who have come to me not searching, just accidentally; a friend was coming and they thought, "Okay, let us go and see what is there." They were looking in a bookstore and they came across one of my books and my picture attracted them; or they liked the title of the book and they became curious, and they have come here. But this search is very, very unconscious. You are not thinking, meditating about your life, about how it should be, what it should be, where it should go.

And each desire, when it takes possession of you, becomes your master. When you are angry, anger becomes your master, takes complete possession of you. It is not that you are angry; you become anger, and you do something in your anger for which you will repent. And this is the irony: one "I" will repent for the act of some other "I." The anger did something, harmed somebody, and then the anger was gone. Now you know you have done something wrong. This is another "I," another desire, another state, another mood. Now you will suffer, and you will go and you would like to ask to be forgiven. This is somebody else; it is not the same person. Where are those red eyes, that violent face, that readiness to kill or be killed? They have all gone.

Once a man spat on Buddha. He was very angry – he must have been; otherwise it is very difficult to spit on a buddha, it looks almost impossible. How could he do it? But he must have been very angry, in a rage.

Buddha wiped it with his shawl and asked the man, "Have you anything more to say to me?"

The man was embarrassed; he could not say a single word. He went away. The whole night he could not sleep. In the morning he came; he fell at Buddha's feet and he said, "Please forgive me. It was sheer stupidity, I was mad."

Buddha said, "*You* were not; that's why you could do it. You were not – so don't feel worried. You were absolutely unconscious, so you are not responsible. So don't repent! That was some other person who had come and spat on me, you are somebody totally different. That man was in a rage, he was mad. You are sane, you are touching my feet. No, no, you are so different that I cannot make a connection."

Man is a crowd in the state of the jungle. Many people live in you, disconnected, fragmentary; you don't have a soul. That's why Gurdjieff used to say a very meaningful thing: that man is not born with a soul. Man is born with many selves, but not with a soul. When all these selves melt into one, integrate into one; when all these selves are changed chemically and become one unity, then you have a soul. When all these selves drop into the ocean and their separateness has disappeared and oneness arises, then you have a soul. No one has a soul; by your birth you have not got a soul – very significant, very meaningful. One has to *become* a soul; one has to integrate this crowd inside you, these selves fighting with each other.

At this stage, the stage of the jungle, people are more interested in answers than in questioning. They are immediately satisfied with any stupid answer given to them. In fact, they have never asked the question. Even before asking, they have taken the answer. That's how somebody has become a Hindu and somebody a Mohammedan and somebody a Christian: before you had ever asked the question the answer was given to you, and you have been clinging to the answer. What do you mean when you say, "I am a Jew" – or a Mohammedan or a Hindu or a Jaina? What do you mean? Have you asked the question, or have you just borrowed the answers? Without asking the question you have believed in Christ, in Buddha, in Krishna, in Mohammed? This is sheer stupidity. How can you get to the answer when you have not even asked, you have not inquired?

In the state of the jungle, people believe in answers without asking. Questioning is arduous, questioning is difficult. Just to believe in borrowed answers is comfortable, convenient. To question, one has to suffer; to question, one has to travel; to question, one has to go within oneself. You just take the answer; you just borrow it.

At this stage people are very knowledgeable: the pundits, the priests. They themselves live in a dark, dense forest, and they go on leading others also toward denser, darker jungles. In this state, the jungle, people are very worldly, although they pretend to be religious. They pretend: they go to church, they go to the temple, the mosque, the *gurudwara,* but it is all formal, they don't mean it. They pay lip service to God, but they don't mean it. It is more of a security measure – maybe God is; it is a "perhaps," and more of a social formality. It is good to appear to be religious.

The Sunday religion is very good; it gives you respectability. These people are not seekers. And these people are very orthodox because they are afraid. They know that their knowledge is false, borrowed, cheap, so they are very afraid. If somebody says anything against them, they immediately pound on him: "You are creating doubt." They don't want any skepticism, they don't want any doubt; they don't want any questions. They want to cling to the comfortable beliefs their parents have given to them – or the society, or the state. They don't want to be shaken. They live in a false world of words, ideologies.

This is the type of person you call straight – the square, the traditional, the conformist. He is past-oriented; he never looks to the future and he never looks in the present. He is past-oriented; the past was golden, the real days are gone. Those days existed when Jesus was walking on the earth, or when Buddha was walking on the earth, or when Krishna was playing his flute. His golden age is always in the past, his utopia is always in the past: "It has been; now we have fallen from it." He believes in a fallen state. He thinks that now there is no future – and he never looks at the future, he clings to the past. He is a dead man and he clings to dead beliefs, dead ideologies. His religion is not a movement, his religion is not dynamic; his religion is codified, organized, dead. His religion is a corpse. This type of person believes in the priest, in the bishop, in the pope, in the *shankaracharya.* This person never goes to seek anywhere else.

I have heard...

The parson of a tiny congregation in Arkansas rashly lit out one night with the entire church treasury, and the local constable set out to capture him. This he did, dragging the culprit back by the collar a week later: "Here is the varmint fox," announced the constable grimly. "I am sorry to say he has already squandered our money, but I drug him back so we can make him preach it out."

Now even this type of priest will do, because religion is just a formality. Even a thief can be forced to preach. Nobody bothers about the priest – his being, his consciousness. No, at the most, his training is needed: that he knows what he is doing. This type of mind, the jungle mind, is very ritualistic. The ritual is religion; the chanting of a mantra the priest has given to you is enough.

The priest himself has not arrived home, and he goes on giving the *guru mantra;* he goes on giving people their mantras, their keys. He goes on distributing keys and he has not yet opened his own door. He is as ignorant as the people he leads. But he has one thing: credit that comes from past centuries and centuries. A Hindu priest can say that for five thousand years his family has been priests; it has a market value, that's all. He has credit. The Hindu can say that the Vedas are the oldest scriptures in the world. Their being old is thought to be very valuable. In fact, the older a book, the more dead it is bound to be.

Religion is fresh, young – like a new leaf, or this morning's dew-drops on the grass leaves. Religion is born every moment; it has nothing to do with the past. A really religious person goes in search of some Buddha who is alive, of some Christ who is still living and breathing, goes to find a Mohammed to whom the Koran is still coming, to whom the Koran is still descending.

But the jungle type never goes anywhere; he clings to the priest, to the religion, to the church in which he was accidentally born. He remains there, he lives in it; he dies in it.

I have heard...

According to a Hollywood journal, a cinema adorable was in the process of getting married for the seventh or eighth time. The offici-ating clergyman, flustered by all the publicity and glamour, lost his place in the ritual book.

The star yawned and whispered, "Page eighty-four, stupid!"

Now even she knows – having got married seven, eight times, she knows which page. "Page eighty-four, stupid!" she says to the priest. This ritualistic religion is just mechanical. The priest knows because he repeats it every day. And you, by and by, become acquainted with it because you go on repeating it every day. It depends on repetition. It is not a revelation, it is not your acquaintance; it has nothing to do with you, it is absolutely disconnected with you. You are not born to it; it has not been born in you. It remains superficial.

I have heard...

An old maid died and her two friends went to have a gravestone made.

"Do you have a suitable epitaph?" asked the engraver.

"We thought: 'Born a virgin, lived a virgin, died a virgin' would be nice," answered the woman.

The engraver answered, "Why not save money? Just put: 'Returned unopened.'"

And that's what happens to the man who lives in the jungle state: he comes here, but never lives. Life is dangerous; he cannot afford it. Life is an adventure into the new; he clings to the old. Life is unknown and unknowable, and he does not want to risk his knowledge. He is returned unopened. He comes, he lives, he dies; but in fact he never comes, and he never lives, and he never dies. His whole existence is fast asleep. He has not yet claimed to be a man.

This type of person is what you call pigheaded. He always has the outlook of "holier than thou" – very moralistic. He thinks he is very moral; he does not know the *ABCD* of morality. But he clings to the social code, he never goes beyond it, he keeps to the rules. Not that he is moral; he clings to an immoral society, how can he be moral?

A moral man is bound to be unsocial; a moral man cannot be social – at least it has not been possible up to now. We can hope that some day, in some future world, the society will be so moral that the moral man may not need to become unsocial, but it has not been so up to now. Hitherto, it has always been so that whenever there is a moral man, he is unsocial.

A Jesus is unsocial, so is Buddha, so is Kabir. Why are real moral people unsocial? – because the society is immoral. If you adjust to the society, you become immoral. How can you adjust to a society which is immoral and remain moral? And the morality that is preached in the society is just hocus-pocus; it is bogus, it is just a show, it is not really moral. It pretends, and hidden deep behind it is all that is immoral.

Christians go on teaching to love your enemy – and they have fought more wars than anybody else, and they have killed many more people than anybody else. The whole history of Christianity is bloody. The very word *Islam* means peace – and Mohammedans have never been peaceful.

It seems simply unbelievable how we have tolerated all these things in the world – how we tolerate, how we are unable to see into them. The church has been one of the calamities, yet still it remains "the protector." It goes on making announcements about what man should do. But everything is put in such words that the man who lives in the jungle is deceived.

For example, now the world is becoming too crowded and abortion is moral, and to go on producing children is immoral, because the world will be more crowded, there will be more famine, more war, more poverty. You will be the cause of it. But the pope goes on saying that no Catholic is allowed to abort; it is a sin. The same is true about the Shankaracharya of the Hindus: he goes on saying, "No abortion."

Now to go on populating this world is going to be one of the most immoral things. This world is already too populated. And if you bring a child into this world, you are not only doing something wrong to the world, you are doing something wrong to your child too: you will be throwing him into a very miserable world. His future will be miserable. But the old ideology is never aware of the new reality. It goes on talking nonsense. Maybe those words were meaningful one day; they are no longer.

A real religion has to change with the time. And this type of man is too pigheaded; he never changes, he's not ready to change. He's very much against change, he's anti-revolutionary. This type of man is a fanatic and a fascist; he is ready to be violent any moment. And all his violence arises because he is not self-confident about himself, and not self-confident about his religion. His religion is not his own experience; how can he be self-confident? If you argue with him, he immediately brings the sword into the argument. His argument is that of the sword. This type of man is very irrational, but he talks as if he is very rational.

His rationalism is nothing but rationalization, it is not true reason.

Remember and watch: somewhere deep in your soul you must have this jungle. A few people have it more, a few less, but the difference is of quantity, of degree. This jungle is in every person. This is your unconscious, your dark night within. And from this dark night arise many instincts, impulses, obsessions, insanities, and they take possession of you. Your consciousness is very fragile; your unconscious is ninety-nine percent and your consciousness just one percent. You cannot depend on it. Watch it, and don't support the unconscious. Take your cooperation away, don't cooperate with it. When anything happens and your unconscious starts taking possession of your consciousness, become watchful, become alert.

For example, anger arises. It arises from the unconscious, the smoke comes from the unconscious; then it spreads to your consciousness and you are drunk with it. Then you can do something you would never have done in your senses. Wait! This is no time to say a single word or do anything. Close your door, sit silently, watch this anger arising and you will have found a key. If you watch this anger arising, you will see by and by the anger has subsided. It cannot remain forever; it has a certain amount of energy, a certain potentiality. When it is exhausted it goes back, and when it goes back and re-settles within yourself you will see a change, a qualitative change in your being. You have become more aware. The energy that was going to become anger and was going to be wasted and was going to be destructive has been used by your consciousness. And now the consciousness burns brighter – from the same energy.

This is the inner method of how to change the poison into nectar. When you are feeling very sexual... I am not against sex, but I am against sexuality. And let me make a distinction: when you are feeling very sexual and being possessed by the passion, this is not the moment to do anything. Close your doors, meditate on your sexuality. Let it arise; let it come out of the dark night within you, out of the jungle. Let it spread – watch, simply watch, become an unmoving flame of awareness. Soon you will see it has settled again and your consciousness is burning brighter than ever. You have absorbed it, it has become nectar.

I am not against sex; when you are feeling very prayerful, very loving, go into sex, nothing is wrong – but never be driven by passion. See the difference: when you are feeling loving, it is a totally different quality. When you are feeling happy, celebrating, and you would like to share your energy with somebody you love, go and make love. But this is not a moment of passion, this is a moment of tremendous warmth, a moment of love – share!

Have you noticed? – people almost always make love after they fight with their woman or with their man. That becomes a ritual. First they fight, they become angry, and then suddenly passion arises. Anger feeds the passion. There are people who will not feel passion unless they are beaten by their woman or by their man.

You must have heard about de Sade. He used to have all his instruments always with him in his bag – who knows where he will find a woman to love? And his instruments consisted of things with which to torture himself, or to torture the woman. But without torture, passion would not arise. When you are whipped, suddenly there is passion.

And there were women who said that once they loved de Sade they could not love anybody else – because first he would whip them and make their bodies hot, and they would become angry, and they would scream, and they would run around; he would whip them to passion and then he would make love. Of course, this is the way to move into the jungle.

And just on the other extreme was Masoch: he would whip himself, he would force the woman to whip him. Only when he was whipped – and he would scream and he would shout and he would become angry, and his face would become red with rage – then he would be potent; otherwise he would be impotent.

In a smaller measure you also do it, unconsciously. Couples fight, they argue, they nag, they create anger; then they make love and then go to sleep. This is moving into the jungle. This is sexuality, not natural sex.

Natural sex is more meditative. There is less fever – more warmth but less fever. Passion is a fever, a state of madness, insanity. Warmth is a state of love. If you can make love fully alert, your love processes will help you toward becoming more and more aware, more and more centered. You have to pull yourself out from the jungle.

The second state is the forest. It is almost like the jungle, with a slight difference: the forest has a few paths, footpaths – not super-highways, but footpaths. The jungle has not even a footpath. The jungle is very primitive. In the jungle, the human being has not yet entered, it is almost animal. In the forest, human beings have entered. A few footpaths are there, you can find a way.

The forest is like dreaming. The jungle was like sleep, the forest is like dreaming. It is like the subconscious: a twilight land, neither night nor day, just in the middle. Things are still foggy, but not dark. You can see a little, you can move a little, you can have a certain amount of awareness. This is the land of the starry-eyed, the hippie, the so-called religious searcher, the drug addict – trying to find any way, any means or shortcuts to somehow get out of the forest. This is the state where the search begins – in a very wavering way, but at least it begins. It is better than the jungle.

The hippie is better than the square, than the straight; at least he searches. Maybe sometimes he moves in the wrong direction. Searching for meditation, he becomes a drug addict – because the drug can give a certain similarity, a certain similar experience – but at least he searches, at least he is moving. He may commit errors, but he is moving. The man in the jungle is not moving at all; he may not commit errors, but he is not moving. And not to move is the greatest error one can commit. Move! Life is trial and error, and one has to learn through errors.

Many paths open in this second stage – in fact too many, and one becomes confused. It is very chaotic. The jungle is very settled, everything is clear. Though it is dark, belief is clear: somebody is a Hindu and somebody is a Mohammedan and somebody is a Christian, and things are clear. The Christian goes to his priest, the Hindu goes to his priest, the Mohammedan goes to his. They have their Bible, their Koran, their Vedas, everything is clear. It is dark but things are clear, people are not confused. People are dead, but not confused. With life, confusion and chaos arise. But out of chaos stars are born.

In the second type come the poets, the painters, the artists, the musicians, the dancers. They are the revolutionaries. The first type is orthodox, the second type is revolutionary. The first type is traditional, the second is utopian. The first is past-oriented; the second is future-oriented. For the first the golden age has passed, for the second it has to come. He looks ahead.

He is just like The Fool in the Tarot cards: he looks ahead into the sky. He is standing on a cliff, one foot hanging in the abyss – but he is so happy. He does not look down, he's looking at the sky, at the stars far away. He is full of dreams. He is near his death, but he is full of dreams. It is dangerous.

But if you ask me what to choose, I will say choose the second. Be the fool, never be the pundit. It is better to be a fool and risk, than never to risk and remain satisfied with bogus, borrowed knowledge. The second is a fool. For the second stage I have a special name: I call it "California-land." Yes, it is the California of the human soul, where a great supermarket, a spiritual supermarket, exists: all sorts of techniques and all sorts of guides and maps.

This is the moment when one starts looking. A man is not satisfied with the church he was born into; he starts moving and tries alien ways, strange ways. This is the moment when a person becomes a student and searches for a teacher. Still the search has not gone very deep, but it has started. The seed has sprouted. One will still have to go very far. One has to go far, but now a possibility exists.

The first type is dead; the second type is too alive, dangerously alive. The first type is at one extreme, the second has moved to another extreme. In the second also there is no balance; the balance will come in the third stage. The first clings to the dead letter, and the second clings to nothing, belongs to nowhere, goes on moving, is a wanderer. The first is a householder, the second is a wanderer. But the second is like a rolling stone: he gathers no moss. He never comes to his own center; he goes on moving from one teacher to another, from one book to another.

The first simply believes in *his* book, and the second becomes available to all the books of the world. He reads the Bible and he reads the Koran and he reads the Gita – and becomes confused and becomes muddle-headed, and he cannot figure out what is what.

The first is very articulate, the second becomes less articulate. Have you talked to a hippie? It is very difficult to figure out what he is saying. And when he does not know what he is saying, he says, "You know?" He does not know himself, and he asks you, "You know, you see?" And he is not seeing anything himself. Rather than expressing in words, he starts expressing in sounds. He starts using sounds, baby sounds; he becomes less articulate.

The first is very rationalized, lives in the head. The second is moving toward the heart, becomes more of the feeling type. The first is not aware, but thinks that his thinking is his awareness. The second has not yet reached the source of feeling, and thinks emotionalism, sentimentalism, is feeling.

The hippie can cry, can laugh; he's eccentric, crazy, but better than the first. The first is political, the second is nonpolitical. The first believes in war, the second starts trusting in peace. The first accumulates things; the second starts loving persons. That's beautiful. The first believes in marriage, the second believes in love. The first lives a sheltered life, the second does not know where he will be tomorrow.

But good – things have started moving. They can move in a wrong direction, true, but they can move in a right direction too. Movement is good; now the right direction is needed. One thing has happened, now the direction will be needed.

The first is very worldly, believes in the bank balance and the life insurance; the first is very greedy for power, money. The second does not believe in security; he trusts life more than life insurance. He believes in love more than in the security you can have in a bank balance. He is not money-minded, he does not hoard. He is not moral in the sense that the first is moral, but he starts having a new sort of morality – a revolutionary morality, a personal morality. The first type's morality is social, the second type's morality is personal; the first type's morality depends on conditioning, the second type's morality depends on conscience. He looks around, and whatsoever he feels to do, he does it. He does his own thing, he is individual.

The first is collective, the unconscious is collective; the subconscious is individual. Have you seen? – when you dream, you dream alone. You cannot share it with anybody; it is individual, personal. You cannot even invite your woman to see your dream. She may be sleeping just by your side in the same bed, but you dream your dream, she dreams her dream – everybody is doing his own thing. That's why I call this state the state of subconscious, the dreaming state.

The first is not interested in the questions or in the question; he is interested in the answer. The Hindu has answers: the Hindu answer; the Jaina has the answer: the Jaina answer, and so on and so forth. The second is still not interested in the question, but he has too many answers. The first has only one answer, the second has too many answers. Still the question has not become the most important thing, the answer still is, but now, too many. This is good, this is a relaxing. The second cannot be pigheaded. He cannot deny outright and say, "The Bible is wrong because I am a Hindu." He cannot declare outright that the Gita must be wrong, "Because I am a Christian." No, he becomes more human, he becomes more universal. He has looked into the Gita and into the Bible, and he has seen glimpses of truth everywhere. He has too many answers.

The first is dogmatic, theological; the second is philosophical. And the third is the garden, the third stage.

The garden is the state of awakening: one is awake. First is sleep, the second is dream, the third is awake. Hindus call the first *sushupti*, the second *swapna*, the third *jagrati*. Now he is conscious, aware; the day has dawned. Books, guides, teachers, have become irrelevant; he has found the master.

The first believes in the priest. The second does not know where to go: he has no compass, he has lost all direction, he goes to anybody. You can train a dog and call him "guru maharaj-ji," and he will go. Just propagate and you will see that the dog has found followers. The second can go to any guru maharaj-ji; he is ready to fall at anybody's feet, he is *too* ready. The first is never ready, the second is too ready. For the first, there is no question of falling at anybody else's feet other than his own priest's. To the second, everybody seems to be the priest. His eyes are very wavering. He can go to anybody, to whosoever claims, to whosoever can shout loudly, "Yes, I am going to be your guide. I am the guide; I am the world teacher. I am this and that." Whosoever claims, he will be ready to fall at his feet.

But the third is no longer interested in teachers; he is not a student. He is interested in personal contact – he is interested in a master, he wants to become a disciple. He is not bothered what the master says, he is more interested in the vibe that the master creates around him. He is not interested in his doctrines, in his philosophy; he is interested in his being.

When you become interested in being, and when you look directly into a person's innermost core, when you start feeling the presence, only then can you become a disciple. You are not in search of any philosophical answer; now the question has become important: "Who am I?" The second is ready to learn, the first is not ready to learn, the third is ready to unlearn.

Let me repeat: the first is not ready to learn – he is stubborn, he thinks he already knows. The second is ready to learn from anywhere, and then he learns too many things – contradictory, foolish, good, bad – and he becomes confused. The third is ready to unlearn. He is not searching for knowledge. He says, "I am in search of a person who has arrived. And I will not listen to whether what he says is argumentatively true, philosophically true. I would like to have an intimate relationship."

The relationship between a teacher and a student is not personal. The relationship between a master and a disciple is personal; it is a love affair. One has to feel, one has to be in the presence of the master, one has to watch. One has not to bring one's mind in; one has to put the mind aside, and one has to look directly, and feel.

One Zen master used to say, "When I reached my master, for three years I was sitting by his side, and he would not even look at me. Then after three years he looked at me, and that was a great joy. Then three years again passed, and one day he laughed at me, smiled, and it was a benediction. Then three years again passed, and one day he patted me on my head, and it was tremendous, it was incredible. Then three years again passed, and one day he embraced me, and I disappeared and he disappeared; there was unity."

To find a master is to find the closest point from where godliness is available, the closest door from where godliness is available: somebody who has arrived. But how will you decide? You will have to feel; thinking won't be of any help. Thinking will mislead you. You will have to feel, you will have to be patient, you will have to be in his presence, you will have to taste, you will have to become drunk with his presence. And by and by, things will become clear. As your mind subsides, things will become clear. Either he is the master or he is not – and it will be a revelation. If he is, then you can drown yourself totally. If he is not, then you have to move. In both ways, you will have come to a conclusion. Sometimes it happens that you may feel he is the master, but not for you. Then too you have to move because a master can help only if you and he fit together, if you are meant to be together, if you are meant for each other.

So sometimes it happens there may be a great master... Buddha and Mahavira both lived at the same time; they were contemporaries. And disciples would come to Buddha, and they would sit with Buddha for years. Then one day suddenly the disciple would be gone. And the same would happen to Mahavira: a few disciples would come to him, would be with him, and one day they were gone and would start following Buddha.

Now Buddhists and Jainas have been arguing for centuries why it happened. Jainas will say that it happened because Mahavira was the true master, so many people came from Buddha; they never refer to the disciples who moved from Mahavira to Buddha. And the Buddhists always talk about the disciples who came from Mahavira to Buddha, and they forget to talk about the disciples who went from Buddha to Mahavira.

Disciples had moved, that's true, and from both sides – and the reason is not that Mahavira was not true or Buddha was not true. The reason is: sometimes you fit with a master, sometimes you don't fit. The disciples who moved away from Buddha touched his feet, thanked him – because this experience too had happened in his presence, that they were not meant for each other. And they were grateful for their whole life toward Buddha. They moved to Mahavira, they attained to their realization in the presence of Mahavira, but they were grateful to Buddha too.

At this stage – the garden – a totally different perspective opens. This is the point where the question, "Who am I?" becomes important, and you don't ask for the answer, you are not ready to accept any answer from without. And the master is not going to give you any answer. In fact, he is going to destroy all your answers. That's what I am doing here. I am destroying all your answers.

If you are a Hindu, I am shattering Hinduism; if you are a Mohammedan, I am shattering Mohammedanism; if you are a Christian, I am shattering Christianity. That's what I am doing, I am taking away all your answers, so you are left alone with your question, pure with your question, virgin with your question. When your question is left there and there is no answer from the outside, you start falling into yourself. The question penetrates like an arrow to the very source of your being – and there is the answer. And that answer is not verbal, it is not a theory that you come across, it is a realization. You explode. You simply know. It is not knowledge; you *know*. It is experience, it is existential.

The first person is dogmatic, sectarian. The second person is philosophic. The third person is religious, existential. And then the fourth state is the home.

Hindus call it *turiya*, the fourth state. At the fourth state you have arrived; you have arrived at the very core of your being, the home: enlightenment, *samadhi*, satori, nirvana. You have come to the point where the master and the disciple disappear, where the devotee and God disappear, where the seeker and the sought disappear, where all duality disappears. You have transcended the two, you have come to one.

This is the place we all have been seeking. And the beauty of it is that it is already there. When you arrive home, you will know that one has arrived where one has always been. Looking backward from the home you will laugh. You will see the jungle was not out there, it was your own unconsciousness; the forest was not out there, it was your own dreaming faculty; the garden was not out there, it was your own awareness.

And the home is your own being, *sat chit anand*. It is you, your innermost nature, *swabhava*, Tao – or call it whatsoever name you like to call it. It is nameless.

These are the four states, and I talked about them in such detail because it will help you to understand these sutras, and other sutras that are going to follow.

Now the sutras:

There is nothing but water at the holy bathing places; and I know that they are useless, for I have bathed in them.

Kabir is talking about the jungle. *There is nothing but water at the holy bathing places; and I know that they are useless, for I have bathed in them.*

One is not purified by taking a bath in the Ganges. It is stupid; the very idea is stupid because your impurity is not of the physical, your impurity is not like dust on your body. Yes, that much the Ganges can do: it can clean your body, it can give you a bodily cleanliness, freshness. But the problem is not there, so the solution cannot be there. The dust is deeper; no Ganges can take it away.

And Kabir says: *...for I have bathed in them.* Kabir says: I have been in the jungle – the jungle of the rituals, dogmas, scriptures, priests, temples, mosques, Sunday religions. I have been there; it is useless.

The images are all lifeless, they cannot speak; I know, for I have cried aloud to them.

And Kabir says: I have been worshipping the images in the

temples – they are dead, they cannot help. *I have cried aloud to them* and they have never answered. They are man-made, and man-made gods won't do. Man cannot create God; God has created man. How can you create God? All symbols are dangerous because there is a possibility you may start thinking of the symbol as the real.

The symbol is not the real. No image represents God, no word represents truth. The word *God* is not God; of course, the word *fire* is not fire. And you cannot eat a menu and be satisfied. The menu is not food.

Remember, all symbols are menu-like, and many people are feeding on menus and suffering and starving, and they wonder why they are suffering. The images, the scriptures, the theoretical formulations – all symbols are useless.

The images are all lifeless, they cannot speak; I know, for I have cried aloud to them.
The Purana and the Koran are mere words; lifting up the curtain, I have seen.

And even books won't help: the Koran and the Purana won't help, the scriptures of the Hindus and the Mohammedans and the Christians and the Jews won't help. Kabir says: ...*lifting up the curtain, I have seen.* I have lifted the curtain of the word and the verbal and the philosophical, and I have come to see the truth has no connection with words; truth is wordless, truth is beyond words. The truth cannot be reduced to a theory; it is vast, and theories are all very narrow. The truth is the whole – how can any theory contain it? Theories are like small boxes, and the truth is like the whole sky – how can these small boxes contain it?

...lifting up the curtain, I have seen.
Kabir gives utterance to the words of experience; and he knows very well that all other things are untrue.

And Kabir says: don't listen to anything else other than your own experience. Only existential experience can reveal the truth to you. The beauty, the good, the truth, all have to be experienced, and experienced by you. Buddha may have experienced but that has nothing to do with you: his experience cannot be your experience.

Jesus has known, but that has nothing to do with you: his experience is his, and untransferable.

I have seen, I have known, and I would like you to share it. I would like it to be given to you – but it is not possible. You cannot see through my eyes, and you cannot feel through my heart, and whatsoever I say will become only a symbol to you. Unless my saying makes you thirstier – not for more words but for your own experience – unless you start looking for experience yourself, you will never arrive home.

And home is not far away. In fact, the farthest is the jungle – closer than the jungle is the forest; closer than the forest is the garden of the master; and just inside the garden, just in the center of the garden, is your home. Your home is the closest point to you – it has to be so. It is your being.

I laugh, says Kabir, *pani vich min piyasi:*

I laugh when I hear that the fish in the water is thirsty...

And Kabir says: looking at you and seeing that you are thirsty, I laugh. I laugh because I cannot believe how this ridiculous thing has happened – that the fish is thirsty in the water. You are thirsty, in the water? You are homeless, and the home is within you! And you are seeking elsewhere, that which you are always carrying within you? You are pregnant with truth, and you are rushing here and there, hither and thither.

I laugh when I hear that the fish in the water is thirsty; you do not
see that the real is in your home, and you wander from forest to
forest listlessly!
Here is the truth!

Now is the truth! *You* are the truth! Truth is your very being.

Go where you will, to Banaras or to Mathura; if you do not find
your soul, the world is unreal to you.

You live in a world of illusion because you have not yet even touched your own reality. Become real, and from that moment the whole world becomes real to you; because you are unreal, the whole world is created on your unreality, it is founded on your unreality.

The man in the jungle lives in sleep; his world is of sleep. The man in the forest lives in dreams; his world is that of dreams. The man of the garden lives in awareness, he is coming closer and closer, becoming more and more aware of the home. He is at the door.

A knock, and the door shall be opened unto you.

That's what Jesus says: "Knock, and the door shall be opened unto you. Ask, and it shall be given. Seek, and you will find."

The third man has come into the garden; now he can see the home, but still he is not in the home. When you come into the home, it is neither *sushupti*: sleep, nor dream: *swabhana*, nor *jagrati*: awareness. It is super-consciousness, or cosmic consciousness. All those three stages have been transcended. You have come beyond.

This is the state of godliness, *bhagwan*, Allah. When al-Hillaj Mansoor said, "I am the Truth," he was in this state. When Jesus declared, "I and my God, my Father, are one," he was in this state. When Upanishadic seers declared, "*Aham brahmasmi*, I am the whole," they were in this state.

The bhagwan is within you, the godliness is within you, the kingdom of God is within you. Now it is up to you to seek, search, discover it. It is not a question of inventing anything, you have it already; you have just to uncover. "Lifting the veil," says Kabir, "I have seen the truth."

I have seen the truth that cannot be expressed; I have seen the truth that is ineffable. Here, I am teaching you nothing other than your own being, I am bringing you closer to nothing other than your own being. I am throwing you back to yourself. You are missing nothing; you have only forgotten the treasure that is within you, you have forgotten the ways how to look withinward. Again, The Fool in the Tarot cards...

If you have looked meditatively at the Tarot card... And they are cards to be meditated upon; they are old secret methods of meditation. The Fool is standing on the cliff, one foot dangling, hanging over the cliff – and he is not aware, he is looking at the stars and he is very happy. His head must be full of dreams. He is carrying four sacred symbols on his back, and he is not aware what they are. He is not even aware that he is carrying four secret symbols on his back. These are the four secret symbols: the jungle, the forest, the garden, the home.

Now it is up to you. If you turn... A 180-degree turn will be needed. That's what conversion is, that's what sannyas is all about. If you turn, you will simply see that you have never lost for a single moment the bliss of all bliss, the delight of all delights. You have never left your home; you were only thinking that you had gone far away.

You are in the home; you never left it. When this is discovered, one becomes a Buddha, one becomes a Christ, one becomes a Krishna. This is your destiny. And unless you attain it, you will never be at ease. Unless you attain it, you will never have rest. A human being has to be restless. A human being is a bridge; he is not a being yet, he is a promise.

Enough for today.

religion is individual flowering

The first question:

Osho,
Why do you refer to God as "he"? The is-ness, the life energy, the totality, the unknowable... Well, wouldn't it be clearer to call God "it"? What bugs me about the "he" is that "he" implies a personality, a will, a judgmental authority, and my ability to love is crippled enough without that obstacle. I see now that the question is an entry to my problem: how can I trust or come to love your authority?

God is not expressible in any word whatever. Call him "he" and the word falls short; call him "she" and the word falls short; call him "it" and the word falls short, very short. If *he* reminds you of a personality, *it* will remind you of a thing. If *he* reminds you of the male, *she* will remind you of the female. All words are created by human beings for human use, and God is not a human creation, so whatsoever you call him is going to be only symbolic.

Choose any symbol you like: if you feel like calling him "it," call him "it." But remember, *it* has its own limitations. *It* is used for

things, for dead things. And it has another limitation: *it* is very neutral. *It* is not responsive; if you say something to it there will be no
response. Only a person can respond, and love needs response. You
can talk to a wall, but there will be no response; it will be a monologue. God is called he so that your prayer can become a dialogue.
Otherwise it will be a monologue – and mad. The it cannot answer it,
the it cannot be responsive, the it cannot care about you. The it is
neutral. Whether you pray or not makes no difference; whether you
worship or not makes no difference; whether you are or not makes
no difference – the it will be very stony. If *he* is creating trouble, *it*
will create more trouble, mind you. How can you love the it? You
can possess the it, you can use the it – but how can you love it?

In that way, "he" seems to be the best, for many reasons. Let me
explain it to you. First, it gives a personality to God: God becomes a
person – alive, with a beating heart, breathing, pulsating. You can call
him, and you can trust that there will be a response. You can look at
him, you can feel him, and you can trust that he will also feel for you.
The personality helps you to commune, to pray, to relate. If God has
no personality it will be so beyond you, it will be inconceivable. You
are a person; you need a God who is a person too, because you can
relate only to a person. Unless you have become an impersonal
being, you cannot relate to an impersonal being.

Religions have existed, particularly in the East – Buddhism,
Jainism – which don't talk about God at all. But then they cannot talk
about prayer and they cannot talk about love. The moment they drop
the idea of God, of a personal God, of a creator, of somebody there
who can look at you, hold your hand, embrace you; the moment
they drop the idea of a personal God, they have to drop the idea
of prayer as a corollary, as a necessary corollary. Worship has to
be dropped, prayer has to be dropped, singing, dancing have to be
dropped. For whom do you sing, and for whom do you dance? There
is nobody, only stony eyes all around.

And existence is so vast. You say, "Why not call it 'is-ness'?"
How will you relate with is-ness? It will be so vast you will not be
able to embrace it.

With the *he*, God becomes as small as you are. You can hold his
hand. The hand of is-ness is not possible. With *he*, he becomes warm.
Is-ness is cold; existence is cold. You will freeze. Jainism, Buddhism
dropped the idea of God because of these problems – philosophical,

philological: problems that arise out of language and grammar and logic. They dropped the idea, the very idea. But then prayer disappeared, and Jainism became poor for that. Meditation remained, a very lonely effort. Have you seen? – you can meditate alone, you can pray together. Prayer is a communion. Christians, Mohammedans, Jews know what prayer is. Jainism and Buddhism completely lost track of prayer. And prayer has a beauty of its own. A meditator seems to be closed in himself; he has no opening. He is thrown to himself in a deep aloneness. He can become silent, but he cannot become ecstatic.

Ecstasy happens only when there are two, love happens only when there are two. When you are alone you can be silent, still, but you cannot be throbbing with joy, you cannot dance. The Sufi dances because he calls God; he can invoke God in a personal way. Jainism and Buddhism became very poor. When Buddhism spread out of India, it started talking about Buddha as a god – through Buddha, again prayer entered. Prayer never entered Jainism, and Jainism could never spread. It remained a very tiny sect, dead. It is inhuman.

Is-ness, existence, totality – big words, but dead. They don't pulsate. How do you relate with totality, tell me? How will you call totality? How will you connect yourself with totality? You will be too tiny and the vastness of totality is so big, you will be lost.

No, God has to be conceived in a human way. To call him "he" is very human. Yes, by and by, when you approach him, you learn him, you imbibe him, one day there will be no need to call him he, you can drop that. Once the contact is made, once your boundaries and his boundaries are no longer separate, when your boundaries and his boundaries have blended into one existence, then there will be no need. You can simply bow down without even using a single word. You can simply sit in silence, and prayer will be there. You will be praying without any prayer. But that is a later development. In the beginning you will be at a loss if you don't call him by a personal name, if you don't make him personal.

Now, there are two possibilities: either you call him he, or you call him she – both have been used. Sufis call him she: the beloved, the feminine. Christians, Jews call him he: the male, the lover. These are the two possibilities; it depends on you. Both have different qualities.

The moment you call him he, it means you need not go in search of him; he will come, he's the male. And that is the beauty of it: the woman can wait, and the lover will come.

Jews say that you are not only in search of God; God is searching for you. That's the beauty of the pronoun *he*. These words are symbolic, significant, can be of tremendous value. Jews say that he is searching for you; you can wait like a woman, you can become a tremendous awaiting, just an opening, ready to receive the guest. And the guest is coming: the male comes in search of the female.

Sufis call him she; then the whole journey changes. Then you have to seek him, then you have to find him. Of course, the journey becomes more difficult. If you have to seek God, it seems almost impossible that you will succeed. Where will you seek him? The address is not known. Even if he comes by, you will not be able to recognize him; he will be such a stranger. You have never cognized him, so how will you re-cognize him? You have never seen him before, so how are you going to decide, "Yes, here is God"? It is going to be difficult. And where will you go – to Kashi, to Mathura, to Mecca, to Jerusalem? Where will you go – to the Himalayas? Where will you go? How will you move? What will your direction be? From the very beginning there will be confusion.

It is better to wait than to go in search of him. It is better to wait and trust and pray, and let him come to you. That is the meaning of calling him he – that he can come. You become the feminine, then he becomes the male – and the play starts. If you become the male, of course then it is your responsibility to seek him. The Sufi goes to God; for the Jew, God comes to him; for the Hasid, God comes to him.

Now it is for you to decide. I am not saying to call him he; it is for you to decide. It appears to me that *he* is more economical, cleverer. But if you belong to the Women's Lib Movement you can call him she – but then you have to understand the implications of it. It is not only a question of grammar, not only a question of philology, language; it is taking a certain attitude. By calling him he, you declare yourself a woman; with that, it is a totally different endeavor. By calling him she, you call yourself a man. Man is aggressive. If you call him she, you will become aggressive, you will start conquering God. Then God will have to surrender to you. How can you surrender to God? Then you will be too much in your male-aggressive mind.

But if you call him he, you have to surrender to him. He has to come and defeat you, and make you victorious in your defeat. He has to come and overpower you and flood you and destroy you, annihilate you – and recreate you.

My feeling is still this: call him he. You will be benefited; you will be blessed.

And the other question is also there in the first question: "I see now that the question is an entry into my problem: How can I trust or come to love your authority?" I have no authority. You need not trust my authority. I'm just a person, a presence; I am not an authority. I am not proving anything to you, I am not arguing for something, I am not advocating any theory or philosophy, I am not trying to convince you about anything whatsoever.

I have no authority because I don't belong to any tradition. Only traditions can have authority. A Hindu has authority from the Vedas, Upanishads, Gita; the Mohammedan has authority from the Koran; the Christian has authority from the Bible, from the pope. Authority comes from tradition. I am nontraditional; I am not claiming any tradition, I am simply here on my own. I have no authority. I cannot say that whatsoever I am saying is right because the Vedas also say it. I cannot quote, I cannot say that whatsoever I am saying is right, *has* to be right, because Jesus also says the same, Mohammed also says the same.

No, I am not taking any support from anybody else: whatsoever I am saying, I am saying. I know it that way. I have no other authority than myself. I am a presence, a person. You need not trust my authority; I am not an expert. I am a rebel – how can I have any authority? My own experience is all that I have. You can look into me, you can look into my eyes, you can feel me, you can drink me, and that will decide.

And this is not going to be a relationship between an authoritative person and one who has no authority. This is not going to be a relationship between a knower and the ignorant; this is not going to be a relationship between a teacher and a student, no. The professor in the university has the authority, and the student has to learn from him. He knows what is right and he knows what is wrong, and the student simply has to yield to him.

I am not in any way authoritative. I am here; I am a declaration, a revelation. Listen to me, imbibe me, drink me. If that very taste decides something, it's okay; if it doesn't, then I am not for you, you are not for me. Then say good-bye to me. Then there is no need to hang around here; it will be futile. This is a love affair. When you love a person you don't ask for the authority. Love is mad; it is crazy.

I am here only for those courageous people who can be crazy with me. I exist for the eccentrics. I exist only for the very chosen few, the eccentrics: those who are ready to leave all the boundaries of safety and security, authority and scriptures and tradition; who are ready to go with me into the dark; who are ready to go with me and risk.

And I am not promising you anything; I cannot promise, in the very nature of things. Truth cannot be promised; you have to feel it. Remember, authority appeals to the head, to the reason. I don't appeal to the reason; my appeal is to the heart. The heart does not bother about authority. When you fall in love with a woman, do you ask for authority? Has she any authority from Cleopatra that she is beautiful? Do you ask for certificates? Has she been certified by experts that she is really a beauty? Do you take her to the doctor to examine her, to the aesthetic philosopher to decide whether she is really a beauty? No, even if the whole world says that she is not beautiful, you say, "I don't care. I love her, and I know that she is beautiful." She is beautiful because you love, not otherwise. You don't love her because she is beautiful; she becomes beautiful because you love.

I become an authority if you love me, not otherwise. If you are asking for the authority, then you will never love me. Then it is better that we take leave of each other – the sooner the better. I am not going to produce any authority; I have none. You have to look into the person himself. You have to look into me, my presence; you have to feel it intimately.

That's why I say that courage is needed, and only the courageous can love. Love is the greatest courage in the world because it cannot depend on anything else. It has to depend just on a hunch, it has to depend on intuition; it cannot depend on intellect. There is no other proof. Love asks for no other proof, and love cannot produce any proof.

Jews had to reject Jesus. Why? – because he could not produce an authority. "By what authority?" they were asking again and again. "By what authority do you speak? Who has given you the authority to speak?" Who can give authority to a Jesus? And whatsoever he said was absurd. He said, "Authority? Before Abraham was, I am."

Now, Abraham is the most respected prophet of the Jews. And Jesus says, "Before Abraham was, I am. Even Abraham cannot make me authoritative. I am not following Abraham, I have preceded him."
Now this is absurd, because the time gap is so vast. Abraham was thousands of years before. And Jesus says, "Before Abraham was, *ever* was, I am. My existence precedes Abraham's. Who can give me authority?" And he is right, because the source that he has touched in himself is eternal. The source he has touched in himself needs no authority to prove it. On the contrary, Jesus becomes the proof that Abraham was right. This is preposterous.
That's what I am saying. I am saying, I am the proof that Krishna was right; I am the proof that Buddha was right; I am the proof that Jesus was right, not otherwise.
So I have no authority. I am here – take it or leave it.

The second question:

Osho,
My understanding is that knowledge *is* understanding. The wisdom of the sages is the wisdom of the ages. Please lead me to wisdom.

In one question there are three questions. First: "My understanding is that knowledge is understanding." No, sir, knowledge is *never* understanding. Knowledge is a deception of understanding. Knowledge is a pseudo coin, a substitute; it is not understanding. Knowledge is borrowed; understanding is never borrowed.
Understanding is yours; knowledge is always of others. Understanding arises out of your awareness; knowledge arises out of your learning. And the processes are totally different, diametrically opposite. If you want to understand, you will have to unlearn all that you have learned. Knowledge functions as a barrier. Knowledge has to be dropped. The known has to cease for the unknown to be.
Understanding is of the unknown, knowledge is of the known. Knowledge is your memory; understanding is your very being. Knowledge is a borrowed light. Knowledge is like the moon, understanding is like the sun. The moon lives on the borrowed light; it reflects sunrays, it has no light of its own. The sun has its own light.
You say, "My understanding is that knowledge is understanding." Then you have misunderstood, sir.

Second: "The wisdom of the sages is the wisdom of the ages." No, not at all! The wisdom of the sages has no relationship with time. It is not the wisdom of the ages; that is a totally different thing. The wisdom of the ages is nothing but the collective knowledge, the collective experience of humanity. People have lived, people have experienced; by and by, they go on deducing some knowledge out of their experience.

The masses... The wisdom of the ages comes through the masses. It is a mass product; it comes out of time, out of experience. And the wisdom of the sages never comes out of time; it comes out of timelessness. When a person goes beyond time, then he becomes wise. When a person moves into time, he becomes knowledgeable. An old man is knowledgeable; an old man is not necessarily wise, remember. An old man is not necessarily wise, and a wise man is not necessarily old.

Shankaracharya was very young – he was thirty-three when he died – but he was tremendously wise. Buddha was nearabout forty when he became enlightened, Mohammed was nearabout forty when he became enlightened. They were facing people older than themselves; that was one of the conflicts.

When Buddha went to his own father... Of course, the father was the father and, as fathers do, he laughed at the stupidity. He said, "What! Do you want to teach me? You are my son. I am older than you; I am your father. I have known the world; I have known life – its miseries, its blessings. Certainly I know more than you know."

And Buddha said, "That's right, sir. You know more as far as knowledge is concerned, your memory is far bigger than mine. But I have not brought you knowledge, I have brought something totally new. An inner light has arisen in me, a flame. And I see you are living in darkness." The father felt hurt. His ego was hurt, he was angry.

Certainly, Jesus was very young. And if the old rabbis were not ready to listen to him, it seemed absolutely okay. Why should they listen to a young man who has not known the world, who has not lived yet? Jesus was only thirty-three when he was crucified. He suddenly started preaching when he was thirty, very young. People had known him working in his father's workshop, cutting wood, polishing wood. He was a carpenter's son. Nobody had ever dreamed that this boy suddenly would become a wise man. Then one day he declares that he is the Messiah, that he is the son of God. Certainly, how could people believe it? They had known him as a carpenter; he was making furniture for them, and he was doing ordinary jobs in the town, and suddenly he declared... He must have gone mad. Remember, it is always wisdom which is crucified on the cross, because the knowledgeable people cannot tolerate it. It offends; it is offensive. Wisdom is always timeless; it has nothing to do with your life experiences. And what you call "wisdom of the ages" is totally different – it is a mass product. People have lived on earth so long and they have experienced many things, and of course they have deduced, they have come to certain conclusions. Wisdom is not a conclusion, it is not out of experience; wisdom is illumination, wisdom is revelation. It is sudden, like lightning. It is unproved; it *cannot* be proved. In the very nature of its truth, it cannot be proved. You have to fall in love with it or not. It is so sudden and unrelated with your life situations and experiences – how can it be proved? What proof can Jesus give to you? He gave his own life, but he could not give any proof.

Do you remember? The last thing he was asked before he was crucified was by Pilate, the Roman governor. Pontius Pilate asked him, "What is truth?" And Jesus remained silent. He looked into the eyes of the governor but he didn't say a single word. Why did Jesus remain silent? He should have said something... But truth cannot be said. And it is foolish to ask a person like Jesus, "What is truth?" because Jesus *is* truth. He has said many times, "I am the truth, I am the way and I am the goal." Now what is the point of saying it? He's standing in front of Pontius Pilate, truth itself is standing there, and Pilate asks, "What is truth?" Jesus is not a pundit, he is not a professor, he is not a philosopher. He is not going to give a theory about truth – he is truth himself. He stood there absolutely in silence; he made himself available, he made his presence available.

But Pilate could not understand it; he could not see truth. He was hankering for a few words, that this man would say a few words. Jesus didn't say a single thing and yet he asserted everything that can be said about truth. He revealed himself, he was there, his presence was there, his vibe was there. If Pilate had been a little perceptive, he would have known what truth is.

Truth is not out of the experience of ages; truth is not an experience at all. When all experiences disappear and only the experiencer is left in pure consciousness... Consciousness without content is what truth is. It is not an experience; it is not that you experience something. No, nothing is left to experience, nothing whatsoever – just a pure sky, no object, only the subjectivity throbbing with totality, dancing, just the subjectivity, just pure consciousness without any content. It is not an experience.

Let me tell you in this way: godliness is not an experience; it is beyond experience. The world is an experience; godliness is not an experience. Experience is possible in duality only. When I am separate from you, I can experience you. When I am one with you, how can I experience you? How will I divide the experiencer and the experience, the knower and the known, the seer and the seen? No, it is not possible. The subject and the object have lost their boundaries, they have become one – now who is the knower and who is the known?

Wisdom is that lightning where the known and the knower become one, when the seer and the seen become one, when all duality disappears and only one remains, only one. In experience the other is needed; experience is other-based, other-oriented.

You say: "The wisdom of the ages is the wisdom of the sages." It is not. The wisdom of the sages is timeless: it is beyond experience, it is transcendental; and the wisdom of the ages is mundane, temporal, based in experience.

And third: "Please lead me to wisdom." That is not possible. If somebody else leads you, it will be knowledge. Again you will be trapped in knowledge. Nobody can lead you into wisdom – because the other will be the cause of knowledge. Only you can be the cause of your wisdom. Then you can ask me, "What am I doing here?" I am not leading you into wisdom. I can do only one thing, a negative thing: I am trying to destroy your knowledge. I am simply removing the hindrance, the barrier; I am simply removing the rock in your path, that's all. And that rock is knowledge. Once that rock is removed you will start flowing. The fountain is there, blocked by the rock.

Your wisdom is with you; it is your life energy, it is your vitality, it is your élan. It is there. Once you become daring enough to drop knowledge, once you become daring enough to be innocent, daring enough to be ignorant; once you can say, "I don't know," once you have gathered that courage to declare, "I don't know, and all that I know is just illusory, all my knowledge is borrowed, bogus, empty" – the moment you drop your knowledge, wisdom arises.

I cannot lead you to wisdom. Wisdom will arise in you, it will well up in your being. Just drop the rock that you are carrying – and that rock is of knowledge. If you think that knowledge is understanding, how are you going to drop the rock? Then you will protect it. If you think knowledge is wisdom, then of course I will look to you like an enemy who is trying to take your wisdom away.

The master can only be negative; the master cannot give you anything positive. Avoid anybody who says to you that he is going to give you something positive. Avoid! The master is just a help to remove the barrier. The master is *via negativa,* he's the path of negation. He simply takes away. He says, "This is not true, this is not true, this is not true" – he goes on eliminating. One day suddenly he has taken all the props away from you; you collapse, you collapse in wisdom. One day suddenly, when all your hindrances have been taken away, something arises in you, pops in you like lightning. That's what wisdom is: it is your innermost nature, it cannot be given to you.

There are three types of teachers in the world: one I call the charismatic, another I call the methodical and the third I call the natural. These three divisions are also the divisions of therapists too. There are three types of therapist: charismatic, methodical, natural. This division has to be understood.

Charisma comes from a Greek word meaning spirit, full of spirit. The charismatic leader is so full of spirit that if you go to him you will become a slave. He is so full of spirit he will overpower you; he will not bother about you, he will start dragging you by his own spirit. He will lead you, he will become a leader.

I am not a leader, I am not a charismatic master, a charismatic teacher, because a charismatic teacher is dangerous: he kills you, you are nullified, your being is effaced. To be under the guidance of a charismatic person is like trying to grow under a big tree – impossible. It is impossible. You may think the tree is protective, but to grow under a big tree is impossible.

You see a big oak. Thousands of acorns fall under the oak and die. They never grow, they cannot grow. They may be deluded because they will be under the mother tree and there will be protection – but the protection is poisonous. The acorn has to go far away, has to be independent, only then can it become a tree. Otherwise it will never become a tree.

The charismatic person is dangerous, and people are very much attracted to them. The charismatic person is never a true master; he becomes a slave driver. The charismatic is more of a politician than a religious person. Adolf Hitler is charismatic, Mussolini is charismatic. Leaders are charismatic: they have to lead people, they have to make slaves of people, they have to dominate and dictate.

The second type of teacher-master-leader is methodical. He uses methods, not spirit. He will not overpower you by his spirit, he will simply give you methods – better than the first, because he will never make you a slave.

The word *method* again comes from a Greek root; it means to follow. The second type of leader-master-teacher will follow the disciple. He will give a method. He will never lead you; he will follow you. The second type of therapist will follow the patient; he will listen to the patient, he will try to find out what the patient's need is; he will listen to the student, to the disciple, he will look at you, and he will help you from behind. He will never be ahead of you; he will push you rather than pull you. He will not drive you, he will simply persuade you.

The second is better. Of course, many people are attracted to the first and very few are attracted to the second.

The third is the natural master, the natural healer: he never leads you, he never follows you, he accompanies you. He simply holds your hand. He is a friend. Buddha has said, "Next time when I come, my name will be Maitreya, 'the friend.'" And it is very significant.

Buddha says in his life as Gautam Buddha he was too charismatic – so full of power, energy, élan, spirit, that he overpowered people. Mahavira was more methodical. And Buddha says, "Next time when I come, my name is going to be Maitreya." *Maitreya* means the friend. Very symbolically he says, "Next time, I am going to accompany you, I will be a friend. I will not lead in front of you, I will not push you from the back; I will just hold your hand as a friend." This is the natural, this is the best. And this is most difficult to find because you attract, you feel attracted toward charismatic persons, miraculous persons, or you become attracted toward the methodical.

The natural is the best but the least attractive. He is very simple and ordinary; he has no charisma, he does not dazzle you. And he is not very methodical, he is not very technological, he is not very scientific; he is more poetic, he's more chaotic. He's more natural, as chaotic as nature is.

I am a natural person. I have no charisma, and I don't believe in charisma. I don't believe in methods – even if I use them, I don't believe in them.

I am a natural person, very ordinary. I can be lost in a crowd and you will not be able to find me. So I don't lead you, I accompany you. I can hold your hand, I can be your friend.

The third question:

Osho,
Karl Marx's philosophy advocates a classless and stateless society. Is he indirectly advocating a religious society?

Directly or indirectly, he is not proposing a religious society. And the way he proposes he is going to bring this classless and stateless society about is really absurd – he proposes through the state itself. He says, "First the state has to become very dominant – dictatorship of the proletariat – and then one day, when the dictatorship of the proletariat has succeeded, it will wither away." That is nonsense.

Nobody ever wants to leave power. Once it is there in your hands, nobody wants to leave it. The state will become more and more powerful. The society may disappear, but the state is not going to disappear. That's what has happened in Russia, that's what is happening in China. All Marx's predictions have proved false.

Through a dictatorship, no society can come to a point where the state disappears. The state will become more and more powerful. And the people who control the state will never like, have never liked... Who likes to lose his power? Power corrupts, and corrupts absolutely.

Karl Marx had no understanding of human psychology, of the human mind. He was acquainted with the structure of the society, with the economic structure of the society, but he was completely unaware of the human structure, of the psyche – and that is more important because finally that is the decisive factor.

He was not aware that Stalin would be born; he was not aware that Mao would be born. In fact, he was thinking America would become the first communist country, and he was wrong. He was thinking that a very affluent society, a capitalist society, would become communist first, because he thought that in a capitalist society the difference between the poor and the rich would be too big, and the poor would revolt.

But just the contrary has happened: two very poor countries have become communist. Russia and China, both are very poor. He could not have even imagined Russia ever becoming a communist country.

Why not America? In fact, the process has been totally different. The difference between the poor and the rich has not increased. In fact, they have come closer: the poor have become more and more rich in America. The difference exists, but the difference is less than ever before. And if American society goes on progressing, one day America will become the first classless society that has been possible.

And the difference is disappearing naturally: affluence is growing, riches are growing. You are so greedy about riches because they are so scarce. When there is so much of something, who bothers to hoard, for what? You don't hoard air, you don't hoard water. If everything else becomes so available, hoarding will disappear. That is the only natural course.

Communism is an abortion; it is unnatural. Capitalism is natural. And capitalism is going to disappear naturally. That will be a natural death, as a man dies on the deathbed, slowly, slowly, slowly. It will not be an accident – a young man suddenly dies of a heart attack or a car accident... Natural death is good because out of natural death, natural life is born.

I am not in favor of Karl Marx. And, in fact, he himself was not a proletarian. He himself was quite rich. In fact, to think about communism one needs to be quite rich. He remained in the British Museum his whole life, sitting, doing nothing, reading books.

I have heard an anecdote...

In the communist heaven, the equivalent of St. Peter stopped one applicant at the gate and asked, "What are your qualifications for entering here?"

"Well," said the man, "on earth my father was a rich industrialist, my mother came from a family of middle class tradesmen. Me? – I was a successful writer, and finally, after inheriting a large sum of money, I married a baroness."

The gatekeeper was choking with rage by this time. "And those are your claims for entering our communist heaven?" he spluttered.

Meekly the applicant added one more line. "I thought my name might help me," he murmured, "It's Karl Marx."

Marx was not a poor man. Even to dream about communism, even to dream about utopias, one needs to be affluent. Communism is a by-product not of the proletariat's thinking, but of middle class people. The middle class people are the most frustrated people in the world. The poor man is not frustrated; he's poor and settled. And the rich man is not frustrated; he's rich and settled. The middleman is very frustrated: he wants to be rich, hopes he can be rich, and he feels the poverty like a shadow following him. He is in limbo.

The middle class man is the most dangerous man. He is both poor and rich, and he does not want to be poor and he wants to be rich. If he cannot be rich then he would like to destroy the whole society. He would like nobody to be rich.

And a miracle is happening in America: the rich are disappearing and the poor are disappearing, and the middle class is becoming bigger and bigger and bigger. The idea of Marx was just the opposite: he was thinking that the rich would become richer and the poor would become poorer, and by and by the middle class would be divided in two parts: those who are rich will move to the rich, and those who are poor will fall down into poverty. The society will be absolutely cut in two – the poor and the rich – and that will be the inevitable moment of revolution. This has not happened, is not happening.

Just the contrary is happening: the middle class is becoming bigger and bigger. The rich are one extreme of the middle class now, and the poor are another extreme of the middle class. The middle class is the only class now. And this middle class is going to become the classless society sooner or later. The classless society is going to come, but not through Marx; it is going to come through a totally natural process of capitalism, not through communism.

And Marx certainly was not a religious person at all; he was against religion. He was not really acquainted with religion. All that he knew about was Judaism and Christianity. He was a Jew. And this is something to be understood. Marx was a Jew, Freud was a Jew, Einstein was a Jew – the three great names of the modern world were all Jews. Jews have suffered so much; they are very angry. And their anger comes in so many garbs. Marx's anger against society is in fact Jewish anger against a non-Jewish world. And he knew only Judaism and Christianity, which are not very developed religions. Had he known anything about Buddhism or Patanjali or the Upanishads, his ideas would have certainly been different. But he was not aware, and he was not in fact even trying to become aware. His religious understanding was very poor; he was an economist.

Religion has nothing to do with society; that's why he was against religion. Religion is individualistic, and he was a socialist par excellence. That's why he said, "Religion is the opium of the masses." Religion is individual because it believes in individual freedom. And the flowering of the ultimate is going to be individual, not social. You have never heard of a society becoming religious, only individuals – a Buddha here, a Jesus there, a Moses somewhere else. Only individuals have become religious.

The society can never become religious because the crowd mind cannot come to that flowering. To be religious is such a tremendous growth. It is the opening of your ultimate potential; it cannot be of the masses. You don't think that one day the masses will become great painters like Picasso or Leonardo da Vinci. You don't think that one day the masses will become great musicians like Beethoven, Mozart or Wagner. You don't think that the masses one day will become great mathematicians like Einstein, Planck, Eddington. No, you don't think that way. Then why do you think the masses will one day become great religious geniuses like Buddha, Jesus, Moses, Mahavira, Mohammed? It is not possible.

The mass lives in a very dark way; it lives in the jungle. Only very few people escape from the jungle and enter the forest and only very few of those who enter the forest ever enter the garden. Many more become much too attached to the forest and they remain there. Let it be this way. Only one person in one million ever escapes from the jungle and reaches to the forest. Out of one million in the forest, one escapes from the forest and reaches to the garden. And out of one million in the garden, one escapes from the garden and reaches into the home. That has been the proportion up to now, and it is going to be the proportion still.

Religion is only for the few. It hurts, because you would like religion to be for everybody. But I cannot help. If music cannot be for everybody, and painting cannot be for everybody, and dancing cannot be for everybody, then – excuse me, I cannot help – religion too cannot be for everybody. And in a communist world, religion becomes impossible because they don't allow individuality, they don't allow freedom; they don't allow anyone to be different from the mass.

I have heard a Soviet Russian story...

A man was seized with a violent cramp in his stomach and sought relief at the modern white structure erected for the purpose in his home town. Upon entering the building, he found himself in a hall with two doors. One was marked "Male," the other "Female." Naturally, he entered the door marked "Male."

He found himself in a room with two doors. One was marked "Over twenty-one," the other "Under twenty-one." Since he was fifty-two, he entered the door marked "Over twenty-one."

He found himself in another room with two doors. One was marked "Serious illness," the other "Minor indisposition." Since he was doubled up with pain by this time, he staggered through the door marked "Serious illness."

He found himself in a room with two doors again. One was marked "Nonbelievers and Godless," the other was marked "Believers in God, the religious." Since he was a believer in God, he entered the door marked for the religious, and found himself on the street.

In a communist world, a religious person cannot exist; he is not allowed. A communist world believes in the society, in the absolute domination of the society. The individual is thought to be a danger. Anybody trying to be individual is looked on as the enemy; one should not try to be an individual, one should follow the crowd, one should be in the crowd. One should not try one's own ways and styles, even about ordinary things. If you go to China, Russia, you will find uniformity even in dress; even in cars you will find uniformity. Everybody has to be just like everybody else. Nobody should try – even in dress – no one should try any individual style because that is dangerous. Communism does not allow the individual; then how can it allow religion? It is impossible.

Religion is individual flowering. Religion can exist only in an individualistic society where freedom is allowed, where freedom to be oneself is allowed, where nobody interferes with you, where you are left alone, to yourself, where you can do anything that you want to do with yourself. The society interferes only when you start interfering with other people's lives; otherwise not. If you are not harmful, nobody will interfere with you.

This is possible only in a democratic country; this is possible only in a capitalist country. I am all for capitalism and I am all for democracy. It is better to be poor but to remain democratic. It is better to remain uneducated but to remain democratic. Otherwise your stomachs will be full but your spirits will be empty; otherwise your bodies will get nourishment but your souls will die, starve.

And the second part of the question:

If not, what type of social order should there be where man will not be exploited by man?

Unless there is more than enough, man will always be exploited by man. It is not a question of communism or socialism or capitalism: unless there is more than enough, man will be exploited. So create more than enough, be creative, use all possibilities to create more. That is the first thing. And the second thing: live in the present, don't think of the morrow. Listen to Jesus. He says: "Look at the lilies in the field. They spin not, they weave not, they labor not, they don't think of the morrow – yet they are so beautiful. Even Solomon, arrayed in his whole glory, was not so beautiful."

Live in the present. The future creates greed, greed creates hoarding; hoarding creates poverty. Only a religious society... And when I say a religious society I don't mean a religious social order. By "religious society" I mean where many, many people are religious, at least striving toward religion; where many people are meditating, praying; where many people are loving, caring, where many people have compassion; where many people are freed from greed and hoarding; where many people are enjoying life in the present, delighting in the play in the present and not bothering about the future; where many people are simply delighted, moment to moment. In that society exploitation will disappear. Otherwise exploitation is not going to disappear.

You can change the structure – in Russia the old exploiters have disappeared but the new exploiters have come, and the new are more dangerous because they are more technologically equipped than the first ones. The rich people were there, they exploited; the czar was there, he was exploiting – but nothing to be compared with Stalin and his company. They were more equipped. The czar was not so equipped; that's why the revolution was possible.

Now there is no possibility of revolution in Russia – impossible! You cannot even imagine a revolution because the grip of the state is so great, and the state is so technologically equipped against the individual, that no individual can even think... It is impossible to talk about revolution; it is impossible to even think of it because they say that the walls have ears. You cannot even talk to your wife frankly because, who knows, she may be an informer. You cannot talk to your own child, to your own kid, because he belongs to the Youth Communist Party. And they are teaching their people to be more patriotic, to be more for the country, against the family. The society is the goal, not the family. The family has to be disrupted completely.

There are no longer any parties, ideologies are no longer available; no possibility to publish a book or a newspaper. How can you think that in Russia a revolution can happen? No, the state is so powerful it will crush anybody in the bud.

And now what are they doing? First they used to murder their enemies. Now they don't; they have more lethal weapons: they brainwash, they don't murder. They simply give electric shocks, insulin shocks, and they brainwash the man. He comes back home from the hospital, not from the prison, completely idiotic, stupid. He has forgotten all that he knew; he cannot even think, he cannot say two sentences logically. He has to learn from *ABC* again. Now, how can you think about revolution?

Sooner or later, in a communist country, it is going to happen that – because children have to be born in the hospital – immediately when a child is born they will put an electrode in the head; that will do. Then the government will even know what you are always thinking – not saying, that is not the question. Then the police station will know who is thinking some wrong idea, your number will show in the police office. Suddenly a light will come to the number thirty-one, thirty-one is caught. It is possible now, technologically possible.

And remember, man is so dangerous: whatsoever becomes technologically possible, he *has* to try it. He is obsessed, he cannot resist the temptation.

The last question:

Osho,
I feel guilty that I can come to you and the poor people cannot.

Don't feel guilty – please stop coming. Let me tell you one anecdote...

Martha was dying. With her last breath she turned to Abe and asked, "Abe, before I die, make love to me just one more time."

Abe answered, "How could you ask me to do such a thing? I will kill you!"

Martha pleaded, "Everyone is entitled to one last request before they die. You should grant me this last wish."

Abe replied, "Okay." He got into bed and made love to her. No sooner did he finish than she hopped out of bed completely cured, and ran downstairs and started to cook a chicken and yelled into the living room, where her children were sitting, that dinner would be ready in an hour.

The children were astounded, and ran up the stairs to their father who was sitting in a chair and crying. They said, "Papa, why are you crying? It's a miracle! Mama is completely cured!"

He replied, "I know, but when I think what I could have done for Eleanor Roosevelt..."

Get it? "I know, but when I think what I could have done for Eleanor Roosevelt. That's why I'm crying."

Don't think about Eleanor Roosevelt, and don't cry unnecessarily. If you feel ashamed, don't come because to feel guilty is very bad, and I don't want anybody to feel guilty. Then go and serve the poor people. If you want to come here, forget about the whole world. If you think about the world you cannot listen to me, you cannot understand me.

Your life is short, your life is really very short. You don't know whether you are going to exist the next moment or not. And don't feel sorry for the poor because, in the first place, the poor may not be ready to come. I know poor people. I have been traveling in this country, I was born in this country; I know poor people. Sometimes when they come to me, they come for some other reasons. They never come for the reason where I can be helpful. They come... Their son is not getting employment, so, "Osho, bless." They come because their wife is ill, they come because somebody is not getting a child, "So bless." They come for some other reasons, not for religious reasons. A poor person cannot really have religious reasons; he is starving. His problem is not religious; his problem is physical. Only a rich person can have religious problems. Religion is a by-product of affluence; it is a luxury.

When your bodily needs are fulfilled, then psychological problems arise. A poor man never has psychological problems; you will never see him going to the psychoanalyst – have you ever seen a poor man...? He has no psychological problems. When your bodily needs are completely fulfilled your problems shift, they take a higher form, they move on a higher altitude – they start becoming psychological.

Indians are very happy that they don't have many psychological problems, and that they don't need many psychiatrists in India. And they are very puzzled as to why America has so many psychiatrists. They feel very sorry for America because they think, "Poor people, they are suffering so much mental illness." They don't understand that a mental illness is a blessing; it simply shows that physical needs are fulfilled; now the person can afford to be mentally ill.

When mental needs are fulfilled, then religious needs, spiritual needs, arise – never before.

So if you are feeling sorry for any poor person, don't feel sorry. It is as if you see a small child playing and you start feeling, "This poor child, he cannot enjoy sex yet." Now, it is for you to feel guilty, and if you want to feel guilty, you are free. And if you want to stop making love to your woman or to your man, stop – because those small children... They cannot make love yet.

They will make love in their own time. Everybody has his own ripening. And if a poor person has really become interested in religion, he will find a way to come to me. Nobody can bar him. There are many poor people here, they will find a way, they will do everything they can do and they will come. Their intensity will bring them. Your pity is not going to help them. Only one thing can happen out of your pity: you may miss me.

Once a Jewish businessman was fishing in a lake when he hauled in a fish of a type he had never seen before. It had golden scales and silver fins which gleamed and flashed as it thrashed about on the bottom of his boat. Suddenly, the fish startled the businessman by speaking!

"Kind sir," implored the fish, "throw me back in the lake and I will grant you three wishes."

The businessman considered carefully and then said, "Make it five and we've got a deal."

"I can only grant three," gasped the fish.

"Four and a half," proposed the businessman.

"Three," said the fish barely audibly.

"Okay, okay," said the businessman. "We'll compromise on four wishes. How about that?"

But this time the fish made no reply at all. It lay dead on the bottom of the boat.

Life is very short. I will not be here forever. Use the opportunity that is available to you, and use it as much as you can. Let your inner flame burn bright, and then you can go to the poor people and help them also. That will be of some help. Right now you will feel guilty, they will not gain anything out of your guilt; and you will certainly miss.

The very, very last question:

Osho,
Is Santa Claus enlightened?

If he is not, then who is?

Enlightenment is fun. It is not a serious thing. Santa Claus is a buddha, is a christ. Santa Claus is humor, and enlightenment is humorous. It is nothing serious; it is joy, it is fun, it is delight.

Enough for today.

CHAPTER 5

sing the glory of existence

O sadhu! Purify your body in the simple way.
As the seed is within the banyan tree, and within the seed are the
flowers, the fruits, and the shade, so the germ is within the body,
and within that germ is the body again.
The fire, the air, the water, the earth, and the ether; you cannot
have these outside of him.
O kazi, o pundit, consider it well: what is there that is not in the
soul?
The water-filled pitcher is placed upon water, it has water within
and without.
It should not be given a name, lest it call forth the error of dualism.
Kabir says: Listen to the word, the truth, which is your essence. He
speaks the word to himself; and he himself is the creator.

There is a strange tree, which stands without roots and bears fruits
without blossoming; it has no branches and no leaves, it is lotus all
over.
Two birds sing there: one is the guru, and the other the disciple.
The disciple chooses the manifold fruits of life and tastes them, and
the guru beholds him in joy.

What Kabir says is hard to understand: the bird is beyond seeking,
yet it is most clearly visible. The formless is in the midst of all forms.
I sing the glory of forms.

Truth is a challenge, the greatest there is. It is a challenge to
inquire, it is a challenge to seek, and it is a challenge to be. It
is not something that you will possess some day, it is something that you have to become. And, in fact, you can become only
that which you are already; you can become only your being. The
challenge of truth is the challenge of your own innermost core,
the challenge to come home, the challenge to come back to the
center, the challenge to recognize yourself, the challenge to know,
encounter yourself. It is arduous.

To face oneself is arduous because we have invested too much in
our ignorance, in our self-ignorance. We have staked too much, so
self-knowledge begins to become very, very difficult. Hence everybody is called, but only a few listen to the call. And those few who
listen to the call, even many of them misinterpret it, delude themselves. Those who listen rightly, even they don't respond rightly.
Those who respond rightly, even they don't persist for long. Hence,
many are called, but very few arrive.

In fact, everybody is called. God's challenge is for everybody; it
is an open invitation. You are here for that challenge – to accept it, to
go through the fire, to be purified through the fire. But it is a gamble;
one has to stake one's all. And this is the irony, that when you don't
have anything, you are very much afraid to stake. The irony is,
when you have, you can have the courage to stake too.

That's my everyday experience: whenever I see somebody who
has something, he is ready to surrender, and whenever I come across
a person who has nothing, he is very afraid of surrender. This is very
mysterious. One who has nothing is very much afraid to surrender;
maybe he is afraid that if he surrenders he will come across his noth-
ingness. If he surrenders his defenses, he will have to know his inner
emptiness, his poverty.

It is better to pretend that one is rich and never look within. It is
better to go on dreaming: "I have much, so how can I surrender?"
But this is my experience, and I have not come across a single
exception to this. It seems to be the rule that those who have are
ready to surrender, they are not afraid. And Jesus says, "Those who

have will be given more, and those who don't have, even that which they have will be taken away."

When you have, you have the courage to stake. And when you stake, you become capable of getting more. And when you stake all, unconditionally, totally, only then are you capable of receiving the gift of godliness. Then Christ is born in you. When you stake all, Christ is born in you. When you go through the crucifixion, when you are crucified, there is resurrection.

I see two types of people in the world; the whole of humanity can be divided into two categories. One thing: all are crucified. Half of them remain crucified, and half of them, or a few of them, have the possibility to be resurrected. Those who remain crucified simply suffer, and they suffer for nothing. Their suffering is meaningless, irrelevant.

Have you seen...? Your suffering is meaningless, irrelevant. For what are you suffering? What are you gaining out of it? You are simply suffering; you are a wastage, a wasteland. Those who simply suffer are crucified; those who suffer for the divine are resurrected. Then their suffering begins to have meaning, significance.

Life is going to disappear, that much is certain; death is going to happen, that much is certain. But are you going to die for the divine? Or will you be simply dying? If you are simply going to die, then you are crucified without resurrection. If you are going to die for the divine, if you are going to become an offering, a sacrifice, then you will be resurrected.

Everybody is crucified, only a few get down from the cross, attain a new life – what Jesus calls "a life of abundance," a life of infinity, holy life, because it is whole. Only very few get down from the cross and become ecstatic. Their death is no longer death; it is the beginning of an eternal life.

Now it is up to you. If you accept the challenge, you can be resurrected. Christ will be born in you, or Buddha or Krishna – these are just names. Remember one thing: Krishna, Buddha, Christ are not names of certain persons. They denote a certain state, the same state. Christ means one who has realized himself, and through that realization has realized the whole; one who has come home, one who can say, "I am God." The same is the meaning of Buddha or Jina or Krishna.

Ordinarily, you are wandering away from yourself, and every

day you go farther and farther away. You go on moving toward the periphery, and you go on creating new peripheries to move into again. You move toward the horizon which is not possible to achieve – because the horizon exists not, it is just illusory. Only the center exists.

That's why Kabir says, "Sadhu! – O monks! – go nowhere. God is here. God is where you are. Seek him not anywhere else, otherwise you will miss." And the challenge is not coming from the outside. The challenge is coming from your innermost core, even if sometimes you may feel it is coming from the outside, because your innermost core has become almost an outside to you. You have become so unaware of it that when your own soul calls to you, you feel as if somebody else has called you. When the master calls you, it is your own inner voice that he is trying to express to you. It is coming via him. The master is not outside.

Just the other day there was a question: "When to listen to the master? When to say yes and when to say no?" If you have really understood the meaning of the relationship between a disciple and a master, then there is no disciple and no master. Then whenever you say no to your master, you say no to yourself. He is you. The question has not to be decided between the master and the disciple; the question has to be decided between your center and your periphery. When you say yes to the disciple and say no to the master, you have said yes to your periphery against your center. When you say yes to the master against the disciple, you have said yes to your center against the periphery. The master and disciple are not separate. We will come to it in this song.

Kabir says: these *two birds*, the master and the disciple. The disciple has decided to enjoy the world of forms, the manifold world of forms, the circumference; and the master sits at the center, at the center of the cyclone, and watches and witnesses. – He is happy, happy even that the disciple is roaming around, enjoying. One day the disciple will come back; he has to come back because on the circumference there is no contentment possible, there is no bliss possible. There is only misery and misery and misery, and misery goes on becoming multiplied every day.

So the first thing to remember: you are being called. I'm a provocation. I am calling you forth. Listen to it, and not only listen, respond; and not only respond, accept the challenge for the journey.

The journey is arduous, it is going to be difficult. It is very inconvenient to go into the unknown because you have to move away from your securities, away from your comforts, away from all that you have belonged to up to now: your identities. But only when you move away from yourself do you come to yourself, because that which you think yourself to be right now is not your real nature. It is a deception that you have managed; it is a hallucination, it is auto-hypnosis.

P. D. Ouspensky talks many times about a certain law he calls "the law of the seeds." It is of tremendous significance to understand it. Have you ever seen a big oak tree? In its lifespan it will create billions and billions of seeds. But not all will become trees; out of a million seeds, maybe one will become an oak tree, others will be lost. Nature produces very extravagantly knowing well that many are called but many don't listen. A million seeds are produced so that one seed can become an oak. Millions of people are born so that one person can become a Christ or a Buddha or a Krishna. Remember this law of the seeds.

Even in man... An ordinary man, a normal man, will make at least four thousand to six thousand ejaculations in his life. Each ejaculation carries millions of life-cells. Out of millions of life-cells, perhaps one will reach to the woman's egg; the woman will become pregnant. Out of millions of life-cells, perhaps one...

You will be surprised: a single male body could populate the whole earth if all the seeds became embodied. A single human body is enough; a single male is enough to populate the whole earth because each ejaculation carries millions of life-cells, and in a whole life there are four thousand to six thousand ejaculations. And I am talking about a normal person; I am not talking about the supernormal or the abnormal. The supernormal has no ejaculations. His energy starts moving into different dimensions. The abnormal is a maniac.

Just a few days ago I received a letter from a bride. She wrote, "I am afraid that I married a sex maniac. My husband never leaves me alone. He makes love to me all day long: while I am in the shower, while I am cooking breakfast, while I am making the beds and even while my back is turned to him. Can you tell me what to do?" Signed, "Exhausted."

The name is given, but I will not tell you the name because the husband is here. And there was a postscript, a small note: "P.S. Please excuse the jerky handwriting."

I am not talking about these jerks!

A normal human being can populate the whole world – what about an abnormal human being? He can populate many earths like this. Abnormal human beings become mechanically sexual. They become sex machines; they simply produce life-cells and nothing else. They don't produce life; they produce only life-cells. A normal person produces life-cells and life. A supernormal person transforms his whole life-energy into attaining higher peaks of life: energy starts moving upward rather than downward. The energy is no longer affected by gravitation; the energy starts levitating, flying. It has a different plenitude now.

But this law of the seeds has to be understood. So many people are born, only a few will attain. And what will happen to other seeds? They simply rot. They simply disappear, or they are thrown back again into the world as seeds, they are again given an opportunity.

Don't miss this opportunity. To be a seed is a great opportunity because to be a seed means to be a possibility, a potentiality – you can grow. But then the seed has to understand many things because there are a thousand and one barriers to be crossed, and a thousand and one obstacles to be avoided, and a thousand and one wrong alternatives to be dropped. Only then do you move toward growth.

Growth is a rare phenomenon. It is natural, yet rare. When the seed has found its right soil, it grows. It is very natural, growth is natural; but to find the right soil – that is the very crux of the matter.

In today's songs, Kabir is giving very clear directions. Try to understand them.

Sadho, sahajai kaya sadho.
O sadhu! Purify your body in the simple way.

This word *sadhu* is very beautiful; it has to be understood. It has become associated with wrong meanings, but the word is tremendously significant. The very word *sadhu* means simple, spontaneous, innocent. The very word means innocent.

But if you look around India, and go to sadhus, you will not find them innocent at all. They are very complex people, more complex than the ordinary, worldly people. From where has their complexity come? They are not spontaneous at all, they are not natural at all. They are doing unnatural things. They are trying to somehow go against nature, to go upstream. They are not moving with the river, they are trying to push the river. Hence, they have become unnatural. They are not sadhus, they are not innocent people.

The first ingredient in a sadhu will be the understanding that one is ignorant. Ignorance brings innocence; knowledge makes you corrupted. If you can honestly, sincerely say, "I don't know," you become a sadhu: the first step.

Somebody asks you, "Does God exist or not?" and you say, "I don't know" – your response is that of a sadhu. In Buddhist literature, whenever somebody came to Buddha and Buddha asked, "Do you believe in God? Do you believe in hell, heaven? Do you believe in the soul?" and the man says, "I don't know, sir," Buddha would say, "Sadhu, sadhu you are innocent, you are greatly innocent, you are tremendously innocent." This is the first step.

Knowledge creates complexity: the more you know, the more complex you become – and the more cunning you become, and the more you start trying to deceive and cheat nature. An innocent person remains in cooperation with nature; a man of knowledge starts cheating nature, exploiting nature. He uses his knowledge to force nature to serve him.

That's how you see science trying to cheat nature. Of course, in the long run, nature is going to take revenge. You cannot cheat nature for long. Finally, your cheating is going to be a destructive step against yourself. That's what has happened: three hundred years of scientific cheating, and now the whole of humanity is coming close to its total death, a global suicide.

To become a sadhu, the first thing is: don't claim knowledge because all knowledge is illusory. You don't exactly know what the case is, nobody knows. Only ignorant people think they know; the wise people know that they don't know.

The second thing: the sadhu will be like a child, he will move with spontaneity. When he is hungry, he will eat; when he is sleepy, he will fall asleep. Have you not seen small children? – even sitting at a dining table, they fall asleep. They are just eating – a bite in the mouth, and the child has fallen asleep.

The second thing about a sadhu will be his spontaneity. But you will not find spontaneity in the so-called sadhus. When they are feeling hungry they are fasting; how can they be innocent and how can they be spontaneous? And when they are feeling sleepy they are keeping a vigilance, they are forcing themselves to remain alert. When they are feeling angry they are trying to smile, and when they are feeling sexual they are talking about *brahmacharya* and celibacy. These people cannot be sadhus – not according to Kabir, not according to me.

The sadhu has to be innocent like a small child. Yes, Jesus' definition is right when he says: "Only those who are like small children will be able to enter into the kingdom of my God." He is talking about sadhus – like small children. But one distinction has to be made: when I say like small children, or when Jesus says like small children, he does not mean childish; he means innocent, yet mature. Innocence has its own kind of maturity: a ripeness of innocence, when innocence has flowered.

What is the difference between a childish person and a person who is like a child? The difference is the childish person has no awareness at all. Yes, he's innocent: when he feels hungry, he feels hungry and he eats; and when he feels sleepy, he sleeps – but his spontaneity has a deep background of unconsciousness. The spontaneity is there, but it is unconscious.

When the spontaneity is there, and in the background of consciousness is awareness; when the awareness is there and still you don't interfere with the spontaneous... You are so disciplined in your consciousness that you don't create any unnatural discipline for yourself; your awareness helps you to be natural, to be spontaneous, non-interfering, non-repressive, but yet you are aware.

These two things have to be understood. There are people who are unconscious and innocent; they are childish. They will not enter the kingdom of God, they are not sadhus. Then there are people who are conscious and have become unnatural; because of their consciousness they have started interfering with their natural life. These people are so-called monks, sadhus; they are also not ready for the kingdom of God.

A new combination, a new synthesis is needed: awareness with spontaneity. That is what Kabir means when he says *sahaj samadhi*. *Sahaj* means spontaneity, *samadhi* means awareness: spontaneous awareness. If awareness interferes with your spontaneity, you have missed. If your spontaneity goes against awareness, you have missed. A sadhu is one who is both together: *sahajai kaya sadho.*

Says Kabir: *O sadhu! Purify your body in the simple,* natural, spontaneous *way.* Don't fight with the body – that is the message. The body is yours, the body is you; don't create any enmity with the body. The Christians, the Hindus, the Mohammedans, the Jainas have all been fighting with the body. Somehow, a very wrong notion has become very prevalent: that the body is the obstacle toward God. It is not so, not at all!

The body has nothing to do with it. The body is a vehicle: if you want to use the vehicle to go to hell, it will take you to hell; if you want to go to heaven, it will take you to heaven. The vehicle is simply available, wherever you want to go. If you want to go outside, it will take you outside; if you want to go inward, it will take you inward. The vehicle is just a vehicle; it is tremendously beautiful, tremendously cooperative. The body is so cooperative that even when you start destroying the body it cooperates. You can take a whip and whip yourself, and your hand will be cooperating. Look at the tremendous cooperation: you can whip your body with your own hands; you can drink poison with your own hands and with your own mouth, and the body will cooperate. Its cooperation is unconditional.

Such a beautiful body, such a friendly body – and you have been taught to be against it. You have been taught that the body is evil, or that the body belongs to the Devil: "Don't listen to the body." You are embodied in it, you are rooted in it. It is your soil; you have to grow out of it, you have to be nourished by it.

The first thing Kabir says is: *O sadhu! Purify your body in the simple way.* Don't fight with it; cooperate with it. Befriend it, and be spontaneous with it. Fulfill bodily needs because the body is a chariot and you can make it go to the ultimate consciousness. It will become your passage, it will take you, you can ride on it. It has been given to you for a particular goal. It is a very valuable mechanism. Science has not yet been able to create anything comparable to the body – and I don't think scientists will ever be able to create anything comparable to the body. The body is the divine's most beautiful mechanism.

As the seed is within the banyan tree, and within the seed are the

flowers, the fruits, and the shade, so the germ is within the body,
and within that germ is the body again.

Kabir says that the life spark is hidden in your body. The germ that
can become a flowering, the seed that can become God – the potentiality is hidden in the body. Don't fight with it because that potentiality is
very fragile; if you fight with the body you will destroy that potentiality.
It is very delicate. If you become aggressive, masochistic, if you start
torturing yourself, that delicacy will disappear.

The body has to be looked after: one has to be very caring about
the body and very loving to the body. And then its very spontaneity
purifies it, makes it holy.

The fire, the air, the water, the earth, and the ether; you cannot
have these outside of him.

And Kabir says this body is not outside of God, it is in God.
Nothing is outside of him. The air, the earth, the ether, the fire, the
water – nothing is outside of him, because *nothing* is outside him. God
has no outside.

Now let me explain it to you in this way: the rock has no inside;
man has outside and inside, both. The rock has only an outside; God
has no outside, he has only an inside. These are the three stages of
growth: matter – only the outside, no inside. There is no soul in it, no
consciousness in it. Man is both outside-inside because he is both
body-soul, both matter-mind. God has no outside; he is simply consciousness, simply soul.

Nothing is outside God, so he cannot have any outer circumference. Matter has no center, God has no circumference, and man has
both. That is the agony of man, and the ecstasy too.

Man is tremendous because he bridges matter and mind, he bridges
the world and God. With one hand he holds matter; with the other he
holds God. He is the bridge. Look at the beauty of your humanity, the
glory... And that is his anguish too – man is always pulled apart, torn
apart. On one side matter pulls him, on the other side the call of God;
on one side material possessions, on the other side love, prayer, meditation; on one side ambition, money, respect, on the other side
silence, beauty, good. And man is torn apart. This is one state.

The other state is: you feel so fulfilled because you are both. In you is the meeting point of God with the world. Man is a crossroads where God and the world meet.

Let me tell you: without you the world will be very empty. Without God the world cannot be. Without matter also, the world cannot be. The world can be without man – but it will be very impoverished.

Let me repeat: without God there is no possibility of the world, and without matter too, the world cannot exist. Without man, the world can exist and God can exist, but both will be impoverished. Without man, the agony will disappear and the ecstasy too. God will not be able to dance and sing, and matter will not be able to reach to peaks and touch the feet of God. Without man, the bridge will be broken.

Man is the greatest glory, the most subtle bridge, the most impossible possibility. It should not happen; it is against all rules that man is. God is simple, matter is simple; godliness is pure consciousness, matter is pure unconsciousness. Man is complex; he's both consciousness and unconsciousness. He is polar. Opposites meet in him and contradictions meet in him.

Remember this: it is up to you to turn it into an agony if that is your attitude. It is up to you to turn it into an ecstasy – that too is your attitude. Agony is ecstasy looked at in a wrong way; ecstasy is agony looked at in the right way. And the poison becomes honey if your vision becomes right.

O kazi, o pundit, consider it well: what is there that is not in the soul?

And Kabir says: *What is there that is not in the soul?* Don't talk about the Vedas, *O pundit*; and don't talk about the Koran, *O kazi*; and don't talk about the Bible and the Dhammapada. What is there that is not in the soul itself? All the Vedas are contained there – because all the Vedas have come out of the soul, flown out of the soul. The source is there within you. All the Gitas and the Bibles are born out of you. Because Christ entered into his soul, the Bible flowered. Because Moses entered into his soul, the Bible flowered. Because Krishna entered into his innermost core of being, out came the beautiful Bhagavad Gita, the celestial song. Because Buddha penetrated his own soul, the Dhammapada was born. All is in your soul. When you seek in the Vedas and the Koran you seek in a wrong direction, and you are seeking a secondhand God, and God can never be secondhand; God has to be firsthand.

When you are seeking in the scriptures you are seeking theories and not truth – and truth is original, has to be original. The truth has to be born in you; it cannot be borrowed.

O kazi, O pundit, consider it well: what is there that is not in the soul? Everything is within him, within God, within the soul – and he is in everything.

The water-filled pitcher is placed upon water, it has water within and without.
It should not be given a name, lest it call forth the error of dualism.

The whole problem has arisen out of language: within and without, God and the world, matter and mind. The whole problem has arisen out of naming things. Don't name; drop language, be in a non-linguistic gap, and suddenly you see there is only one. Sometimes try a nonverbal approach.

That's what meditation is all about: looking at life without verbalization. Sit by the side of a tree and just look at the tree; don't even call it a tree, don't say what kind of tree – casuarina, pine, cedar. Don't call it any name, drop the names.

Sometimes look into somebody's eyes and don't call them any names – man, woman, yours, friend, enemy, young, old, beautiful, ugly – don't bring names in. Just look into the eyes, try to avoid verbalization, and suddenly you will come to a leap, a quantum leap, where you will be surprised to see that the observer has become the observed, that the observed has become the observer. Then you don't know who is "I" and who is "thou." These are the moments from where God enters you; his first footsteps are heard.

At least for one hour drop out of language. And to drop out of language is to drop out of society; to drop out of language is to drop out of religions; to drop out of language is to drop out of all that is man-created. Have you seen? – language is very, very significant. Animals are silent, trees are silent; they don't argue, they don't have any scriptures. A tree is neither a Christian nor a Hindu nor a Moham-medan; it is simply there in its beauty, with no name. It does not even know its own name; those names are given by human beings. Your society is created through language, your knowledge is created through language. Just think, if suddenly a miracle happened and language disappeared from the world, what would be the difference between man and animal? What would be the difference between a Hindu and a Mohammedan? There would be no difference. All distinctions are language-created.

So make it a small discipline. When I say discipline I say it with great fear, because you can misunderstand the word *discipline*. When I say discipline, I don't mean force it upon yourself. The word *discipline* means learning. When I say discipline yourself, I mean learn.

Sit by the side of the tree, look at the rose, and don't utter words, out or in. Just be present. Let the rose open in your presence, and let your presence shower on the rose. Let there be a meeting with no language. As the rose is silent, so you be silent; the rose is not saying anything about you, so please, don't say anything about the rose. The rose is not saying how beautiful a man you are. The rose is not saying you are man or woman, black or white. The rose is not saying anything; the rose is in tremendous silence, pulsating in silence. So should you pulsate. Sit by the side, look into the rose, just watch. Don't let language arise. If words come, put them aside. Just remain indifferent to words. They will come; they are your old habit, they will not leave you so easily. You have been using them so much, exploiting them so much, you have been so dependent on them that they will not leave you so easily; they will hover around, they will buzz around, they will bug you. They will come and say, "Beautiful rose..." Remain indifferent, don't cooperate. I am not saying start fighting, simply don't cooperate – that will do. Fighting never helps. The moment you fight you are getting into the mess, the confusion.

If you fight with a word, you will need another word to fight it with, remember. You cannot fight with a word without words. A word comes and you say, "I am not supposed to have any words. Osho has said, 'Sit silently.'" These are all words. Or you say, "Don't you know I am meditating? Don't come to me." But this meditation is again a word.

You can fight only with words. To fight with words you will need more words, and you will get into the whole rut again. No, no need; let the words pass, let them float; it's okay. Be indifferent; be neutral. They will buzz around for a few days, and then by and by they will feel they are neglected. By and by they will feel you are no longer interested; by and by they will feel that they are not welcome. And when words start feeling they are not welcome, when thoughts start feeling that they are not welcome, they start disappearing. You are no longer a host to them.

One day suddenly you will be surprised: a few moments have passed – the rose has been there, the sun has been there, the green trees have been there, you have been there – and not a single word has crossed. You have tasted, for the first time, what meditation is. You have tasted Tao. You had a glimpse into the being of Kabir and Krishna and Christ. You have tasted Osho. You have come to see something of tremendous import, for the first time; and once tasted, you will welcome it more and more. Whenever you find time, you will sit silently. And there is no need to go to a rosebush; you can sit silently in your room – the walls are as beautiful.

It is said about Bodhidharma that for nine years he sat facing the wall – doing nothing, just facing the wall. Sometimes sit facing the wall; just look at the wall, the plain white wall – nothing to distract, nothing much to say. You can create the interval, the gap anywhere. When two thoughts have a gap between them, in that gap take a jump, dive in.

Language is society, language is civilization, language is communism, language is Islam, language is Hinduism, language is Christianity; and in the gap is Christ, in the gap is Mohammed, and in the gap arises the Koran.

It is said that when Mohammed heard for the first time – of course, it is a parable – when he heard that a messenger from God was standing and telling him to recite, recite the name of God, recite his glory… The word *koran* means recite; that's where the name Koran has come from – because the first thing that Mohammed heard was, "Recite!"

He was very much puzzled, and he asked, "How to recite? I don't know!"

The angel said, "That's why! Recite, because those who know cannot recite."

And Mohammed said, "I am very illiterate, and I don't even know language rightly. I cannot write and I cannot read."

The angel said, "Precisely! That's why I say recite; those who know and can read and write are lost in their knowledge. You are pure in this moment, recite."

In this purity, God has spoken. In this purity, his own innermost soul has spoken. In this very purity the beautiful Koran was born.

Now, you need not go to the Koran. You can go to your inner interval, and again the messenger will come and say, "Recite!" I say it so to you because it has happened to me; it can happen to you.

Whenever there is an interval, God's messengers are around you. When there is tremendous silence, God is within you. You are fulfilled.

It should not be given a name, lest it call forth the error of dualism. The moment you give a name to something, you have created the world as dual; you have brought dualism, you have brought a subtle schizophrenia into the world. Whenever you say, "This is beautiful," you have brought ugliness into the world. Don't you see it? Whenever you say, "I love," you have brought hatred into the world. Whenever you say, "You are my friend," you have brought enmity into the world. Whenever you say, "This is good, right, moral," you have brought immorality into the world, you have brought the Devil into the world. In deep silence, when you don't know what is good and what is bad and you don't utter any labels and names, in that silence the duality disappears, the schizophrenia disappears, the split disappears. The world becomes one.

That oneness is God. And to live in that oneness is to be a sadhu, is to be a sannyasin.

Kabir says: Listen to the word, the truth, which is your essence.

When you are listening to your concepts, labels, names, language, you cannot listen to the ultimate word, you cannot listen to the *logos*. Kabir calls it *sabad*, the word. It means exactly the same as when the Bible says: "In the beginning was the word" – it was not human, because it was in the beginning; humanity came long afterward – "and the word was with God, and the word was God."

Kabir uses the word *sabad*. *Sabad* means the word, the logos, that which was before man was ever there, and that which will be there again when man has disappeared. It has nothing to do with our words; it is not linguistic, it is not part of language; it is *omkar,* it is om, it is the soundless sound of existence. It is what Zen masters call "the sound of one hand clapping" – un-struck, not by the clash of two. When you clap hands it is a struck sound, a created sound, and it is out of conflict, it is out of two.

No, there is a sound of one hand clapping – not out of conflict but out of such ultimate harmony, out of one. That is the word, the *sabad*, the truth. But you have to drop your language before God can speak his language. You have to be utterly silent before he can convey his message.

But we have a very wrong notion: we think if we have to pray, we have to talk to God. No, prayer is more listening than talking, better listen rather than talk. You cannot improve upon God. Whatsoever you say is meaningless, whatsoever you say is ridiculous. He knows it already, so what is the point? Keep quiet, remain in silence. Rather, try to hear. Be sensitive; don't use the tongue, use the ear. Prayer is more concerned with the ear than the tongue. The prayer that comes out of the tongue is foolish, meaningless. You are advising God: you are saying, "Do it this way. Whatsoever you are doing is going wrong." You say, "My wife is ill; make her well again. And I am getting old – give me more strength and a longer life," and so on and so forth. All your prayers are your advice to God about how things should be.

A really prayerful man cannot advise God. He will say, "Thy will be done, thy kingdom come. Whatsoever you are doing must be right. Maybe I cannot see why it is right, I cannot even see that it is right – that is my ignorance. But don't listen to me. Even if in my ignorance sometimes I say something to you, please never listen to me; go on doing whatsoever you are doing."

Real prayer is not talk; it is listening, deep listening. One simply sits silently, open, sensitive, alert. Have you seen, sometimes waiting for your beloved, your lover, your friend, a slight murmur in the trees, the wind passing by, or old leaves of the almond falling, and you rush out: "Maybe she has come, maybe he has come." And it is nothing – just wind playing with old, dead leaves. You go again, again you wait, again something else: the postman moving in the neighborhood, footsteps, and you are again at the door.

Just as you watch for your lover, for your beloved, you remain alert for small indications, in the same way a prayerful mind remains alert for God, for his word to arrive. And it arrives! The moment comes when the Koran arises in you; the moment comes when you start feeling the reality of the Vedas and the Gita. And when you have felt it at your innermost core, then scriptures are beautiful; then you can read... Read as many scriptures as you can. It is fun, because then all the scriptures become real. You know, you become a witness of them.

Vice-versa is not true: you can go on reading the scriptures, but just by reading the scriptures you will not arrive at truth. But if you have arrived, then all scriptures become true. Truth is first; scriptures are shadows, echoes.

Kabir says: Listen to the word, the truth, which is your essence. He speaks the word to himself; and he himself is the creator.

And there are not two persons: when God speaks, he speaks to himself; there is no other. Be so silent that only God is; then he speaks to you – but then he is speaking to himself. It is a monologue, there is no other, he talks to himself, he whispers to himself.

That is possible only when you have completely effaced yourself. If you exist as the other, he cannot whisper; or, he may go on whispering, but you will not be able to hear. As the other you are blocked, as the other you are deaf. Drop the otherness: that is the meaning of surrender.

Just the other day somebody asked, "What is the meaning of surrender?" This is the meaning of surrender: drop your otherness. Don't think of yourself as the other, put aside your separateness. Don't say, "I am"; let him be, and let him be so totally that you are drowned in that totality, absorbed, lost. Be a wave in the ocean, but don't claim that you are separate from the ocean – that is the meaning of surrender.

There is a strange tree which stands without roots and bears fruits without blossoming; it has no branches and no leaves, it is lotus all over.

Now Kabir says God is the original cause. Of course, he cannot have another cause. God is the creator, and you cannot ask who has created him. He is the uncaused cause.

There is a strange tree – this God, this existence, is a strange tree – *which stands without roots...* Try to understand it; it is simple. The whole cannot be rooted in anything else because it is the whole;

nothing exists outside it. The whole is rooted in itself. Now this will be a very strange tree – rooted in itself. A tree has to be rooted in the earth; how can the tree be rooted in itself? But the whole has to be rooted in itself, there is nothing else.

There can be no cause of God; God is the ultimate cause. That is what we mean by God: the ultimate cause, the uncaused one, which has always been, which will always be. There is none before it and none after it. God has no past and no future; God has only the present. God is eternal.

There is a strange tree, says Kabir, *which stands without roots and bears fruits without blossoming.* It is very illogical, he says. Existence is illogical. Or, there is logic to its illogicalness. It is very strange, mysterious. It is not reducible to human syllogisms. It blossoms *...and bears fruits without blossoming; it has no branches and no leaves, it is lotus all over.*

How is it possible – *...lotus all over?* It is only lotus and lotus and lotus: no roots, no leaves, no branches. It is simply ultimate flowering. God is the ultimate, that which has already happened; there is nothing more to happen to it. God is not a seed. The seed is something which is not yet a flower; something has to happen to the seed. God is that which has already happened; there is nothing more to happen to it.

That is the meaning when we say God is perfect: there is no more growing; it has grown. It has always been in that state, the state of perfection: *...it is lotus all over.*

Two birds sing there; one is the guru, and the other the disciple.

Now God has divided himself into many forms and goes on playing the game, the *leela*. Somewhere he is the man and somewhere he is the woman, and they lure each other, and they sing songs of love, and they dance dances of love. Somewhere he is the guru and the disciple – the same polarity. Somewhere he is matter and somewhere he is the mind. And somewhere he is the sound and somewhere he is the soundlessness; somewhere he has become life and somewhere he has become death...but the same polarity. *The disciple* and *the guru* mean the yin-yang, the male-female.

The disciple chooses the manifold fruits of life...

And both are within you. The master is your innermost core, the witness; and the disciple is your periphery, your world, the *samsara*.

The disciple chooses the manifold fruits of life and tastes them, and the guru beholds him in joy.

And the master inside you, the center inside you, beholds you in joy, in all your games. Have you watched it? Sometimes shift yourself to the standpoint of the master and see yourself playing, how many games you play: the game of love, the game of ambition, the game of anger, hatred – all are games, *all* are games. But if you become too absorbed, you have become the disciple; if you become alert, you have become the master.

This is the only change, the only transmutation that is needed, the only alchemy. Watch. Kabir is not saying, "Stop the games"; he is saying, "Just watch from the master's standpoint too." Sometimes simply become the watcher, the witness, and see the disciple playing the games. You are talking to your woman and saying beautiful sweet nothings – watch. Enjoy from the master's side. For a moment, shift your whole consciousness to witnessing and see how beautiful a game you are playing.

If you can shift from the master to the disciple, from the disciple to the master, you will never be caught in any game. Then the game will remain the game: you can play it as much as you want, to your heart's desire, but you will never be caught, you will never become identified. You will always remain free, free in the world: *jivan mukta* – free in life, dreaming and yet not dreaming.

The game that you are playing with me, of being a disciple – watch it. And sometimes, let your center become the master, let the game be introverted. I am the master and you are the disciple; we are playing a game. It is an extroverted game: I am just trying to train you so that one day you can introvert the whole game. It is easier to play on an extroverted stage, a projected stage – it is easy. I am the master and you are the disciple, so there is not much confusion. Things are simple: you have one role; I have another role.

One day you have to shift it inside; you have to close the eyes and let your center be Osho, your master, and your periphery the disciple. And then play the game, the same game, and there will be tremendous energy released. A great understanding will dawn over you: the morning, the sun has risen... You will see your own game. And remember, don't be tempted to stop it, there is no hurry. If you are tempted to stop it, you again become identified with the master.

Identification has to be dropped. One has to be free to move from the master to the disciple, from the disciple to the master. This is freedom, this is liberation: to move between the polarities. It is very easy to get identified with the disciple; you are the disciple. Then there are masters who are identified with the master. Both are in the same rut, in the same boat. Both are in a deep illusion. The real master is one who is not identified with either, who knows, "Both are my being, both are my polarities."

The master sits at the center, the disciple goes on playing and the master does not even interfere. He does not say, "Don't do this!" It is a game; in a game everything is allowed – yes, sometimes cheating too. In a game... In a game everything is allowed. The game is a game; one is sincere, not serious about it – it is a game. But the witness remains. And then, by and by, the game continues and yet, on a deeper layer, it has stopped. The game continues on the surface, the waves go on playing on the surface, and the ocean is totally silent at the center. This is the state of being a Christ or a Buddha or a Krishna. That's what Krishna is trying to say to Arjuna, his disciple: "Don't be worried about the game. Play! If it has come to be your part to play the game of a warrior and fight this war, fight. Just remain at the center and go on watching that this is a game, and there is nothing to be serious about."

You will be surprised that Krishna is the only great master in the world who is known to have cheated. And Hindus call him the most perfect master. He is. Rama is not that perfect; he is very much afraid of cheating, he is too sincere. Sincerity is his bondage. He is not relaxed. He is a perfect saint: he has denied all that is wrong – but that is seriousness, and that shows that you are still taking the game very, very seriously. You are not taking it as a game.

Krishna is totally different. It is a game: he promises one day and forgets another day. He is really liberated; his liberation is perfect, without flaw. His liberation is without flaw because he knows all is a game. When all is a game and all is a dream, then why be bothered? He is not worried or bothered; he plays it and remains unattached.

Kabir is again a perfect master. He never left the world – he remained in the world, he remained a householder; he had a wife and children and he continued to do his work. He was a weaver, a poor man; he continued to weave, he continued to sell his cloth in the market. He lived a very ordinary life. He had thousands of disciples, and they would come and they would say, "Master, why do you go on doing these things? Simply sit, simply meditate, simply rest. We are here, why should you do anything?"

But he would say, "No. Whatsoever game God has given me, I have to play. It is good and I enjoy it. I will miss it very much if I stop. I will miss my customers in the market – they wait for me, I weave for them, and God comes through them to purchase it. No, they will miss me very much. And who will weave such beautiful clothes for them? Nobody can do it as beautifully as I can do it."

He would weave the whole day, and by the evening he would go to the market – as in India weavers go to the market to sell their clothes, whatsoever they have manufactured. And to each customer he would say, "Rama. So, God, you have come? You were waiting? For you I made a really beautiful piece. And it is going to last. And I have not only woven it, I have put my whole heart in it. Take care of it; it has been made through love."

He continued. He remained ordinary, and yet with tremendously extraordinary awareness.

The master is within you, your center; and the periphery is your disciple. When your center has arisen, then the outer master is just a reflection. Then you are grateful to the outer master because he has pointed to the inner.

The disciple chooses the manifold fruits of life and tastes them, and the guru beholds him in joy.
What Kabir says is hard to understand: the bird is beyond seeking, yet it is most clearly visible.

The center is beyond seeking. You cannot seek it because it is already there; it cannot be sought, it just has to be discovered. It is already there.

A beautiful anecdote Prembodhi has sent me – a joke by Dick Gregory, the black American comedian...

You white folks must be really crazy – like when you came to America you claimed you discovered a country that was not only being occupied at the time by someone else, by the American Indians, but actually being used by them. And you say you discovered it? You must be crazy.

It is like me and my lady meet you and your lady, as you come down the street in a beautiful, brand new Cadillac, and my lady says, "Wow! What a beautiful car! I wish it was mine."

And I would say, "Martha, let us *discover* it."

Just the American way: let us discover it.

The inner bird, the eternal bird, is there; you have to discover it in the American way. It has never been lost; it is already occupied, and you are already using it! You may not know it; you are already using it, you are centered in it. Without it you will fall to pieces; it is holding you. So you have to discover it in the American way: "Martha, let us discover it!"

It is beyond seeking because in fact it is the seeker – how can the seeker be sought? And it is the sought. It is the journey and it is the goal; it is the beginning and it is the end. It is the disciple and it is the master.

...the bird is beyond seeking, yet it is most clearly visible. The
formless is in the midst of all forms. I sing the glory of forms.

And Kabir says: *I sing the glory of forms* – because I cannot sing the glory of the formless. You cannot sing the glory of God; that is not possible. It is difficult to reduce him to a song, it is difficult to reduce him to words. So Kabir says, "Okay, it is impossible to sing the glory of God? – I will sing the glory of the manifold forms. I will sing the glory of the roseflower, I will sing the glory of the human eye. I will sing the glory of the river in the night, I will sing the glory of the white cloud, I will sing the glory of the sun and the stars."

So let us sing the glory of the manifold forms and that will be an indirect praise of God. God cannot be praised directly; one has to be very indirect. You can offer your praise to God through a roseflower, through the beautiful rock, through a beautiful woman or man. You have to sing the glory of existence.

And that is the only way to worship God. Don't go to the mosque and don't go to the temple and don't go to the *gurudwara*. Sing the glory of this beautiful cosmos around you, sing the glory of the new leaf on the tree and sing the glory of the new dewdrop on the grass; sing the glory of the stars and the sky, sing the glory of human love. Create poetry, create sculpture, create songs – be creative because that is the only way to offer yourself unto the feet of the creator.

Kabir says that only when you are creative are you close to the creator.

Enough for today.

CHAPTER 6

the inner trinity

The first question:

Osho,
The Steiner School of Anthroposophy teaches one to have a strong will. This is a departure from traditional Eastern thought. What is this will? How does this will relate to the ego?

The East and the West, up to now, have worked as polar opposites: the West through the will, the East through surrender; the West through the ego, the East through absolute egolessness. The way of the West is that of the male, and the way of the East is that of the female.

The East believes in passivity: God comes to you when you are absolutely passive, receptive, a nothing, just an awaiting, a prayerful awaiting, with no effort at all on your part. The way of the West is aggressive: the way of the male. Man has to seek, man has to go, man has to conquer. Even God has to be conquered, nature has to be conquered, truth has to be conquered.

Both have failed, because both are partial; they had to fail. The East has failed tremendously, as tremendously as the West has failed – because man is not only male and man is not only female. Man is both, and more. Man is both the yin and yang. And a greater religion, a far more synthetic religion is needed in which the East and West will lose their old conflict.

Steiner is the representative of the Western mind. He revolted against theosophy and created a new school, anthroposophy. Theosophy was Eastern: Blavatsky, Annie Besant, Leadbeater and Alcott. They had searched in the East, in the old scriptures, traditions, old masters, and they had come to a certain conclusion about the East: that if you surrender, God happens.

Theosophy means: *theo* means God, *sophy* means love. You simply live like a woman. You wait, you remain in a welcoming mood. Only that welcoming mood is needed, and God penetrates you. You become the feminine and he becomes the male. That is the allegory of Krishna and his girlfriends. Krishna is God, the male; and the seeker, the devotee, is a female, a girlfriend, a *gopi*. One has to become feminine to reach to God – that has been the essential core of Eastern thought, religion, philosophy.

Steiner revolted against it. First he was a theosophist, but by and by he became aware that it was not possible for him to accept it. He created a new movement against theosophy, a new school. He called it anthroposophy. *Anthrop* means man, *theo* means God. Theosophy is love of God; anthroposophy is love of man. He placed man in the very center. God is not in the center of his thinking; man is at the center.

For theosophy, God is at the center: Krishna playing on his flute and man dancing the dance around him – the girlfriends, the *gopis*. Man is on the periphery; God is at the center. Steiner turned the whole thing upside down: he put man in the center, man becomes the central thing. In the West, man has remained the central thing. In the East, man is peripheral.

Now, both efforts have failed because both are partial; man is both male and female together. It has to be so: you are born of a mother and a father – how can you be just man or just woman? Within your soul your mother continues to live, and your father too. And you have to be a deep harmony of the two.

I call that man religious who has come to a great harmony within his own self, the harmony between his mother and father. They are still quarreling within you, they are still fighting. It is not only that when you were a child your mother and father were fighting; they are still fighting in each of your cells.

So there are two possibilities. A man who is still in conflict and has not come to a deep understanding of his polarities has to choose. Either he becomes an egoist if he chooses the man, the yang; or if he chooses the woman, if he chooses yin, the woman, then he becomes surrendered. But in both cases one part will suffer, the unchosen part will suffer, and you will never be whole. And how can you be holy if you are not whole? The part that is neglected, rejected, will take its revenge. The part that you have rejected will become your unconscious. The unconscious is nothing but the rejected part of your being.

There is a possibility in the future of a humanity where the unconscious does not exist. If we stop rejecting, the unconscious will disappear; man can become absolutely conscious. And that's what we mean by a buddha, the awakened soul. It means that now there is no rejected part; you have absorbed your totality, you have accepted all your facets, you have become multidimensional. Now the polarity is no longer in contradiction; it has become complementary. Your woman inside helps your man, your man inside helps the woman. They have fallen in love with each other, conflict has disappeared. They have become one, they are wedded together. This is the spiritual marriage, and only out of this marriage will you be born. Only out of this inner meeting of the contradictions will you be born.

This is the whole philosophy of the concept of the Trinity. The concept of the Trinity is beautiful and has many meanings: God the Father, the Son and the Holy Ghost. Of course, the Holy Ghost is not the right name – people who coined that must have been male chauvinists. The Holy Ghost is not right, but the Mother – the Father, the Mother and the Son. Then it is perfectly true, factual.

The father and the mother are in you; the son is still missing. Your father and mother have not met inside you; they have met outside you, so your body is created. When they meet inside you, your soul will be created, the son will be born – and that is the birth of Christ.

The East has suffered because the East became feminine. That's why anybody could conquer it: it lost willpower, it lost zest, enthusiasm to live, it lost energy. It became very fatalistic, it became very relaxed. The whole history of the East is the history of being conquered by others – a history of poverty, a history of no science, no technology. It is not a beautiful history.

Yes, a few beautiful people happened: Buddha, Mahavira, Krishna, Kabir, Nanak, Dadu – a few beautiful people, but they are exceptional, they cannot be counted. The greater mass, the greater humanity, has lived in a very ugly way, a miserable way, in deep anguish. At this cost, if one Buddha happens and one Kabir and one Nanak, it is not of worth. The cost is too much.

The West has suffered from male-orientation: conflict, struggle, violence, fight, and no rest, no possibility of any relaxation; a great tension in the mind, hankering for speed, ambition; competition, a cut-throat competition, each fighting with everybody else – a very hostile atmosphere. Of course it has created mad people, neurotic people. Still, a few beautiful people have existed on the fringe: a Christ, a Saint Teresa, a Saint Francis and an Eckhart. But this cannot be said to be a success: the philosophy has failed. The East and West have both failed.

That's my whole effort here: what I am trying to do is to bring East and West closer. The twain can meet. Kipling was wrong when he said, "East is East and West is West, and the twain shall never meet." I say they can meet; they *have* to meet. Now everything will depend... Even the possibility of a future humanity will depend on that meeting. Kipling has to be proved wrong. They have not met up to now, that's true. Kipling is right about the past, but wrong about the future – has to be wrong, otherwise humanity cannot exist. Both are suffering: the East from outward poverty, the West from inner poverty. Both have failed tremendously – grand failures, but failures.

A man has to be a synthesis of will and surrender. A man first has to grow his willpower, his ego. My approach is that if life is going to be for an average of seventy years, then thirty-five years, the beginning of life, should be devoted to strengthening the ego and willpower – and one should listen to Nietzsche and one should listen to Steiner and one should listen to Freud. The ego has to be strengthened, made very integrated.

After the thirty-fifth year, one has to learn relaxing and dropping the ego and becoming more and more surrendered to the divine. The West, the first part of life; the East, the second part of life. Life should start Western and should end Eastern. One should first go into the world; in the world, will is needed. One should go and fight and struggle, because struggle gives you a sharp intelligence, but one should not continue fighting and fighting to the very end. Then what is the point?

Fight, sharpen your intelligence, know the ways of the world, wander all over the world, be a conqueror, and then... Then move inward. You have known the outside; now try to know the inner. And to know the inner, one has to relax, one has to forget anxiety, anguish, tension. One has to be noncompetitive; will is not needed. To conquer the world, will is needed; to conquer God, will is not needed.

To conquer God means to be conquered by God; to conquer God means to relax and surrender unto his feet. Now this will seem very difficult, very illogical. I am an illogical person. My understanding is that only strong egos can surrender; weak egos cannot surrender.

Every day I come across weak egos. Whenever a weak ego comes, he hesitates: to surrender or not to surrender, to take sannyas or not to take sannyas. And why is he afraid? He is afraid because he knows he has a very weak ego; if he surrenders he is gone, he will not be able to stand. He is afraid of his inner weakness. He pretends on the outside, but he knows his inner reality – that he is ready. So he becomes defensive, he defends.

Whenever a person of strong ego comes he says, "Okay, let us see. Let us try this too." He knows, he is confident enough that even if he goes into some unknown path he can still protect himself. And if he decides to come back, he can come back; he has enough trust, enough self-confidence, he has enough will.

Remember, surrender is the last and the greatest act of will. Surrender is not a cheap and easy thing. It is not that because you cannot stand you surrender; you were already falling so you say, "Okay, I surrender" because you were not able to stand on your feet. Surrender is not impotence.

Surrender is not out of impotence; it is out of tremendous power. You have lived the ways of the will and you have found nothing. You have looked into all the possibilities of the ego and you have only suffered; it simply hurts. Then you decide, "Now let us try the ultimate: dropping the ego."

To drop the ego you will need a great will; otherwise it is not easy. It is the greatest act in the world, the last. Only very courageous people can do it. You will be surprised: in India, all the great saviors, avatars, are warriors. This is not coincidental. Both Krishna and Rama belong to the warrior race, kshatriya; Buddha, Mahavira, the twenty-four *tirthankaras* of the Jainas are kshatriyas. This has to be not only a coincidence. Why have all these great people come from the warriors – and they talk about surrender? And they say, "Surrender is the way." They had the will to surrender. A brahmin has not yet come to the state of a Buddha or Mahavira. Why? The brahmin has no will. He has thought, from the beginning, of surrender. He has not arrived at a will from where he can surrender.

Or take it from a different angle: a poor man wants to renounce – what will he renounce, what has he got to renounce? What does his renunciation mean? Then a Rockefeller decides to renounce: his renunciation will mean something. It carries weight; he has something to renounce.

If a beggar declares, "I have renounced the world," people will laugh. In the first place, you had nothing to renounce. If a king renounces, then the renunciation is meaningful. This man has known what wealth is, this man has known what power is, this man has known what will is – and knowing it well, he has understood that it cannot be the last thing in life. Good for the beginning, good for the young people to play with as a toy, but for those who are becoming mature, useless – they have to drop it.

We give small children toys to play with. The day they become a little more mature they throw the toys away, and they start asking for the real thing. We give them a toy train and they say, "Forget about it." We give them a toy airplane and they say, "Throw it away. I want a real car, a real airplane. I want the real thing."

Ego can only give you toys to play with. But it is needed, otherwise you will never grow and never become mature. One day you understand, "Now I need the real thing" – and the real thing is God. And for God to happen, you have to surrender.

Steiner is wrong because his philosophy is half. So is Annie Besant; she's wrong, her philosophy is half. I am talking about a total philosophy.

Up to the age of thirty-five, move in the ways of the world, the ways of will. Strengthen your ego as much as you can by knowledge, by power, by money, by ambition. Live it, because that is the only way to know it. Go into the deepest hell the world can make available to you. Know it – because only by knowing is one liberated.

And then suddenly a light will dawn on you. You will see the whole absurdity of it. You start returning home; you start returning toward the source. For thirty-five years go into the world, and then for the remaining part, come back to yourself. First lose yourself so that you can gain; first sin so that you can become a saint. If you are a saint from the very beginning, your sainthood will not be of much value.

I am not against sin; I am not against anything. I say for you to use everything, go into it. God has made this whole world available to you for a certain purpose: the purpose is learning. Sin is a lesson, is a must. If a child is a saint from the very childhood, is forced to be a saint, he will not have any spine. Let him first know what sin is. Let him become aware, and let him drop it on his own accord. Don't force him, don't discipline him. Give him freedom to move, so one day he can see with his own eyes, feel with his own heart. And he can realize that Buddha is right, that Kabir is right, that Christ is right. But this has to come from your own understanding; otherwise it is borrowed. And God never wants anybody secondhand. Be first-hand. Let your experience be original.

So this is what I say to you: will and surrender have to become part of your life, together, because you are man and woman together, and you are East and West together. The world is one, the earth is one village. All distinctions are just utilitarian, not real. What is East and what is West? And what is surrender and what is will? They are both part of the one wave. They are not two, they are a quantum, one. They are two aspects of one thing, one phenomenon.

So grow in will, and don't be afraid. Become a strong egoist, don't be afraid. Let it hurt, let it become a self-torture, let it become a cancer in your soul – then one day drop it. And that dropping is out of your own feeling, own experience. Then it is beautiful.

There is a danger that I must make you aware of. The danger is that rather than coming to a synthesis, the danger is we may change roles: the East may become West and the West may become East. That is more possible. Seeing the stupidity of human beings, that seems more possible.

The East is trying to become the West: more technological, more scientific, more materialistic, more communistic. In fact, the Pune people simply laugh at you: "What are you doing here? What is here in the first place, meditating? What nonsense!" They want to go to the West to know more engineering, to know more about electronics, to know more about computers, to know more about hydrogen and atom bombs, to know more about how to create spaceships, how to create wealth, more wealth. They want to become more materialistic, more productive. "And you are coming here – have you gone crazy?"

And when they go to the West, you cannot believe what they are doing there. You are fed up with your materialism, and what are they going there for? – to know better technology, to destroy their natural atmosphere, to pollute it, to destroy the ecology. For what are they going to the West? The West is getting fed up with technology. The modern mind is trying to move away from technology – at least the new generation is absolutely against it. The new generation in the West can understand Buddha better than Einstein. The new generation can understand Mahavira, a naked Mahavira, better than all the Darwins and Eddingtons and Rutherfords. But in the Eastern universities, colleges, the new generation is hankering after Rutherford, Einstein, Max Planck – how to know more about science.

The possibility is that the East may become the West and the West may become the East – and the old foolishness continues: again you are far apart, again the meeting has not happened. The meeting has to happen, that is the only hope for humanity. And the meeting has to happen in each individual. It cannot happen in books and philosophies; it has to happen in each individual.

That is what Tantra is all about. Tantra is the oldest science to help you to come to an inner harmony, an inner wedding, an inner orgasm. Your woman and man meet inside and give birth to the child, the child Christ. Then you become a trinity: the father, the mother, the child. And when you are a trinity, you are blessed, you have come home. You know what life is, you have achieved the goal.

The second question:

Osho,
I am a gambler in life. I have brought suffering to almost everybody who came close to me. My eyes have deceived everybody up to now, and when people, out of their suffering caused by me, sometimes said, "You are a good soul," then it was part of my game to deceive myself and feel good about their statement. And now, in my first *darshan*, Osho, you looked into my eyes and you said I am a very good person. But now as you, you

the master, are saying this, I can't deceive myself any longer, and I can't accept these words from you. What are you doing? I'm so puzzled, so lost. Have you also been deceived by me? Or are you gambling with me? Please don't gamble; please help me to drop the games. My whole being is hurt because, Osho, how could you be deceived?

I am not deceived; that's why I said to you that you are a good soul. I wanted to settle it from the very beginning. I wanted to bring it to the surface. That has been your problem, and I am here to bring your problem to the surface of your consciousness. I have not missed – you were caught. I am not deceived.

I don't ordinarily say so: it is very rare I say to somebody, "You are a good soul," because people are not! It is very rare that I say so. But I had to say it to you because this is your old game, and it is very good, from the very beginning, to be clear that this game has not to be played here.

Every individual has a particular weakness, and the weakness persists because you remain unaware of it. I wanted it to be perfectly clear to you. And it did the work.

It was your first *darshan* with me, and I wanted to start from the very beginning. I talked about your goodness because I wanted to create the problem, so you can face it. And it is good that it created anxiety in you. It is good that it created a question in you. It is good that you became puzzled. It is good that you became confused. That is one of my ways of working on you: to confuse you. When you are clear your ego is in control; your clarity is nothing but your ego in control. When you are confused your ego is thrown off-center; then you don't know what is what.

When you come to me, the first thing is that I should confuse you. I should throw you off balance, so your old ego-control is no longer in control – so you don't know what to do. When you don't know what to do, only then do you ask me. And it is good that you have asked.

You say, "Please, don't gamble with me" – I am not gambling – "Please help me to drop the games." That's why I have started this game of calling you a very great, good soul, a really good soul. It is to help you drop your egoistic attitudes.

This is going to happen; you *are* going to become a good soul.

You are not, that's true – but to realize, "I am not a good soul," is the beginning. To realize, "I don't know" is the first step. To realize, "I have yet to grow, I am yet far away," is the first step.

If you continue to think that you are a good soul and you are not, then there is no hope for you. It is as if an ill person thinks he is healthy and well and he never goes to the doctor. What is the point, he is healthy. He thinks he is healthy – and the disease goes on spreading.

You have come to me, and I have diagnosed your disease absolutely. This has been your disease: you have been thinking you are good, you have been deceiving about your goodness, and when people trusted you and they were deceived, you were deceived by their deception. And this is how it went on feeding itself; it became a vicious circle.

You are not good, but you can pretend to be. And through pretension you can deceive others. When they are deceived, of course, you look at your image in their eyes and you feel very happy. This is how things grow: when you feel very happy, you try to be better; when you try to be better, of course the person thinks you are a really great soul, a mahatma. Then in his eyes you can see your reflection – more decorated, still more beautiful. You are again deceived. Now you have to try harder because this person is there, and the game continues. This is how it happens in everybody's life.

You meet a woman or a man – you look at the woman, she looks at you. You look with adoration; she looks into your eyes at her adored image. She feels very good. She was hankering for somebody to pay attention to her, and you are paying attention. She feels very good; that's why she looks at you with adoration. When she looks at you with adoration, of course you look into her eyes; you have never seen your image so beautiful. You feel tremendously good, enhanced. Your ego is strengthened. You try to be more loving... And this way the game continues.

You fall in love. Ninety-nine percent of your love affairs are simply foolish. What you call romance is nothing but stupidity. You feed each other and you help each other. One day you are going to be shocked. Now you want to remain close, more close to each other; you want to be together twenty-four hours a day. Then you are ready to get married, then you go for a honeymoon, and then you become acquainted with each other, and then the reality asserts.

Reality cannot be denied for long. That's why your so-called great people, or so-called great saints, don't live in the marketplace; they go to the Himalayas. If they lived in the marketplace it would be impossible; sooner or later the reality would assert. Reality cannot be defeated forever. You can create a fiction for a few days, a few moments, but you cannot live in the fiction forever, that is not possible. The fiction is bound to collide with reality and will collapse.

If you really want to love a woman, never get married to her. If you really want to adore a man, escape as far away from him as possible. Then you will always love. But if you want to crash the whole love affair, get married, the sooner the better. Go for a honeymoon, and by the time the honeymoon is finished, everything is finished. Suddenly one morning you look at her – she is an ordinary woman.

Have you heard the old story? A princess found a frog, and the frog said, "Lady, I have been cursed, and for five thousand years I have remained a frog. If you take me with you and if you allow me to sleep with you in your bed, by the morning I will become a beautiful prince." You must have heard... This type of story is there. The princess took the frog and in the morning he became a beautiful prince.

But reality is just the opposite: you bring a beautiful prince, in the morning he becomes a frog! Every prince turns to being a frog in the end. And then you are puzzled: "What happened? What went wrong?"

Nothing went wrong. The frog is a frog; the prince was your idea, it was your wish fulfillment. You wanted to have a prince, so you had him. You were longing, you were projecting, you were dreaming.

When you come to me you are going to be shocked in many ways, and you are going to be confused in many ways. I have to dismantle your mind completely. It hurts, and it is not a very kind job. It is surgical. That's why I insist that first you become a sannyasin before I start the surgery – because if you are not a sannyasin, there is every possibility that you will escape in the middle of the surgery. And that will be more dangerous because then you will be mad: the work incomplete, something dismantled and nothing created. That's why I insist you first become a sannyasin, because then I can trust that you will at least lie down for the time the operation takes. You will be on the operating table; you will not escape. You will trust me. Otherwise, I dismantle a part of you, and you escape; then you will be in a worse state than you ever were before. The work has to be completed.

You will be thankful only when you have been completely renewed: you have been killed and you are reborn – only then. Before that there is going to be much pain. Growth goes through pain, much suffering. Growth is not cheap.

So, in fact, I have started the work on you. By calling you a good soul, I have thrown my net. You may think I have missed. I have not missed.

Let me tell you an anecdote...

The knife-throwing expert and his beautiful young assistant stood in front of their tent at the state fair while the spieler described the wonderful act that would be performed within.

Mrs. Silas Hawkins was attracted by the knife-thrower, and Mr. Silas Hawkins detected in the assistant a few curves he had never seen before. They paid their two slim dimes – the tenth part of a dollar – and entered the tent. Finally the assistant stood against a wooden wall and doffed her spangled robe.

Silas Hawkins gasped audibly, then the knife-thrower stepped on the platform, and it was Mrs. Hawkins' turn to gasp. The knife-thrower pulled back his right arm, and a steely blade went zinging through the air. It buried itself in the wall one-eighth of an inch from the assistant's shell-pink ear. Silas Hawkins jumped to his feet with a cry. "Doggone!" he said. "He missed her."

I have not missed. It has hit you exactly where I wanted it to hit you. It has created all the turmoil in you. It has brought all the unconscious rubbish to the surface. The work has started. Now, if you allow me, more shocks will be coming. The more you allow, the more shocks will be needed. It is arduous. To be reborn is going to be arduous – and this is the real birth.

Even in physical birth there is pain and there is trauma and there is suffering. This is a spiritual birth. One birth you have received from your parents, your father and mother; another birth you receive from your master: you are born as a spiritual being. Much has to be cut. Much has to be dropped. Only the very essential has to be saved. The nonessential has to be completely destroyed. And you don't know the essential; you are identified with the nonessential.

So I will have to cut your old identities, by and by. By saying to you that you are a good soul, I have made you aware of a certain fact: that this has been your game up to now. No longer! I am not gambling with you. But things should be clear from the very beginning; you should be alert to what is going to happen. I am not here to console you. I am not here to give you any consolations whatever. I am here to destroy you utterly because that is the only way to give you a new birth.

Mulla Nasruddin was leaving his office at his usual quitting hour, three-thirty, when he noticed a truck driver at the curb struggling unsuccessfully with a heavy case of books.

"I will give you a hand," volunteered the Mulla. The two seized opposite ends of the case and huffed and puffed several moments, to no avail.

"I am afraid it is hopeless," gasped Nasruddin. "We will never get it on the truck."

"On?" screamed the driver. "I am trying to get if off!"

So let it be clear from the very beginning: you will try to save yourself, and I am trying to destroy you. And I could see you directly, because the chief characteristic is such that you cannot hide it.

When disciples used to go to Gurdjieff, he would look into them; he would create situations to find out what was their chief characteristic. Unless the chief characteristic is known, work cannot start. Somebody is greedy, his problem is greed, and if you talk about anger, that is not his problem. If you talk about sex, that is not his problem.

You will be surprised to know: greedy people have no sexual problem. That's why Marwaris have to adopt children. Greedy people don't have sex energy; their whole energy moves into greed. Money becomes their love object, they don't care a bit about women. So if you tell a Marwari to take a vow of celibacy, he will be ready; it is not difficult. But don't tell him about renouncing his money or wealth: that is his problem.

A politician does not bother much about women; his whole thrust, his sexual thrust, is his politics. He wants to reach Delhi, Moscow, Washington; his whole energy is involved in that. His ambition is his sex. He wants to penetrate the capital; the capital is his woman. His ambition is phallic. He can avoid women, he will not be very interested. Once he has reached Delhi he may start thinking about women, otherwise not.

This has happened in India. Before the freedom, all the politicians were great mahatmas, sages, servants of the people, celibates, a great readiness to sacrifice. Then suddenly, when they came into power, all that disappeared; their energy was released. Their energy was involved in reaching Delhi. They had reached Delhi; now what to do? The energy was there, something had to be done with it. Then they got involved in a thousand and one things.

The chief characteristic has to be known. Somebody has anger as his chief characteristic, somebody has deception, somebody has ego, somebody has greed, somebody has jealousy, somebody has possessiveness – different people... But if you come to a master he can just look into you directly, and your chief characteristic is almost your soul. You don't know what else your soul is, but your chief characteristic is there, burning.

Sherlock Holmes once confronted Dr. Watson with the statement, "Oh, my dear doctor, I see you have not donned your long winter underwear."

"Amazing," Watson is supposed to have replied. "How did you deduce that?"

"Elementary," explained the peerless Holmes. "You have forgotten to put on your pants."

And remember, as far as I am concerned, you are always without pants. There is no way to deceive me. I am not deceived. Sometimes I may not be so rude, sometimes I may be polite; I may not say to you what I am seeing in you. Sometimes I may feel it is not the right time. But whenever you come to me – and that is the meaning of *darshan* – whenever you come and encounter me, you are absolutely naked to me. I may not say anything about it, I may wait for the right time; or I may not ever say, and start working without saying it – that depends... But there is no possibility of deception.

If you can deceive me, then I cannot be of any help to you. I can be helpful only because you cannot deceive me.

The third question:

Osho,
Organizations have always frightened me because I felt there was a
inbuilt evilness, and maybe a necessary evil. The Osho foundation
is an organization, and has every possibility of becoming a very
powerful organization. Can you tell me why the organization is
necessary?

Yes, because evil is necessary.

The fourth question:

Osho,
Why do we wear one hundred and eight beads on our *malas*? Does
this belong to the world of ritualistic religion?

Yes, it belongs to ritualistic religion. Don't become ritualistic, but
don't become anti-ritualistic either. A little ritual is beautiful. To
become ritualistic is wrong, but a little ritual is just fine. A little ritual
adds spice to life. It gives salt to your food; it is tasteful. A life without
any ritual will be a very poor, impoverished life.

You meet somebody on the road and you say, "Hello" – it is a
ritual. And he says, "How are you?" and you say, "Fine" – it is a ritual.
You are not fine: he knows, you know, everybody knows. You meet
somebody on the road, you smile; it is a ritual. Just watch: you will
find that life needs a little ritual. It makes life run smoothly, it is lubri-
cating. If the whole of life becomes ritualistic, then it is dangerous;
then you are only eating salt. A little salt in the food is good, but
to just feed on salt is dangerous. You will die. But to drop salt completely is also dangerous. And always remember this: I am never
totally against anything, and I am never totally in favor of anything. I
always keep a balance.

The orange robe, the *mala*, the locket: innocent ritual, but it adds
spice. It gives you a feeling of community. And man needs a few
fictions to live. The truth is too hard. Yes, one day you will become
able to live with the truth, but right now, no. You have to pass through
many stages. Only in the ultimate jump can you drop all fictions.
Then too you may not drop them because they are beautiful in themselves. They are not true, but they are beautiful in themselves.

I am not against ritual. I am simply saying that ritual is not religion; ritual is ritual. And a little ritual is always good – it keeps you in balance, it keeps you sane. Otherwise people start moving to extremes. There are a few people whose whole religion is ritualistic – there is no reality at all. Then there is Krishnamurti: his whole idea is non-ritualistic. There is no poetry, no fiction, no myth, no prayer, no meditation, nothing – just a bare, naked statement of truth.

I don't believe in extremes. I would like you to remember the tightrope walker. Always keep in mind the tightrope walker. He is a symbol of life. He leans to the left, feels that now if he leans a little more he will fall; immediately he balances by leaning toward the right. Then he starts falling toward the right; immediately he balances himself again, leaning toward the left. He continuously leans from left to right, right to left. And that's how he keeps himself in the middle. This is the mystery: to keep in the middle he has to lean to the left, he has to lean to the right. To keep in the middle he has to be very illogical, because the middle is not static, it is dynamic. Life is not static.

So, if you want to keep yourself balanced, healthy, sane, you will always have to lean to both sides: sometimes a little ritual, sometimes no ritual; sometimes a little scripture, sometimes no scripture; sometimes a little worship, sometimes no worship; sometimes a little prayer, sometimes no prayer. In this way you will become a tightrope walker.

And remember – again I repeat – the middle is not a static posture. You cannot just stand there. You cannot say to the tightrope walker, "Why do you go on leaning this way and that? Why all this effort? Just stand there in the middle!" Then he will fall. If you are static you will die.

Life is a process, dynamic, riverlike. Go and watch a river: sometimes it flows to the north, sometimes to the east, sometimes to the south, and goes on leaning to both sides, and one day reaches to the ocean.

Everything is accepted in proportion.

The fifth question:

Osho,
I hear there is a room here called The Office of the Grande Seducer of the Oldies. How old is an oldie?

Now, it is a very technical thing, but I will try to give you a layman's conception. And I will give you the right address where you can find a more informed and expert opinion.

Yes, there is a secret organization here called SIN, *S-I-N*. *S* stands for seduction, seduction into neo-sannyas. That is the name of the organization, SIN. And there are three branches of the organization: for the babies, for the oldies, and for those who are in-between. For the babies, up to the fourteenth year – because by that time sexual maturity happens, and the baby is no more a baby... In fact, he is ready to create new babies, so he cannot be a baby. So you can demark the line: fourteen years is the line for the babies; after birth, fourteen years. Before death, fourteen years is the limit for the oldies. If seventy is the average lifespan, then fifty-six is the demarcation line for the oldies. And in-between is everybody else.

So three departments exist, three branches of SIN: for the babies, Siddhartha and Purva take care; for the in-between, Teertha and Maneesha; for the oldies, Paritosh and Parijat.

But this distinction of the oldies, in-betweens and babies is applicable only here. In America there are only two: the babies and the oldies. The in-betweens exist not. That is a strange thing that has happened in America. People try to remain babies for as long as they can. They go on pushing the line: fifty and still they are babies, fifty-five and still they are babies, and fifty-six and still they are babies. And it is the thirty-first of December, they are fifty-six, and they are still babies!

When they cannot push any longer, when it is impossible, they simply become oldies. They go from babies to oldies directly.

I have heard about a door-to-door salesman who was succeeding, and all his colleagues were surprised because they were selling the same goods, but not so successfully. He was earning almost ten times what they were. So they gave him a party, and asked him, "Please tell about your secret."

He said, "There is nothing much, it is simple. Even if an old hag, a sixty-year-old woman, rotten, opens the door, I say, "Baby, is your mother at home?" That works, and I am immediately welcomed."

America has gone crazy. All natural limits have disappeared. From infancy, people simply move into senility. That's why the great problem of the generation gap has arisen. There is no in-between to link them; the bridge is broken.

Americans are crazy, just as the old Italian said. But I should not anticipate. First I must tell you the anecdote.

Wallace Reyburn, author of *Some of It Was Fun*, entered Naples, Italy, with the victorious troops who threw the Nazis out near the end of World War Two. A grateful native offered to introduce him to a sister at home.

"Is she beautiful?" asked Reyburn.

"Ah, *bella! bella!*" enthused the native.

"Young?"

"*Si! Si! Si!*"

"Is she pure?" persisted Reyburn.

The native turned from him in disgust, remarking, "These Americans and Canadians are all crazy."

Natural limits are forgotten, natural things are forgotten. In America this distinction may not be applicable, but here... And except for America, everywhere in the world these are the three demarcations: the babies who are not yet interested in sex; and the oldies who have grown out of it; and the people in-between who go on wavering, who are still on the tightrope.

And of course, babies can convert babies, so Siddhartha, little Siddhartha and Purva... Right now little Siddhartha is traveling in America, trying to convert babies there, because that is the country where the greatest number of babies exist. And for the in-betweens, Teertha and Maneesha are in charge of SIN; and for old people, Parijat and Paritosh.

So, if you really want a very informed, expert opinion, you go to Paritosh. He is in charge. And right now he is very busy because many parents have come for Christmas, and he is seducing them into neo-sannyas. To help people, somebody has put a notice on his door; that's how this question has arisen. Somebody has put a notice on Paritosh's door: Office of the Grand Seducer of the Oldies – just to help people, so those who want to find the office can find it easily.

The sixth question:

Osho,
What is your attitude to money?

I have lived without money, I have lived with money, and I have one confession to make: it is always better to live with money than without. Money is useful. One should not be used by it, that's all. I'm not against money; it should be used – it is a good, utilitarian invention. It helps. It is tremendously useful; but use it, don't be used by it.

Money should not be your master; you should be the master, that's all. And if you have to choose, then my suggestion is to always choose to be with money. It is better to be with money than without money. I am not saying that you will be happier; I am only saying that you will have more choice to choose your misery according to your heart.

A poor man has not much choice: he has to be miserable, whatsoever the misery happens to be. A rich man has much more choice. The poor man has to suffer in a limited way. The rich man suffers unlimitedly: he can suffer here, he can suffer in New York, he can suffer in London, he can suffer in Beijing. He has the whole world to suffer in, and sooner or later he will be suffering on the moon and Mars. He has more freedom, and freedom is good. If you are poor you have to suffer one woman; if you are rich you have to suffer many women. It opens doors.

So if you ask me, I will suggest that if you are trying to choose to live with money or without, I would say to live with money. It will give you more experience, it will bring you to godliness sooner because you will be tired sooner.

A poor man is never tired of money, remember, because he has no money. How to be tired of something you don't have? A poor man always hankers and desires and dreams about money. Only a rich man is finished with money. In fact, that is the definition of a rich man: one who is finished with money, he is the rich man. He has known, he has seen what money can give, and now he would like to have something more that money can never give.

I am not saying money can give you God or peace or happiness, but there are foolish people...

A mahatma came to see me a few years ago, and he said, "I have renounced money because through money you cannot have bliss."

I said, "Who told you, in the first place, that you will have bliss? Through money you can have a beautiful house. Who told you that you will have bliss? Who has told you that you will have happiness? You will have a big car."

There are foolish people who expect that bliss is going to happen through money. Then one day they become disillusioned. Money is not wrong; their illusion, their projection is wrong. Money is not at fault. If you go and try to squeeze oil out of sand, and oil does not come out of it, will you say that the sand is at fault? You were foolish, you were stupid. In the first place, who had told you that by squeezing sand you would get oil?

Money cannot give you bliss, cannot give you peace, cannot give you God, cannot give you paradise. But to come to know this, one has to have money. Then you become clearly aware of what money can give and what money cannot give.

When a person has known what money can give, his efforts start moving beyond money, beyond the world. Money is a beautiful invention, one of the most important inventions man has ever made, next only to language – the first is language, the second is money. These are the two most important foundations for civilization, society, culture.

I am not against it; I am simply saying what money can give and what money cannot give. If you think that by hoarding money, one day you will suddenly become meditative, then you are a fool. By hoarding money are you not going to become meditative. And remember, by renouncing money are you not going to become meditative. These are both foolish people. First they think that through money they will get God, then one day they think that by renouncing money they will get God – but in both cases they remain money-oriented.

God has nothing to do with money. You can have God with as much money as you want, and you can have God without money, as much without money as you want. God has nothing to do with money. A rich man can become meditative, a poor man can become meditative. But my understanding is this: that if a poor man wants to become meditative, he will need tremendous intelligence because he will have to see the futility of money which he does not have. He will need tremendous intelligence.

Kabir must have been tremendously intelligent – I think more intelligent than Buddha and Mahavira. My reason for saying so is that Buddha had money, Mahavira had money. If they became fed up, it is simple, it is logical – it is as simple as two plus two are four. If Buddha had not renounced the palace, then it would have proved only one thing: that he was stupid. If he renounced, that does not prove that he was very intelligent, that simply proves an average intelligence.

But Kabir, Christ, Mohammed, are more intelligent people. They didn't have money, they didn't have anything, and still they became aware that money is useless. They didn't have a great kingdom, and without having it they renounced it. They must have been very sharp people, tremendously alert. They could see through things that they didn't have. Their transparency, their clarity, was tremendous, incredible.

If a poor man wants to be religious, he will need great intelligence. If a rich man wants to be religious, he needs only average intelligence. So, if a poor man becomes religious, he is a great sage. And if a rich man does not become religious, he is a fool, stupid.

The last question:

Osho,
Each day when I leave Chuang Tzu Auditorium, I see three white
robes hanging in the laundry room. Yet I never see you wearing
more than one robe. I have a suspicion that you are actually one of
triplets. This would explain how you go on contradicting yourself in
successive lectures, and appear in more than one place at the
same time.

So, you have found it out! Now keep it a secret and don't tell it to anybody. It is true. I have to confess. Now you have found out, I have to confess. It is true – I am a trinity, the trinity I was talking about: the father, the mother, the son.

And yes, it is true. That's why it is so easy for me to contradict myself: sometimes the father is speaking, sometimes the mother, and sometimes the son. You will find three rivers meeting in me. It is a *sangam;* it is a meeting point of three rivers, a *treveni*, a trinity, a trimurti. I have three faces.

That's why it is so easy for me to move through all the traditions – there are only three traditions in the world. Three is a very basic unit: the father, the mother and the son. That's why it will be difficult for you to make a coherent philosophy out of my assertions. You will have to have great intelligence to see the coherence; otherwise the contradiction is very obvious.

When I speak as a father, I speak as a father: authoritative. When I speak as a mother, I speak as a mother: nonauthoritative, loving. When I am a father, I order you, command you; then I am a Moses with Ten Commandments. When I am a mother, I persuade you, I don't order you; then I am not a Moses, then I am more like a Krishna. He persuades Arjuna, he persuades in a thousand and one ways, very friendly, very lovingly. By and by, he brings him in. And when I am the son, I speak rebellion, revolution; then I speak as Christ, as Buddha.

I am all three, and I would like you also to be all three. To be one is not to be very rich. To be all three together is to be very rich.

And the very last question:

Osho,
What is this astonishing nonsense about you having no charisma?

True, it is astonishing and it is nonsense. How can it be: I, having no charisma? But now things can be easy. Now you have understood the principle of the trinity. And I told you that there are three types of master: the charismatic, the methodical and the natural. The father is the charismatic, the mother is the methodical; the son is the natural. The word *natural* comes from a root which means "out of birth."

Certainly so, you are right: it is amazing and it is nonsense. One of my parts is charismatic, one of my parts is methodical; one of my parts is natural. And that's how it should be. A perfect master should be all three, simultaneously.

So please, if I say something, you can now sort it out. You can have three drawers: the father, the mother, the son, and you can go on collecting, and everything will be sorted out, figured out easily, simply.

And don't ask me, "Why did you say that one day?" because

you are not asking the same person, and it is not so easy as it is in this anecdote.

Let me tell you...

In Nathan Asubel's *Treasury of Jewish Folklore* appears the story of a famous preacher of Dubno whose driver stopped en route to a lecture date and said, "Rabbi, do me a favor. For once I'd like to be the one receiving all the honors and attention, to see what it feels like. For this one engagement, exchange clothes with me. You be the driver, and let me be the rabbi."

The preacher, a merry and generous soul, laughed and said, "All right – but remember, clothes don't make the rabbi. If you are asked to explain some difficult passage of the Law, see that you don't make a fool of yourself."

The exchange was affected. Arrived at their destination, the bogus rabbi was received with tumultuous enthusiasm, and obviously loved every minute of it. Finally however, there came the dreaded moment when an extremely tricky question was put to him. He met the test nobly.

"A fine lot of scholars you are!" he thundered. "Is this the most difficult problem you could ask me? Why, this is so simple, even my driver could explain it to you!" Then he called the preacher of Dubno: "Driver, come here for a moment and clarify the Law for these dull-witted fellows."

It is not so easy for me because when I am here, the other two are not. I cannot call, "Come and explain this for me." So please, never raise any questions about contradictions. Whatsoever I have said another day is finished; I am finished with it. I don't look backward; I go ahead.

And there is no need to worry about it. Whatsoever I am saying right now is the truth. The present is the truth; the past is dead. All those assertions of the past are dead. The next moment, again, the truth will have its own form. Then don't carry this moment with you.

My whole teaching is not to carry the past and to just remain true to the moment. Then there will be no contradiction. There is none – the contradictions appear only because you are trained too logically, and I am an illogical person. My whole logic is that of illogic. I am an irrationalist.

Yes, I am three, but please don't tell it to anybody.
Enough for today.

a harmony of love and renunciation

*I have stilled my restless mind, and my heart is radiant: for in
thatness I have seen beyond thatness, in company I have seen the
comrade himself.*
*Living in bondage, I have set myself free: I have broken away from
the clutch of all narrowness.*
*Kabir says: I have attained the unattainable, and my heart is
colored with the color of love.*

*That which you see is not: and for that which is, you have no
words.*
*Unless you see, you believe not: what is told you, you cannot
accept.*
*He who is discerning knows by the word; and the ignorant stands
gaping.*
*Some contemplate the formless, and others meditate on form; but
the wise man knows that Brahma is beyond both.*
*That beauty of his is not seen of the eye, that meter of his is not
heard of the ear.*
*Kabir says: He who has found both love and renunciation never
descends to death.*

It was a beautiful morning and the sun was just rising on the horizon. The first rays of the sun were playing with the almond leaves, and I saw an owl settling on the almond tree. He said, "Getting dark! Is this a good place to rest until dawn?"

Only a rabbit was listening to him. The rabbit said, "Sir, it is dawn! The sun is rising. You have it the wrong way round."

The understanding of an owl is totally different: the night is day for him and the day is night, and in the morning he settles for the night. Evening is his dawn. This much gap exists between the mystic and the non-mystic. What is dawn for a mystic is a dark night for you, and what is a dark night for the mystic is all that your life consists of – hence, the misunderstanding.

Mystics have always been misunderstood. They say one thing; we understand something totally different. Misunderstanding is so natural between a mystic and a non-mystic that understanding seems almost a miracle. And whenever it happens that understanding flows between a mystic and a non-mystic, the non-mystic is no longer a non-mystic; he is transformed by that very understanding.

"Kindly let me help you or you will drown," said the monkey, putting the fish safely up a tree.

Now, he is trying hard to be compassionate, trying to save the fish from drowning. He is bound to kill it out of compassion. This has to be taken in very deeply; it will be the turning point.

Now, Kabir is a mystic, one of the greatest. What he is trying to say, in the first place, is much distorted the moment he says it because he has known it in a state where words never penetrate, where silence is eternal. He has known it, experienced it, encountered it, but in a moment when he was not a mind.

Then he wants to convey it: the mind has to come in, the mind has to take a certain role. The mind tries to convey it, but in that very effort it is distorted. Now the silence has to enter sound, the silence has to enter its opposite; the wordless has to become confined to the word, the indefinable has to be reduced to a definition, and something mysterious has to become an explanation. All is lost. If not all, then almost all. Only a flicker of truth remains, just a ripple. While in his experience it was a great ocean, now it is just a ripple.

Still the mystic has to say it. He has to share it; it is part of his experience to share it. It is just as a flower opens and shares its fragrance: it has to be done; nobody can contain it in himself. He owes it to humanity and to all those who are still struggling in the dark. Maybe he cannot convey the whole light, but even a reflection of it may be helpful to many. Even a distorted form of it may help many to seek, to search, to inquire. It may make many thirsty for it. So the mystic has to say it, and whenever a mystic says it he cries because he can see what it was in his experience, and what it has turned out to be in his words. Ninety-nine percent is lost. And then when you hear the word, you translate it again according to your experience.

First, the experience; then the mystic has to translate it according to his mind. And the mind is given to him by the society, the mind is conditioned by the society. The mind is nothing but an experience of living with people. He has to translate it: that which is known in tremendous aloneness, that which is experienced in absolute solitude, has to be brought into the mundane world, has to be reduced to a mass language, a mass medium. Much is lost.

And then you hear the word, and rather than listening to the wordless you catch hold of the word, which is the nonessential. The essential is lost again. And then you translate the word according to your own mind, according to your own experience. Now you are a thousand miles away from the original experience.

I have heard...

A great Zen master, Sosan, was asked to explain the ultimate teaching of the Buddha.

He answered, "You won't understand it until you have it."

But then what is the point in understanding it? When you have it, you have it; there is no need to understand it. When you don't have it, you cannot understand it, and the need exists to understand it. This is the paradox: you can understand it only when you have it. There is no way to understand it before this; only the experience will explain it to you. Nothing else can do that work, no substitute is possible. But then there is no need – when you have it, you have it. When it is there, it is there. There is not even any desire to understand it. It has happened; you have known, it has become you.

It is just like when you eat. When you eat food, you don't become food. Have you seen it? Otherwise you would have become a banana. You eat a banana – you don't become a banana, the banana becomes you. And exactly the same happens when you have known God: God becomes you. When you have known truth, truth becomes you. Digested, it runs in your blood, it becomes your bones, it becomes your marrow; it becomes your presence. There is no need to understand it. In fact, there is nobody to understand it; nobody is left behind it, you have become it. Your understanding has become it. The need exists because we don't understand. So we go on seeking for explanations, and no explanation can explain it.

This is the paradox of religious experience: those who know, need no understanding about it. They are tremendously contented knowing it; it is more than enough. They may dance, they may sing, they may laugh, but they are not in any way seeking to explain it. They may live it, they may keep quiet about it. They may sit silently, or they may become madly ecstatic about it, but they don't bother to explain it.

That's why all the great scriptures of the world – the Upanishads, Tao Te Ching, Jesus' sayings, Buddha's Dhammapada – are simply statements, not explanations. The Upanishads don't prove God, they simply assert. They say: "It is so." It is not an argument; they are not proposing any hypothesis, they are simply declaring it is so. It is a declaration. They don't produce any proof for why they declare it, why they declare that it exists. They simply say, "It is so. Take it or leave it, but it is so." And there is no need for any proof; they are the proof.

But for those who are still in the dark night of the soul, stumbling, groping, some explanation is needed. It will be very, very far away from the truth, it will be a lie – but still it is needed. So mystics speak. They have to speak, they have to outpour their beings, knowing that it may help a few. It helps only a very few people. It helps only those who are ready to trust; otherwise it never helps. If you argue it is lost – a mystic cannot argue, he cannot convince you. In that way, the mystic is very fragile; in that way, logically, he is very fragile: he cannot argue and he cannot prove. You can come close to him, you can feel his being, you can look into his eyes, you can hold his hand, you can fall into his love. You can trust this madman, the mystic, you can go with him on an unknown journey. It is going to be a courageous adventure of trust. If you doubt, suddenly you are cut off. If you doubt, then there is no possibility of any bridge. One has to trust.

If you trust the word of the mystic, there is a possibility it may create a little ripple in you. Otherwise, with doubt, even that ripple disappears. Listening to Kabir or to Christ or to Krishna, remember it. They have to be listened to in a certain way; it is no ordinary listening. They have to be listened to in such love, trust, so that you don't stand separate from them, that you become all ears; that you become feminine, that you become just receptive, that you simply drink. You don't have any ideas and you don't try to translate it. Rather than being in a hurry to translate it inside you, to interpret it, and to think whether it is right or wrong, you simply listen as you listen to music.

When Ravi Shankar is playing, you don't bother about whether he is right or wrong. What do you mean by right or wrong? Music is music – good or bad, but not right or wrong. You don't bother; you simply listen, and because the music has no language, you cannot translate it. You are simply in the presence of the music, surrounded by it, overwhelmed by it, taken off your feet to a faraway journey by it. But you are not deciding whether it is right or wrong, whether it appeals to your logic or not. You listen from the heart.

The mystic has to be listened to as if you are listening to music. And yes, I say to you, it is music, far deeper than any musician can create. Once you start translating it, things become difficult.

Even these beautiful translations of Rabindranath Tagore are not true – cannot be. Kabir's sayings are in Hindi; then they were translated into Bengali; then from Bengali, Rabindranath translated them into English. They are faraway echoes, and much is lost. For example:

I have stilled my restless mind, and my heart is radiant: for in thatness I have seen beyond thatness, in company I have seen the comrade himself.

I have stilled my restless mind – chalat mansa achal kinhi. Now, the original has a totally different taste to it. If I have to translate it, I will say, "My Lord, so you have done it? You have made my moving mind unmoving?" That is the meaning of it: chalat mansa achal kinhi. "The mind that was always moving, always moving… My Lord, so you have done it? You have made it unmoving?" That would be truer to Kabir.

Chalat mansa achalkinhi. Kabir is amazed! Kabir says, "My God, what have you done? I have been trying and trying and trying, and I could not still it, and you have stilled it? It was so difficult, not even conceivable. Even a single thought was so difficult to drop, and now it has dropped completely, now it is nowhere. I cannot find it. All those vibrations of the mind, all those waves, continuous waves, all those thoughts, thought-processions – all have disappeared. So you have done it" – *chalat mansa achal kinhi.*

Rabindranath translates it, "I have stilled my restless mind." Now he has missed the whole thing. He says, "I have stilled my restless mind." No, Kabir is not saying that. The sentence can be translated this way too. So I am not saying that the translation is linguistically incorrect; it is mystically incorrect. *Chalat mansa achal kinhi* can be translated this way too, because Kabir is not saying anything about who has made it unmoving, I or you; he has not said anything. It can be translated as: "I have stilled my mind." But that is impossible because "I" is the mind, so "I" cannot still itself. That will be pulling yourself up by your own shoelaces – operation shoelaces! You are bound to fail, it is not possible. Only God can still. So I say it is linguistically correct, but mystically incorrect.

Only God can still the mind. It is a gift. It is a grace that descends on you; it is not something that *you* do – because whatsoever you do, *you* will remain. Your doing cannot dissolve you. Your doing will strengthen you more and more. Your effort will become food to your ego.

How can you still your mind? Who is this one who is going to still the mind? It is mind itself. It will be just like a dog chasing its own tail. Hence, I say it is mystically incorrect. I don't know much language, but I know what mysticism is. I may not be well informed about mysticism, but there is no need to be well informed about mysticism, it is my experience.

Information is knowledge received by tuition; knowing is knowledge unfolded in intuition. I am a mystic; I am not a poet. Rabindranath was a great poet, and he has seen to it that the translation should remain poetic, linguistically correct, but he has missed something of tremendous value.

Let me repeat it: *chalat mansa achal kinhi.* "Oh my God, it is amazing! It is a miracle. I could never have believed that it could happen. It is incredible! So you have done it, and I am simply

amazed. I cannot believe it, and it has happened. I am nowhere. You
have stilled me. Your grace is great."

Kabir is grateful. This is a song of gratefulness. And Kabir does
not believe in methods, he does not believe that man has to do
something to attain to God. What can man do? Human hands are so
small; their reach cannot be very big. Our reach will be *our* reach,
how can we reach God through our human reach? It is impossible.
Only God can reach us. We can be available, that's all. We can bow
down, surrender, that's all.

Kabir does not believe in effort, he believes in effortlessness.
That's what he calls *sahaj samadhi*, spontaneous ecstasy. Kabir is a
lover; his path is the path of love. Love knows no effort.

Have you not observed it in your own life? Can you do anything
about love? If I say to you, "Go and love that man," what will you do?
You will say, "What nonsense! How can I go and love like that?" You
cannot command anybody to go and love somebody. If love happens,
it happens; if it doesn't happen, it doesn't happen. There is no way to
produce it to order. And that is one of the miseries of the world: we
have all learned to produce it on order, so of course it is false.

The mother says to the child, "Love me, I'm your mother." And
the child is helpless. He is so dependent that rather than becoming a
lover of his mother, he becomes a politician. He starts pretending,
"Yes, I love you." He smiles. We corrupt small children, we corrupt
them into politicians. He does not mean it at all, but he has to do it.
The mother says, "I am your mother and you have to love me." Now,
how is one supposed to love? What can you do to love somebody?
You can pretend, you can act, you can play a game of love, but it will
not be love at all. And the child starts playing a game of diplomacy.
He becomes political. When the mother comes he smiles. The smile
is just on the lips; you cannot force the heart to smile. You can, at the
most, exercise the lips. And he looks at the mother with adoring eyes
– false, and he says again and again to the mother, "I love you," and
so on and so forth.

He has to love the father and the brothers and the sisters. He
really hates all the brothers and all the sisters because they are com-
petitors. In fact, every child wants to be alone; he hates the siblings,
he has to compete with them. But he has to love: "This is your
younger brother," so he has to love. He hates this younger brother;
he wants to kill this younger brother: because of this younger

brother he is no longer as important as he used to be. He is no longer the center of attention of the family. He is discarded on the periphery; this younger brother, this enemy, has taken the central place. Now the younger brother manages, dictates and dominates from the center stage. He himself is now not more than a secondary character. How can he love this younger brother? But he has to show love; otherwise he will be in difficulty. And this is how love is falsified from the very beginning.

Then for your whole life you will go on loving in the same false way. You will go on pretending, and you will never allow real love to take possession of you. And you will always be afraid of real love, because real love will look like a flood – dangerous, coming from the unknown, uncontrollable. You have learned a trick.

Of course, your love is so small that it can be controlled. It is so false it can be controlled. It is in your hands, you can do whatsoever you want to do with it. Real love is greater than you; it is huge, enormous. It simply floods over you; you are simply taken away. You are no longer standing anywhere. You lose your being in a real love; it is great, it pours from the heavens.

And the same is true about meditation. Real meditation pours from heaven. It is not something that you do; it is something that happens. On your part only one thing is needed, and that is that you have to remain receptive, flowing, ready to go with God. If God is going north, you go north. When the weathervane points to the north, it does not make the north wind blow, remember. When the weathervane points to the north, it does not make the north wind blow – it simply records that the north wind is blowing.

And so is meditation, and so is love, and so is prayer: it does not make God flow toward you, it simply records that God is flowing toward you, that God is blowing toward you. Meditation is not a method – not for Kabir. That is the difference between Patanjali and Kabir. Patanjali is methodical, he believes in methodology. Kabir believes in love. What Patanjali calls *samadhi* Kabir will call artificial samadhi. Against Patanjali, Kabir says, "Think of the *sahaj*, the spontaneous, the simple, that which is not created by you, that which is not manufactured by you – because whatsoever *you* manufacture is going to be useless, worthless. *You* are worthless, so whatsoever you manufacture is going to be naturally worthless. Your signature will be on it."

Sahaj samadhi means: it is not made by you, it is not homemade;

it is God-given. The signature is not yours; it is God's. That's why I say the path of Kabir is the path of love.

I have stilled my restless mind... No, "The mind has become still. I have seen my mind becoming still. I have watched it happening. My God, you have done it? And my heart is radiant."

When the mind is silent, the heart is radiant. When the mind is chattering, the heart is dead. You cannot exist in the heart if you exist in the mind. If you exist in the mind... The mind is very jealous and very possessive; it does not allow you to move toward the heart. The mind is a very jealous wife, it absorbs you totally; it does not leave a single moment to move toward the heart. And even if you start thinking about the heart, the mind creates a false heart in the head. The mind even starts manufacturing feelings.

Sometimes somebody comes to me and says, "I have fallen in love with you, Osho." I say, "Really?" He says, "I think so." Now, a feeling cannot be a thinking. Either you have fallen in love with me or you have not fallen in love with me, but you cannot *think* that you have fallen in love with me. Thinking is a false thing, but the mind produces pseudo-coins to deceive you. It says, "You need love? Okay, have it" – and it creates a thought of love, it creates a thought of feeling. The mind is tremendously inventive; it can go on playing games. And this has to be watched; otherwise you will always be lost in the head. The head is very tricky and it goes on tricking you again and again. It is a tremendous trap; it can create anything. It is very efficient in producing false goods.

One young man was saying to me that he could not cry, his tears had dried up. And he said, "I'm trying hard because now I have understood that crying is needed, that crying will relax me, that crying will make me more available to feelings. So I am trying hard."

I said, "If you try hard, you may succeed – and that is the danger. The mind can even produce tears. It can force the eyes to flow in tears, and it will not have any relationship with your heart. And once you have succeeded in forcing the eyes, you will think that now you have succeeded, the mind has deceived you."

One has to be very, very watchful. Kabir says that only when God stills your mind does it happen. So what is to be done on our part? Kabir says: on our part we have to be receptive ends. On our part we have to be just welcoming, watching, waiting. On our part we are not to do anything – because any doing is our own undoing. And this is difficult. Try it. It is very easy to do something; the most difficult thing in the world is not to do anything. Not to do is the greatest achievement. Zen people call it *zazen:* sitting silently, doing nothing.

I have come across a very beautiful Zen story. Listen to it attentively; it is *your* story...

Behind a temple there was a field where a lot of squashes were ripening. One day a fight started. Now, you know, squashes are squashes... A great fight – the squashes split into two groups and made a big racket shouting at each other. And of course they used to live in a temple, they were growing in a temple, so those two groups must have been religious: Christian and Jew, Buddhist and Jaina, Hindu and Mohammedan – something like that. A great theological debate arose.

The head priest heard the uproar. He yelled and scolded them saying, "Hey, you squashes! The idea of fighting among yourselves! And in a Zen temple! Everyone do *zazen*. Sit silently, doing nothing."

The priest taught them how to do *zazen*: "Fold your legs like this; sit up and straighten your back and neck." While the squashes were sitting in *zazen*, their anger subsided and they settled down. Then the priest said, "Everyone put your hands on the top of your heads."

When the squashes felt the top of their own heads with their hands, they found some weird thing on their heads. It turned out to be the vine that connected them together. They started laughing. They said, "This is really ridiculous! We are one, and we were fighting unnecessarily."

Sitting in *zazen*, one finds that the universe is one. Sitting silently, one finds that there is no conflict anywhere, that the enemy exists not; that enmity is just our own illusion, created by us; that tension, ambition, struggle, is all just a mind game. There is nobody to struggle against; the whole is one.

When you come to know that the whole is one, that we are connected with each other, that we are together, that I am part of you and you are part of me, that we are members of each other, then suddenly you have opened. This understanding comes not through any effort, but just sitting silently, effortlessly, just waiting – alert, of course, because you can fall asleep and then nothing will happen.

Two things are easy: doing something is easy or falling asleep is easy. Whenever you are not doing something, suddenly you feel sleepy. You know only two ways: either do something – then you can remain awake; or don't do something – and you start feeling sleepy, you start feeling like falling asleep. Just between the two is the thing: don't do anything, be as quiet as you are in sleep, and yet as alert as when you are doing something – as alert as if you are fighting your enemy with a sword, and as quiet as if you have fallen asleep. Where sleep and awareness meet together, there is *sahaj samadhi*, there is that spontaneous ecstasy. And in that moment you suddenly feel your whole energy has shifted toward the heart. The head disappears; you become headless.

Just the other day, Savita was saying that she was very puzzled: she had seen me in a sort of dream or reverie, without a head. I said, "Perfectly true, Savita. You have achieved a great satori, a great experience. I *am* without a head! And you are also without a head, everybody is without a head."

This happens when the energy starts moving toward the heart: one day suddenly you realize that there is no head. Not that your physical head disappears – it is there, but no longer the center of your being; it is there, but no longer on the center stage, no longer the controller, no longer the manager, no longer the boss.

The mind settled, the moving has become nonmoving. The mind, when it is not moving, is a no-mind because movement is the mind itself. When your mind is not moving, where will the mind be? Thought, to be, has to move. If there is no movement in your mind and all thought processes have stopped, mind has disappeared: mind is nothing but a thought process. When the mind is not, ...*my heart is radiant*... Then suddenly a sun rises in your heart. You are full of light, you are full of joy, you are full of love.

...*for in thatness I have seen beyond thatness*... And there you come across the beyond. There, through that moment, you come to see that which is the reality.

Through the mind you have always come across your own projections. Through the mind you never come to the real. The mind goes on creating ideas about the real. You never face reality as it is; there is always a screen of thought, and the thought always goes on distorting the reality. You never see that which is, you are not objective. Your imagination goes on working, your wish fulfillment goes on working, your desires go on coloring things. You can never see things as they are unless the mind is completely put aside. When you see through the heart, you see the reality.

...for in thatness I have seen beyond thatness... In that tremendous light, radiance of the heart, I have looked into the depth, I have looked into the beyond.

...in company I have seen the comrade himself. And now I know that whosoever is around me is nobody else but you. *...in company I have seen the comrade himself:* now my wife is no longer my wife – it is God playing the role of my wife. And my son is no longer my son, and my husband is no longer my husband – it is God playing the role of my husband or my son. Even the enemy is no longer the enemy, but God playing the role of my enemy to make life a little more exhilarating, to make life a little more rich, to make life a little more creative, dynamic. To enrich life, God has taken so many forms.

...in company I have seen the comrade himself.
Living in bondage, I have set myself free...

Now there is no need to go anywhere. Kabir says: *Living in bondage, I have set myself free...* Now this is a far greater freedom than the freedom that exists against bondage. This is true freedom; it is not against bondage, it is simply beyond bondage. If you can be free even in a prison, then are you free. Then your freedom has a spiritual quality. Then you can be chained on the outside, and still, deep inside, you are as free as a bird in the sky. And then you are not fighting, even with chains.

I have heard...

Once, Diogenes was caught by a few robbers. Diogenes was a very healthy mystic. In the West, he seems to be the only person who can be compared to Mahavira in the East. He used to live naked, and he had a beautiful body; it is said that even Alexander was jealous of him. He was a naked fakir; he had nothing other than his glory, his own beauty.

He was caught: he was meditating under a tree in a forest, and a few robbers caught him. And they thought, "It is good. We can get a good price for him. He can be sold in the slave market." But they were afraid because he looked very strong. The robbers were at least half a dozen, but still they were afraid. And they approached very cautiously because he could be dangerous: he alone seemed to be enough for six people.

Diogenes looked at them and said, "Don't be afraid! Don't be afraid, I'm not going to fight you. You can come close to me, and you can put your chains on me."

They were surprised. They chained him, they made him a prisoner, and they took him away to the marketplace. On the way he said, "But why have you chained me? You could have just asked me, and I would have followed. Why make such fuss about it?"

They said, "We cannot believe that somebody is so willing to become a slave!"

And Diogenes laughed and said, "Because I am a free man, I am not worried about that." They could not understand. Then, in the marketplace, standing in the middle of the market, he shouted, "A master has come to be sold here. Is some slave desirous of purchasing him?"

Look what he said: "A master has come to be sold here. Is some slave desirous of purchasing him?"

A master is a master. Real freedom is not against bondage; real freedom is beyond bondage. If your freedom is against bondage, you are not really free. You can escape to the Himalayas just because you are afraid of the marketplace and the wife and the children, but you are not really a free man. The Himalayas cannot become your freedom. You are afraid of the wife; and if the wife comes to see you in the Himalayas, you will start trembling. Your henpecked husband will suddenly be there.

It is said about Swami Ramateertha that he traveled all around the world preaching the message of the East. He was a great thinker, a great mystic. Then he came back. He was staying in the Himalayas with his disciple Purna Singh. One day, Purna Singh reports in his diary, Ramateertha's wife came to see him. And Purna Singh says, "I have seen Ramateertha meeting thousands of people, men, women of all sorts, but suddenly I felt a shadow falling on him – the wife – and he became a little afraid."

And he said to Purna Singh, "Tell my wife that I don't want to see her."

Purna Singh was shocked. He said, "Sir, if you are afraid of your wife, then I would also like to go away from you. Then you are no longer my master. Why should you be afraid of the poor woman? And she has come from a faraway village, from Punjab. You left her, you left her with the children, and she has been carrying on somehow in poverty, in tremendous need, with no complaint. She has come just to touch your feet, just to see you, and she will be gone by the evening – and you don't want to see her? There must be some subtle fear in you; you are still afraid of her. Then you are still a husband, you have not become a real sannyasin."

Ramateertha listened to Purna Singh's words, became aware, and said, "You are right. Call the woman. Not only will she touch my feet, I will touch her feet too. This may be a message from God. This may be my last fear; it must be somewhere in my unconscious. You are right."

"Since that day," Purna Singh wrote in his diary, "Ramateertha had a luminosity that was never there before."

Since that day he was really free; he *was* freedom. The last shadow of bondage disappeared. He accepted his wife too. Now there was no grudge, no complaint, no fear, no escape.

That's what I mean when I say freedom should be beyond bondage, not against bondage. A freedom against bondage is afraid of bondage, and a freedom which is afraid is not freedom at all. Freedom and fear never exist together. Fear is the death of all freedom, and freedom is possible only when all fear has disappeared, utterly disappeared.

That is the meaning of Kabir: *Living in bondage, I have set myself free...*

Now there is no question. Now this freedom has no conditions about it: "I should live in the Himalayas, then I will be free"; "I will live in a Catholic monastery, then I will be free"; "I will avoid women, then I will be free"; "I will not touch money, then I will be free" – all nonsense, all rubbish, created by the cowardice of man, created by fear.

Living in bondage, I have set myself free: I have broken away from the clutch of all narrowness.

This is freedom: to be free from *all narrowness.* If you are a Hindu you cannot be free; you are very narrow, you are in a tunnel called Hinduism. If you are a Mohammedan you are not free. If you think you are man or you are woman, you are not free – tunnels, all tunnels, all of them. If you think you are a Negro or a white man, then you are not free – tunnels, all tunnels, all of them. If you think you are a communist or anticommunist, if you have some ideology to define you, you are not free.

Freedom means no definition. You are undefined, as vast as existence itself. And that is the truth, you *are* that. *Tattvamasi*: you are that. You are the whole, not an iota less. The part is the whole – let me declare it. It is very unmathematical to say that the part is the whole, but mysticism is unmathematical. If you go to the mathematician he will say, "How can the part be the whole? The part has to be the part. The part can never be the whole, and the part can never be equal to the whole, and the part has to be smaller than the whole." Certainly, it is mathematically right, but mystically it is nonsense.

The part is the whole, *equal* to the whole, not a little smaller, not a single iota less. Because the part is not separate from the whole, how can the part be smaller than the whole? Just think of a wave: the mathematician will say, "The wave is less than the ocean." The mystic will say, "The wave *is* the ocean!" How can it be smaller than the ocean? Can you take the wave away from the ocean? Can you take it away? Can you hold it in a box? Then you will know that the moment you take the wave away, it is no longer a wave. The wave exists only in the ocean, as the ocean; it cannot be taken away. The wave is nothing but the ocean waving.

The wave is an activity of the ocean. It is not separate, there is no division. The wave is the ocean, the part is the whole. And when you remember this, then you declare, like Christ, "My God and I are one"; or, like al-Hillaj Mansoor, "*Ana'l Haq* – I am the truth"; or, like the Upanishads, "*Aham Brahmasmi* – I am God, I am absolute, I am the whole."

I have broken away from the clutch of all narrowness.
Kabir says: I have attained the unattainable...

Listen to the beauty of it:

...I have attained the unattainable, and my heart is colored with
the color of love.

Why call it "unattainable" if you say, "I have attained"? That's where logic and mysticism go their separate ways; they part company. The logician... If you go to Arthur Koestler and you ask him about this sentence where Kabir says, "I have attained the unattainable," he will say, "Absurd! If it is unattainable, then certainly, how can you say you have attained it? If you say you have attained it, then how can you say, in the same breath, it is unattainable?" He will say this is mystification, this is madness.

But listen, it is not mystification. Kabir is trying to say something of tremendous value. He has to use this absurd expression because that is the only way to express it. Truth can be expressed only through paradox!

...*I have attained the unattainable*... What does he mean then? He calls it unattainable because you cannot attain it. You cannot achieve it, you cannot make it a goal, you cannot make any effort to attain it. There is no methodology to attain it, there is no way to attain it – hence he calls it unattainable. But still it is attained. One day, suddenly, it comes as a gift, not as an attainment. Not that you have attained; you are simply amazed, you cannot believe your own eyes: it is there, it is showering all around you. And the paradox is: the more you try to attain it, the less will be the possibility for the gift to come to you.

When you drop trying to attain it, when you forget all about attaining, when you have understood that it cannot be attained, when this understanding has penetrated to the very core of your being, and you are relaxed, and there is no desire to attain, to go anywhere, to be somebody, to have something – some experience of God, *moksha,* nirvana – when all these desires have disappeared... Because you know it is unattainable, it cannot be desired, it cannot be made an object of ambition; all objects of ambition will create ego – and through ego it is not possible. How, through the ego, can you become vast? The ego is the tunnel; how can you remain in the tunnel and yet attain to the vast sky? Impossible!

Understanding "I am the root cause of my misery, I am my confinement," one relaxes. When the relaxation is perfect, when the realization is *utter*, then it comes as a gift.

So Kabir says, "*I have attained the unattainable...* Not that I have attained it – I have been given it, it is a grace. God has descended on me."

That's why I say Rabindranath has not translated it rightly.

Chalat mansa achal kinhi – "So, my God, you have done it? I had lost all hope. I had even stopped praying for it; it was meaningless. For thousands and thousands of lives I was searching for it, and then I dropped the whole search. And now that I have dropped all searching, you have done it? You surprise me! When I was trying, you were frustrating me. And now I am no longer trying, you have done it? When I was thinking I was capable of having it, when I was thinking I deserved it, you never listened to me. You were so far away. And now that I think I don't deserve it, that I am not worthy of it, suddenly you are here?"

...I have attained the unattainable, and my heart is colored with the color of love. Only when God has happened is your heart colored with the color of love, never before. Or, when your heart is colored with the color of love, God is attained, never before it. And please don't make a puzzle out of it, don't start asking which is first, the hen or the egg. Don't ask that.

Either move through love and you will attain to God, or move through God and you will attain to love. They come together; it is one package. The hen and the egg are not separate – the egg is nothing but a way for the hen to produce more hens, and the hen is nothing but a way for the egg to produce more eggs. They are not separate. The egg is the hen unmanifest, and the hen is the egg manifest. They are two ends of one thing, of one phenomenon. So are God and love.

That's why Jesus says, "God is love." And I say to you, love is God. Both mean the same. God is one end of the same energy, of the same vibration, and the other end is love. You start from anywhere.

Please start; don't just sit and think, "Which is first? From where should I start?" People who think about from where they should start never start. Thinkers never start. Only nonthinkers take the jump.

Somebody comes to me and I inquire, "What about sannyas – are you ready to take the jump?" The person says, "I will think about it." Thinkers never take any jump. Thinking means making everything certain before it has happened. Thinking means trying to make the unknown known before going into it. Thinking means, "First I should make all the arrangements. I am not moving into some gamble." Thinking is cowardly. Thinking is cowardly; thinkers are cowards. What can you know in this mysterious life? What can you know? Nothing is known.

I have heard...

In a jam-packed bus, a young secretary was having difficulty fishing for a quarter in her purse to pay her fare. A stalwart gent standing next to her volunteered, "May I pay your fare for you?"

"Oh no," she stammered, "I could not let you do that. After all, you are a total stranger."

"Not really," he told her. "You have unzipped me three times."

But that's what we call acquaintance, knowledge. Do you know your wife? Do you know your husband? Do you know your child? Do you know your mother? Do you know me? What do we know? All knowledge is so superficial. But still, the thinker thinks that first he has to make everything certain, first he has to become knowledgeable in every way. He has to have the map, the guide, the possibilities, the dangers, the benefits, and then he will move. Then you may move into anything, but you cannot move into sannyas: it is a gamble. Then you cannot move in God; it is the ultimate gamble.

That which you see is not...

So what will you think? And what *can* you think?

That which you see is not; and for that which is, you have no words.

That which is you cannot see because of your thinking. Thinking is the greatest foolishness of man. Then you carry ideas in your head, and you are always looking through those ideas.

I have heard...

Commuters from Connecticut have become used to horrendous railroad service, but when a local limped into Grand Central an hour and a half late on a scheduled forty-minute run, even one meek little schnook from Mount Vernon protested.

The conductor reminded him, "We are always late when it is snowing."

"I know that," persisted the schnook. "But this morning there is not even a cloud in the sky!"

"We are not responsible for that," concluded the loyal conductor. "Snow was predicted."

That is the way of knowledge. You go on looking for things which are predicted, but not for things which *are*. You go on looking for things for which you have been trained, but not for those things which are. You go on looking for that for which society has prepared you, but not for that which is the reality. No society has yet been able to prepare you for reality because society is a myth, society is a fiction, society is a lie.

I have heard a very rare incident, and it is true; reliable sources say it is so...

When a famous explorer came across a small island on his journeys, they were traveling on a very big ship. The islanders had never seen such a big thing. They had known only very small boats where two persons, at the most, could sit – just fishermen's boats. When this big ship landed near the island, the explorer reports in his diaries, the islanders did not see it! Nobody was attracted. People were working on the shore and fishing – and such a huge ship, and nobody even looked...

They were surprised: "What is the matter? Are these people mad?" They should have run, they should have gathered in a crowd. The whole small island should have gathered there; that's what the explorer was expecting.

When they went on land and they inquired, then by and by the islanders became aware of the ship. And then the chief said, "Because we have never seen such a thing, we never expected it."

Unless you expect something, how can you see it? When you expect something, you start seeing things. If you are moving through a monastery and you don't know that it is a monastery, you may see something else which is not there. If you know it is a monastery – it may not be a monastery – you may start seeing things which are not there. If you go through a cemetery and you don't know, you will not see ghosts. But if you know that it is a cemetery – it may not be, you may be misinformed – you will start seeing ghosts. Your vision is clouded by what you expect. Your vision is not clear.

That which you see is not; and for that which is you have no words.

*Unless you see, you believe not: what is told you, you cannot
accept.*

Kabir says, "I know whatsoever I am saying you cannot believe
because you have not seen it." How can you believe it? I can understand your difficulty. When I tell you, "Take the jump into sannyas,"
I know your difficulty. You have not seen it; how can you trust it? You
don't know me either; how can you trust me? You don't even know
yourself; how can you trust yourself? I can understand your confusion, your difficulty. And those who take the jump have not taken
the jump through any conclusion on their part. They have taken the
jump in spite of all the fears, doubts. In spite of their minds they
have taken the jump. It is not that they have become convinced;
there is no way to become convinced. What I am talking about is
something you experience – only then do you know. So how can
you become convinced about it? There is no way to make you convinced a priori, beforehand.

Kabir says: "I know."

*Unless you see, you believe not: what is told you, you cannot
accept.*
*He who is discerning knows by the word; and the ignorant stands
gaping.*

For one who knows, even a slight hint is enough: even a word
will give him the message of the wordless. But he knows already; he
is the discerning one, he has awakened.

Kabir and Farid met once and didn't talk. For two days they
remained silent together. Sometimes they laughed, sometimes
they hugged each other. Holding hands, they sat there, looking at
the moon and the sun. And the disciples were very worried: "What
has happened to them?" They were both usually always talking.

Farid was a great master; so was Kabir. And Farid was traveling
around the country, so his disciples said, "Kabir's ashram is close by. It
will be a beauty to see you together. It will be a great experience for
us." And they were hoping secretly that when the two met, there would
be some communication between them, a dialogue, and they would be
benefited tremendously.

So Kabir's own disciples said to him, "We have heard that Farid is passing by. We should invite him. It will be a great event for the "ashramites" to see you both together, having a chitchat. We will be benefited tremendously."

Kabir laughed. Farid was invited. Farid stayed in Kabir's ashram for two days, but not a single word was uttered by the two. The disciples became very, very bored. They were expecting much; they were frustrated, of course. They kept watch day and night because maybe when they were gone the two might talk. So they never left them, they never went to sleep. Even when Kabir and Farid were sleeping, they were waiting, but not a single word was exchanged.

Then Farid left. Kabir went to say good-bye, and even then not a single word was uttered. They hugged each other and departed. The moment they departed from each other, the disciples jumped. Farid's disciples jumped on him and they asked, "What happened to you? We had never known that you are such a dumb fellow! Why did you keep quiet? Why did you torture us so much? That silence was very heavy, and we were waiting for some communication between the two of you."

Farid said, "But what to say? He knows."

And so was the case with Kabir. He said, "What to say? To say something to him would simply prove that I don't know. He knows, I know, and we know the same thing. We looked into each other's eyes, and it was finished. What is the point of repeating? It would be a repetition, and meaningless."

When somebody knows, even a word is not needed – or even a word is enough.

Some contemplate the formless, and others meditate on form; but the wise man knows that Brahma is beyond both.

A few think God has form – *saguna;* a few think God is formless – *nirguna.* Kabir says that God is beyond both, and God is within both, and the within is the beyond. He is in forms, and yet formless. He manifests himself in so many millions of forms, and yet remains unmanifest.

That beauty of his is not seen of the eye...

If you want to see him, these eyes won't be of any help. *That beauty of his is not seen of the eye...* In fact, you will have to close these eyes. You will have to open the eyes of your consciousness, of your awareness. These physical eyes will not do.

...that meter of his is not heard of the ear.

That melody, that music, that meter, that song, is not heard by these ears. You will have to move withinward. He is singing there within you, not outside. These ears can hear only the outside music. You will have to move withinward; the singer is there, the musician is there. He is continuously singing a song. That song is your very life.

But you have to listen in a totally different way, and you have to see with a totally different quality.

Kabir says: He who has found both love and renunciation never descends to death.

Remember, the highest harmony is between love and renunciation. Look at this tremendously seminal sutra: love and renunciation, together. That's my whole teaching too.

People come to me and they say, "If you simply teach meditation, it would be enough. Why do you teach love too? We have never heard saints talking about love. Why do you talk about love? Or even if saints talk about love, they don't talk about ordinary human love."

One day when I said, "God is love, and don't write love with a capital *L*," one woman wrote a letter of protest. She wrote, "Why? Why not write the letter *L* with a capital? Why do you insist that the *L* should be written in lowercase?" I can understand her protest. With a capital *L*, love is something divine, not human. With a capital *L*, your love is dropped out of it; it is the love between Krishna and his *gopis*, the love between God and his devotees – not the love that happens between you and your child. That is a lowercase *l* love. Yes, it is good if I say love with a capital *L* and say it is God. "But ordinary love, human love, you call divine?" That is difficult, that looks like a sacrilege – but that is my whole effort here.

There is no capital *l*. Even God should be written with a lowercase *g* because this whole existence is divine, the whole existence.

In the very ordinary, the extraordinary is present. Look into the lowercase *l*: the capital *L* is present.

In the ordinary pebble, in the ordinary rock, he is as much present as in a Kohinoor. There is no distinction for him. The whole of existence is precious with his presence.

Kabir says: He who has found both love and renunciation... Very difficult to understand: the very extreme of illogic. We can understand love, but then what about renunciation? We can understand renunciation, but what about love? They seem to be the greatest contradictions possible. When you love, how can you renounce? And when you renounce, how can you love?

Try to understand it. Ordinary love is a sort of sleep: you become attached to the object of love, you start feeling jealous, you become possessive. Your possessiveness and your jealousy really poison the whole of love. They destroy it. Love is destroyed by jealousy, possessiveness. The moment you try to possess your love-object, you have denied love; you have already denied. You have declared that you don't love.

Love is possible only if there is no possessiveness and no jealousy. That means love has attained to renunciation. You love the person, but you renounce possessiveness; you love the person, but you renounce jealousy; you love the person, but you don't want to make a slave out of him or out of her; you love the person, but you respect his or her freedom; you love the person, but your love does not become an imprisonment. You love, and yet you remain unattached. You love, you love tremendously, but still you don't cling – that is renunciation.

Love the world and don't be attached. Be in the world, but don't be of the world – that is what renunciation is. That's what I call sannyas: a great harmony between love and renunciation; a great harmony between this world and that; a great harmony between God the creator and the world, the created; a great harmony between the body and the soul; a great harmony, with no conflict – the disappearance of all conflict.

If your love is so great that it can contain renunciation, only then is it love. If your renunciation is so great that it can contain love, only then is it renunciation. A man who can be loving and yet in renunciation, is the greatest growth, the destiny. That is the destiny we are seeking. And unless it is attained, you will never feel fulfilled. God is the lover and the sannyasin.

Look: he loves the world, otherwise the world could not be. He loves the world, and yet you cannot find him anywhere. He is completely absent; his renunciation is utter. He loves the world – he goes on creating it. He loves tremendously, otherwise why should he create? He cares tremendously, but is so unattached that he never comes in the marketplace to declare, "Look, I am the creator."

He has no I. He is the creator without ever feeling, "I am the creator." His renunciation is total; his love is utter.

A sannyasin will be a miniature of God; his love will be total, his renunciation too. And Kabir says: *He who has found both love and renunciation never descends to death.* He goes beyond death; he becomes deathless. He has attained to the nectar of the divine. He has attained to the elixir. For this elixir, the alchemists all over the world have been searching and searching. This elixir can happen in you. Just one combination is needed, one great synthesis: the synthesis between love and renunciation.

Enough for today.

CHAPTER 8

freedom to choose

The first question:

Osho,
Is there life after death?

This is a wrong question, basically meaningless. One should never jump ahead of oneself: there is every possibility that you will fall on your face. One should ask the basic question, one should begin from the beginning. My suggestion is, ask a more basic question.

For example, you can ask, "Is there life after birth?" That would be more basic because many people are born but very few people have life. Just by being born you are not alive. You exist, certainly, but life is more than mere existence. You are born, but unless you are reborn into your being, you don't live, you never live.

Birth is necessary, but not enough. Something more is needed; otherwise one simply vegetates, one simply dies. Of course, it is a very gradual death – and you are so unaware that you never know it, you never become aware of it. From birth to death, it is a long progression of death. It is very rare to come across an alive person.

A Buddha, a Jesus, a Kabir is alive. And this is the miracle: that those who are alive never ask the question "Is there life after death?" They know it. They know what life is, and in that knowing, death has disappeared. Once you know what life is, death exists not. Death exists only because you don't know what life is, because you are as yet unaware of life, its deathlessness. You have not touched life, hence the fear of death exists. Once you have known what life is, in that very moment death has become nonexistential.

Bring light into a dark room, and the darkness disappears; know life, and death disappears. A person who is really alive simply laughs at the very possibility of death. Death is impossible; death cannot exist in the very nature of things: that which *is* will remain, has remained always. That which is cannot disappear. But you have to come to this experience existentially, not theoretically.

Ordinarily the question "What happens after death?" remains in the mind, whether you ask it or not, because nothing has happened *before* death. Life has not happened even after birth, so how can you believe and trust that life is going to happen after death? It has not happened after birth, how can it happen after death? One who knows life knows that death is another birth and nothing else. Death is another birth; a new door opens. Death is the other side of the same door you call birth: from one side the door is known as death, from the other side the door is known as birth. Death brings another birth, another beginning, another journey.

But this will be just speculation to you. It will not mean much unless you know what life is. That's why I say to ask the right question. A wrong question cannot be answered, or it can be answered only in a wrong way. A wrong question presupposes a wrong answer. I am here to help you to know something, not to help you to become great speculators, thinkers. Experience is the goal, not philosophizing – and only experience solves the riddle.

You are born, but not yet really born. A rebirth is needed; you have to be twice-born. The first birth is only the physical birth; the second birth is the real birth, the spiritual birth. You have to come to know yourself, who you are. You have to ask this question: Who am I? And while life is there, why not inquire into life itself? Why bother about death? When it comes, you can face it and you can know it. Don't miss this opportunity of knowing life while life surrounds you.

If you have known life, you will have certainly known death – and then death is not the enemy, death is the friend. Then death is nothing but a deep sleep. Again there is a morning, again things will start. Then death is nothing but rest – a tremendous rest, a needed rest. After the whole life of toil and tiredness, one needs a great rest in the divine. Death is going back to the source, just as in sleep.

Every night you die a little death. You call it sleep; it would be better to call it a little death. You disappear from the surface, you move into your innermost being. You are lost, you don't know who you are. You forget all about the world, and the relationships, and the people. You die a small death, a tiny death, but even that tiny death revives you. In the morning you are full of zest and juice again, again throbbing with life, again ready to jump into a thousand and one adventures, ready to take the challenge. By the evening you will be tired again.

This is happening daily. You have not even known what sleep is; how can you know death? Death is a great sleep, a great rest after the whole life. It makes you new, it makes you fresh; it resurrects you.

The second question:

Osho,
The owner of the Grand Hotel where I am living would like an answer to this question: "Why did God create this world?"

First, never bring anybody else's questions to me. Bring the questioner because I cannot answer anybody else's question. The questioner has to be here, in my presence, because deep down my presence is the answer – not what I say, but what I am. Never bring borrowed questions. If it is not yours, it is meaningless. Tell the owner of your hotel, "You can come," and if he is really interested, he should come. I don't think he is interested in God or in anything – maybe curious, but curious people are just stupid. Any stupid person can be curious. To really be an inquirer, one needs great intelligence.

Now, if he is interested, I am here in Pune, and he runs a hotel here. You are here from faraway countries, he has not come. He is not interested, he is just curious. He is not ready to stake anything, not even coming here. It is not very costly to come here; he could have come. And he knows you are coming here every day, and he knows that you are a sannyasin. He knows that you have staked your life, you have gambled with your life, and he has not even become interested.

Never bring such questions to me. This type of question is foolish; it cannot be answered because unless you ask intensely, unless you ask from the very core of your being, the question is irrelevant. The question becomes relevant only when you are behind it and you are ready to do something for it: you are ready to pay for it.

God is not available to such people. They are not ready to pay anything. They want God very cheaply. They want God secondhand. Now, you will listen to my answer, and then you will go and tell him. First, you don't know; you will not listen to what I say. You are bound to carry a wrong message. Of course, your mind will come in, you will distort it, you will add something, you will delete something from it, you will color it with your own mind, with your own interpretation, and then you will take it to him. It is already dead; you have killed it, and then you go and give it to him.

If inquiries are possible in this way, then books are available. He should go and consult a library; all the answers are written there. And he must have read something, otherwise the question would not arise. He must have heard the word *God*.

Never do these things. If somebody asks such a question, drag him to me. Tell him, "Come and face this man directly." But I suspect that the question is yours, and not the owner of the hotel. But you are not courageous enough to say that it is yours. People are so ashamed, even of asking authentic questions. Why are people so ashamed? – because to ask a question proves that they are ignorant. So people would like to hide behind somebody else's back – and this "owner of the Grand Hotel" is a perfect place to hide. People feel a little ashamed when they ask a question because the very idea "I am asking a question" means "I don't know."

Once it happened...

A man came to me and he said, "My friend has become impotent. Can you suggest something?"

I said, "It would be better for you to send your friend and he can say the truth: that his friend has become impotent. Why have you bothered? You could have sent the friend, and he could have told the truth: that his friend has become impotent. You are not even potent enough to ask a question? Why bring this friend in?"

The first thing when you ask a question is to recognize your ignorance. From there the inquiry starts. A question is beautiful when the questioner knows that he doesn't know. Then a question is healthy – because the mother is healthy, and the question is your child. When you say, "I don't know, and I ask because I don't know," then the question is tremendously healthy, alive, its heart beating. It breathes. And I love a living question; then something can be done.

Now, you bring a dead question because you cannot accept the fact that you don't know. You know perfectly well that this owner of the Grand Hotel does not know that he is asking. That's why I am going to answer – because I know it is your question.

"Why did God create this world?" First thing: it may be a surprise to you that God never created this world. This world is your creation. God has created a world, but you don't know about that world at all. *This* world he has not created at all; this world where Richard Nixon exists, where Vietnam exists, where Idi Amin Dada exists. This world God has not created: this world of Adolf Hitlers and Mussolinis, and fascism and communism, and Stalin and Mao. This world God has not created: this world where such tremendous poverty exists because people are so greedy, because people go on hoarding; this world where such ugly life exists, where not even a shower of love happens: desert-like, loveless, people just competing, fighting, conflicting, where such immense violence exists... This world, God has not created. This is your world. You are the creator of it. You are this world. This world is your projection; this world vibrates on your ugliness.

So the first thing: God has not created this world. Please don't make him responsible for it; he is not. Otherwise he would be the greatest criminal if he had created this world. At least I for one declare that he has not created this world – this is your creation.

But you will say, and logically too, that he has created us, and if we create this world then finally he is responsible. No, still I say he is not responsible because he has created you as freedom. That is the thing to be understood.

This ugly world wouldn't exist if God had created you as slaves. If God had created you as robots, mechanisms, then this ugly world would not exist. Then you would all be buddhas, but meaningless buddhas. If a buddha cannot be an Adolf Hitler, if the very possibility is denied, then the buddha is just a statue, meaningless. If you have to be good, and there is no freedom to be bad, then what is the point of being good? The world would have been good if God had not created you free. If he had forced you to be just mechanical repetitions, gramophone records, then you all would have been delivering a Sermon on the Mount, or a Bhagavad Gita. But a gramophone record is a gramophone record.

God has created you as free. Of course, in freedom the opposite is implied. You can do good if you choose, you can do bad if you choose that way. The choice is yours. God has given you complete freedom to choose.

That is the glory of man, and the agony – the glory, because man is free. Can't you see it? A tree is not free; a rosebush is a rosebush. Whatsoever is going to happen is already predestined. The rosebush is not free. If it decides not to grow roses, nothing will happen; roses will still come. If the rosebush decides to change the color of the roses, nothing will happen; the rose will remain of the same color as before. If the rosebush decides to become a lotus, nothing will happen; the rosebush will remain a rosebush. It is destined to be a rosebush. It is beautiful, but not free.

That's why I say nothing can be compared to man's beauty. Even roses are nothing compared to man's beauty; a rose has to be a rose, it is in a sort of bondage. It cannot do otherwise. It cannot go astray; it has to be a saint. It has to be a Jesus, it cannot be a Judas. That's why a rosebush is just a rosebush – good to look at, but nothing to be compared with the beauty of human beings. The beauty comes because a person can be a Jesus or a Judas, and everybody carries both possibilities: Jesus and Judas.

Everybody is totally free. And the range is big – the whole spectrum. Man is a rainbow, all the colors. Man is not predestined. Hence we have created this world out of our freedom. The responsibility is ours. If you want to become a Buddha, you can become one. Nobody can force you to become a Buddha. If you want to become a Genghis Khan, you can become a Genghis Khan; the choice is yours. God is not dragging you anywhere. He has given you enough rope; you can go astray, you can come back. Because of this possibility of going astray, this world exists. This world can be changed, can be utterly changed. Once we change our consciousness, this world can become a totally different affair.

You ask, "Why did God create this world?" So the first thing: he has not created this world, he has created you, he has created human freedom – and one should feel grateful that he has made you free. Otherwise, if you are forced to become a Jesus, then to be a Jesus is mechanical, meaningless; there is no significance, no poetry in it.

Because you can miss the target... The Christian word *sin* is very significant. Its original root means missing the target. The original root for the word *sin* comes from "missing the target." You can miss; it is up to you. Sin is missing the target, it is going astray. And God will not prevent you: his love is so infinite that he will love you even if you have gone astray. He loves the sinners as much as the saints. And if you listen to Jesus, Jesus says he loves the sinners even more because they need more love.

Have you not seen? If a child is ill, the mother cares more about the ill child than the healthy child – naturally so. It is justified. The healthy is healthy, so there is no need for the mother to be over-careful. But the ill is ill: the mother sits by the side of the bed, massages the child, takes more care. Jesus says God cares more for the sinners, those who have missed the target. He goes on showering his mercy on them.

This world is our going astray, our sin. It has nothing to do with God.

The second thing: why did God create this world? The second thing is that in the Christian, in the Judaic, in the Mohammedan world, a very wrong conception exists about God, as if he is separate from his creation; as if one day he created the world and then forgot all about it. It is as if God is a painter – the painting is finished and the painting becomes separate from the painter. No, the East knows far better. The East says that God is not separate from his creation; the creator is not separate from his creation. He is involved in it, he is in it, he *is* it. The creator is the creation.

That's why I insist again and again, don't call God "the creator," call him "creativity." God is a dynamic creativity. The creator is a dead concept – as if one day he finished. That's what Christians go on thinking: in six days he created the world and the seventh day he rested. In six days, finished? Then what has he been doing since then? He must be getting very tired, not doing anything. He must be getting fed up. He must be bored – have mercy on him.

He is not finished yet – the creation is never finished, it is an ongoing process. The creation is never complete, and God goes on and on and on. He is not finished with it. If he were finished with it, then that would be the end. He is still involved, he is still in love. He is still painting, he is still sculpturing; he still hopes.

Rabindranath has said, "Whenever I see a newborn baby, I look at the sky and say, 'God still hopes.'" A new baby is a hope. Of course, he failed with the old generation, so he creates a new generation. He says, "Let us see; maybe this time I will succeed." His optimism is infinite. He is like a poet who goes on composing new poems every day. Every day he feels a little satisfied and a little dissatisfied – satisfied because something has happened in the poetry, something has been caught, a ray of light; but something is still missing. Tomorrow morning, another try.

Rabindranath had written six thousand poems, and when he was dying an old friend said to him, "You can die peacefully and in deep contentment because you are the greatest poet."

Rabindranath opened his eyes and said, "Stop this nonsense! Right now I am telling God: 'What are you doing? I have been trying and trying, and I have not yet succeeded! Much has happened, but I am not satisfied. And just now I was getting closer and closer, and this is the time to take me away? I was just getting closer and closer, and I was feeling that just round the corner it is there – the poetry for which I have been trying. My six thousand poems are my six thousand failures. Maybe the six thousand and first...? And is this the time to take me away? What are you doing? My whole life I have been trying and trying and trying, and now I feel the crescendo is coming and I am coming to the peak, and this is the moment you withdraw me?'"

God is not yet finished; God still hopes. Hence, we can also hope. In his hope is our hope too. He has not utterly failed. He still trusts you, he still goes on creating. So this concept of a dead creator somewhere in the past...

Christian theologians are so foolish that they have even decided the date, the year: he created the world four thousand and four years before Jesus Christ – on a certain Monday of course. Early, at six in the morning, when you start the Dynamic Meditation, he started this whole dynamism. Early in the morning, six o'clock – he must have fixed the clock with an alarm! It is all foolish.

Creation is timeless: it has always been there, it will always be there, because God is creation, God is creativity. So I never call God a painter, I call him a dancer.

When the painting is finished, the painter and the painting are separate. In dance, it is totally different. Dance is the most spiritual phenomenon because the dancer and the dance are one. You cannot separate them, the duality does not exist. There is a tremendous oneness: the dancer is the dance, the dance is the dancer. If you take away the dance, the dancer is no longer a dancer. If the dancer stops, the dance stops – they are not two. God is as involved in his world as a dancer is involved in his dance. Hence I tell you to revere the world, never condemn it; God is involved in it, God is present everywhere.

That's what Kabir goes on saying: "Feel the awe, the reverence, the wonder, because he is everywhere, still working. You can catch hold of him, still painting, still sculpting, still dancing. It is not something that happened sometime in the past, it is happening right this moment: he is speaking through me; he is listening through you. The creation is still going on. It is never going to end, it is an endless journey."

In fact, existence has no goal. It is a pure journey. The journey in itself is so beautiful, who bothers about the goal?

Saint Teresa has said, "Heaven is all the way to heaven. Has he not said, 'I am the way'"? Such a beautiful assertion, of tremendous import: "Heaven is all the way to heaven" – don't wait for some heaven as a goal – "Heaven is *all* the way to heaven. Has he not said, 'I am the way'"? God is the way, not the goal. God is here, not there. God is now, not then. God is in you, in me, all around. *Only* God is.

So you cannot ask this question: "Why did God create this world?" He never created it, he is still creating, and if you really want to know why, go to the artists. Don't go to theologians and don't go to philosophers and don't go to pundits; go to the artists. Go to a van Gogh when he is painting and ask him why he is painting. Go to a dancer, hold his hand and ask him, "Why are you dancing?" Go to a singer and ask him, "Why are you singing?" and you will know the answer.

The painter will shrug his shoulders; he will say, "What else can I do? I love painting. Why? There is no why. I love painting. It is the way I am. It is the way I feel happiest to be. This is the only way I feel tremendously blessed, that's why. There is no other why."

Ask a dancer, "Why are you dancing?" and he will say, "What else can one do? Life is to dance." Or ask a lover why he is in love. Have you ever loved somebody? And if somebody comes and asks you why, what will you say? Will you really have any answer as to why you love? You will say, "Why? There is no question about it. That's the way I feel the best, at my very peak. That's the way I feel blooming. That's the way bliss happens to me."

Now, there is no question about bliss. If you are happy, you are happy; nobody asks you why you are happy. Yes, if you are miserable, a question is relevant. If you are miserable, somebody can ask why you are miserable, and the question is relevant because misery is against nature, something wrong is happening. When you are happy, nobody asks why you are happy, except for a few neurotics. There are such people; I cannot deny the possibility.

I have heard about a patient – the psychiatrist was bored with him. Of course, he was getting enough money out of him, but by and by he was getting bored: three, four, five years of psychoanalysis, and the man was repeating the same, again and again and again. The psychiatrist said, "Do one thing: go to the mountains for a few days. That will be very helpful."

So the patient went to the mountains, and do you know what? Next day a telegram arrived for the psychiatrist. The patient said in the telegram, "I am feeling very happy – why?"

Feeling very happy – why? An explanation is needed? No, happiness needs no explanation; happiness is its own explanation. God is creating because that is the only way he can be happy, that is the only way he loves, that is the only way he sings, that's the only way he can *be* at all. Creation is his innermost nature, no why is needed.

The third question:

Osho,
What is the difference between a monastery and an ashram?

A lot of difference, a great difference! The difference is as much as between West and East. The difference is as much as between will and surrender.

The monastery is a Western concept. You should never translate *ashram* as *monastery*. That is corrupting the word *ashram*, destroying its whole meaning. A monastery is on the path of will: people are trying hard to know the truth, struggling hard to find God. The monastery is strenuous, tense.

The very word *ashram* means rest, relaxation. The very word *ashram* means tremendously relaxed. An ashram is a place where you go to relax; the monastery is a place where you go to seek, to search. A monastery is aggressive, male; an ashram is female, passive. An ashram is effortless; a monastery is nothing but effort. In the monastery you are working to achieve God, and in an ashram you are playing: that's the difference. The ashram is fun; the monastery is very serious.

The word *monastery* comes from *monk*. The monk is a very serious man: he has renounced the world, renounced the wife, renounced the children, renounced this and that. The monk is very dry; hence all the old Western monasteries existed in the deserts. The great monasteries existed in the deserts – dry, dry inside, dry outside, no rest, no shade of a tree, no greenery, no flowers flowering, just effort and effort and effort, no oasis of rest. The word *monk* means a person who has decided to be lonely.

The word *monk* means lonely, one who has decided to live on his own. That's why from the same root come *monopoly, monogamy, monotony* – the same root: one, alone. A monastery is a place where many people live in their loneliness, but they don't live together. There is no togetherness. A monastery is not a community. People are there, many people may be living there, but each is living alone. Together, they are lonely. It is not a community. Each is seeking God; great effort has to be made: one has to be ascetic, one has to continuously flog one's own body, one has to torture it, one has to fast, one has to destroy all attachment to the world. How can you relax? The world is sin and you are born in sin – how can you relax, how can you rest, how can you celebrate?

You will be surprised: the word *celebration* comes from a root *celere*, and *celere* means fasting. In the old Western monasteries, when the monks were fasting, it was called celebrating. Now, a feast can be a celebration, but how can a fast be a celebration? But that's how fasting was imposed – as celebration. Torture, self-torture, was thought to be prayer. The world is thought to be against God, so you have to leave the world if you want to achieve God.

The ashram has a totally different perspective. The ashram means a community, a communion of people, of souls who are alike. You will be surprised: remember, the modern Hindu ashram is not really Eastern. The modern Hindu ashram is so influenced by the Christian monastery that it is not Hindu at all. If you really want to have a glimpse of a Hindu ashram, you will have to go to the days of the Vedas. The master was there, but the master was not a monk. He was a married man: he had a wife, he had children, the ashram was his family. That's why the ashram was called *gurukul*. *Gurukul* means the family of the master. He had children, he had a wife, he lived a relaxed life, deep in the forest, deep in nature: a spontaneous way of life, unhurried, not searching, but waiting; not putting God against the world, but enjoying the world because God is in it. And the disciples who lived with him were his family, *gurukul*. It was not an institution; it was a family. They were children to him, his own kids. They may have been older than him – that is not the point – but they were his kids.

This community lived in a very deep, relaxed way – dancing, singing, feasting, celebrating, enjoying nature: the stars, the moon, the sun, the morning, the evening, the day, the night, and listening to God's voice in nature. Hence, the master had moved to the forest. Remember, it was not against the world. When the Christian monk moves out of the world, he is against the world. When the Eastern sage moved to the forest, he moved because he was all for the world, and in the marketplace the world had been corrupted and destroyed so much. Know the distinction, it is tremendous.

The Eastern sage used to move into nature because there, God is more present. Man has not yet interfered. It is difficult to find God on an asphalt road, howsoever hard you look. You will not even find a glimpse. It is very difficult to find God in a factory – difficult, very difficult – because the human noise is too much. The mechanical, the technological, is too much; the natural has gone far away.

I have heard that there was a survey in London, and a million children reported that they had never seen a cow. Now this is too much: a million children have never seen a cow? How will they ever be able to understand what God is if they have never looked into the eyes of a cow? God is more crystal-clear in the eyes of a cow than in the eyes of a pope or a *shankaracharya*. One million children have not seen a cow? Now those one million children will suffer tremendously. There are thousands and thousands of people who have never seen the Himalayas, the snow-covered peaks, the eternal snow: virgin, never trodden upon. There, God is still more present, is more throbbing, alive; man has not destroyed yet.

The Eastern sages moved into the forest, not because they were against the world but because they wanted to really know the world that God has created, un-interfered with by man. When the Christians move to a monastery they move against the world, because the world is a place of sin. They both move, but they move for different reasons, diametrically opposite.

The Eastern word *ashram* is beautiful: it means rest. You have lived in the world; you have known the world, now to rest you go to an ashram. You have seen the world: the ugliness of it, the futility of it, the uselessness of it, the meaninglessness of it – now you would like to rest. Now you go deep into the forest, you sit under the shady trees, you listen to the murmur of the brooks and the song of the birds, and you see the sunrays playing on the treetops in the morning, and you watch the silent stars. You relax. By and by you relax into your nature with the help of nature outside you. It becomes a harmony: the inner nature and the outer nature. You start playing with the outer nature. It is not a seeking; a Hindu ashram is not for seeking, it is a place to rest.

Seek, and you will never find because the very seeking makes you tense. The East says, seek not, and he will find you. Seek and you will never find; seek and you will seek in vain. Blessed are those who can rest in prayer, who can rest and trust, and who can say, "Okay, whenever you feel like coming, come. I am not in a hurry." The East is not in a hurry, the East has no consciousness of time. It says, "Okay, if in this life, good; and if you decide to come next life, good. You will still find me here. There is no hurry."

The West is in too much of a hurry. In the West, the concept of one life has made such a tense knot in the human mind – only one life, seventy years, three score and ten years, and finished? And of those seventy years, twenty-five years are lost in education, for almost twenty-five years you will be sleeping, and for the remainder, shaving and going to the office, coming from the office, and the traffic and the conflict and the children and the wife and the court and the divorce – all these things. What is left? If you count everything, you will be so surprised: not even seven minutes are left for God. A great hurry arises, move fast, do something! Otherwise, how will you find God?

God is not something to be found. It is something you relax into; it is an inner space. When you are not, it is there. And when you are not... You are only not when you are not a seeker. The seeker holds you as an ego. *Who* is seeking?

The ashram is a totally different concept: you relax, you just be. You do small things. You feel hungry, you eat; you feel tired, you go to sleep, with no hurry, with no worry. You just allow God to come in his own way, and in his own time. This is the concept of an ashram. If you really want to know a real ashram, my ashram is the only one because all other ashrams are absolutely corrupted by the Christians. They think they are Hindu but they are not; there is a certain attraction in the Christian argument, it appeals. First, the very idea of will appeals – you have to work hard.

The Christians have given a work ethic to the world. Work! Play? Forget about play, play is for children. You work, you are a grown-up; you work hard, you work for your whole life, and then in the end, like a carrot dangling, you will have your reward. In the end! And that end never comes. You work and work and work and you die working. One day you fall into your grave.

In the East we don't have that work ethic. We say relax, enjoy, play, fool around, have fun, don't be serious. And the end is not in the end, and the end is not in the result; it is in the process itself. Let me repeat: "Heaven is all the way to heaven. Has he not said, 'I am the way'"? This relaxed attitude by and by helps you to disappear, to disappear utterly. And when you are not, suddenly one day you see God is there. And you see... You are amazed that he has always been there. If you were not seeking him, you would have known him at any time. Your very seeking was the hindrance because the sought was hiding in the seeker, and you were rushing hither and thither.

The monastery is the West; the monastery is the argument of the West. The ashram is the East, the argument of the East. And I say to you that all the other ashrams in India have become Christian, because Christianity appeals very much. The modern world was made by the West; the East is no longer East.

Will helps you to feel more egoistic. Everybody wants to feel that he is somebody, and you can feel that you are somebody only if

you do something. Just fooling around, you cannot feel like somebody. Just having fun, you cannot feel like somebody. You have to
do something to prove that you are somebody. And then the
Christian ethic says: religion is service, so go and serve people.

The Eastern attitude is: religion is not service. Service may come
as a by-product but it is not synonymous with religion. Religion is
meditation, prayer, relaxation; religion is going into yourself. If you
have arrived deep in your own being, maybe – and that is a maybe –
perhaps, you may start serving people. But the service will not be a
duty; it will be just a sharing. The East says it is just a "perhaps,"
because it may not happen to everybody in the same way. Each is so
unique. When it happened to Meera, she started dancing; she forgot
all about service. Of course, there were poor people, and it would
have been more economical if she had served poor people, but she
simply started dancing and singing.

And I say she did well. If she had served a leper or a poor person,
or if she had opened a school and had made a hospital; that would
have been a great loss because her songs are so tremendously beautiful. Her dance has changed the whole quality of human existence,
she has pulsated a new tune. No, it would not have been good. It is
good that she allowed her own expression. There have been people
who never went anywhere when they became enlightened; they
remained under their trees. That's how it happened to them.

In the East we accept the uniqueness of the individual. We don't
enforce any ethics on top of him. We simply say that when you have
come home, whatsoever happens is good. Whatsoever God wills
through you, let it be so. Amen! You don't interfere. If he wants to be
silent in you under a *bodhi* tree, then let him be silent. Through
silence he will create pulsations which will change the centuries, the
coming centuries. For thousands of years those pulsations will help
people to attain higher states of consciousness, altered states of consciousness. So don't bother and don't interfere. If he wants to remain
quiet and silent, let him be. If he wants to dance in you, let him. If he
wants to go and serve poor people, let him. If he wants to become a
Meera, good, if he wants to become a Chaitanya, good, if he wants to
become a Buddha, good; whatsoever he wills, let his will be done.

But the Christian argument is important: the world is poor,
people are suffering, and you are meditating? Go and serve people!
It is logical, it appeals to reason. The ashram has disappeared.

I am trying to create a new commune – new in the sense that it no longer exists; otherwise it is the most ancient one. It existed once, now only the memory remains – not even the memory. It has disappeared, faded away: a commune where people are simply relaxing and doing their things, moving through feeling, not through reasoning; functioning through the heart not through the head, and taking it easy.

Yes, the very word *ashram* means: take it easy.

The fourth question:

Osho,
You crafty old bugger! Will I ever learn your ways?

There is no possibility, sir because I have none. I *am* the way. If you see through me, through and through, only then will you find. If you listen to my words – and that's what you are doing; the questioner is not a sannyasin – if you are just standing outside me... To become a sannyasin means to stand inside me, to become part of my family, to belong to me. I am the way. I am not preaching some way to you, I am simply preaching myself. I am not giving you some method, some way, handing over some technique to you. And if you are trying to figure it out, you will become more and more confused. I can drive you crazy. Either be a sannyasin, or escape.

If you are a sannyasin, then your madness has a method to it. If you are not a sannyasin, then you will become more and more confused. You will become mad without a method. And when you have become too confused, if you escape from here that won't help; I will go on haunting you.

You ask, "Will I ever learn your ways?" There is no possibility, sir. It is impossible because there are no ways that I am preaching here. In fact, I am destroying all ways. I am trying to take all ways from you. Here, my whole effort is to create anarchy in you, chaos, because *your* ways are hindrances to God. When you are in an anarchic state – not knowing who you are, not knowing where you are going, not knowing what is what – in that beautiful chaos, freedom exists. Only in that freedom is God possible.

I am trying to create a space here, not a way. I am not making a superhighway so people can follow on it. No, I am throwing you into the wild where no map exists, and I am not going to give you any guide. Here I am not teaching you a certain doctrine – no, not at all. I am trying to take away all the doctrines that you have already learned. Here, I am trying to help you unlearn, to unlearn the ways so that the way can exist. And the way is not one of the ways; the way has nothing to do with your choice or with your mind or with your reason or with your logic. When you are completely at a loss the way exists, God exists.

Here, it is not a question of any theology; it is a question of love. If you stand outside just like a spectator, an observer, you will get something, but that will not be the true thing, and you will get it in a very fragmentary way, and you will get it according to you. And you cannot get me according to you, remember, make it a point: you can get me only according to me, not according to you. That is the meaning of becoming a sannyasin – that you say, "Okay, now we will take you as you are, according to you." If you take me according to yourself, that will be simply a misunderstanding. Then we are poles apart.

I have heard...

A very voluble preacher was working himself into a frenzy during a sermon on hell and damnation. A little four-year-old boy in the congregation could not take his eyes off the wild figure in the pulpit. Finally, he whispered to his mother, "What will we do if he ever gets loose?"

Now, a child has his own understanding. He is there, listening, but with his own understanding.

If you are trying to understand me from your own understanding, you will not understand me at all. You will get some wrong conceptions, notions, and whatsoever you carry from here will be a burden to you rather than a relief. It will disturb you, and it will always create trouble for you. Never be anywhere halfheartedly. Either be or don't be, but never be halfhearted; otherwise you are committing a wrong against yourself.

You can hear me, certainly, without becoming a sannyasin; you can meditate here without becoming a sannyasin. You can remain an outsider, aloof, neutral, and you may think that you are very clever – but you will get into trouble. And I am warning you; then it is at your own risk.

The trouble will be that something will start happening, and it will never be the right thing because I don't trust much in techniques – techniques are just devices to bring you closer to me. Techniques are just devices for you to play with, so that you remain occupied.

I talk to you, but talking is not the goal. I have to deliver something which cannot be talked about. I can deliver that only when I feel that your heart is open. Till the heart is open, I will go on persuading your mind – but whatsoever I am doing with the mind is not the real thing. The real thing has to be delivered to you when your heart is ready, when you are in a deep trust, when you have accepted me. And remember, you will think, "That's what I'm thinking: whether to accept you or not." If you accept me through your rationalizations by thinking, it will not be acceptance.

You will still be accepting yourself, your own thinking. If you decide, "Yes, this man seems to be right, and now I am going to take the jump," it is no longer a jump at all. You have missed the jump. Now you are still trusting your own thinking, you have decided, concluded, "This man is right. Now I go into the journey." You are still not going. The step has to be taken in innocence, not in cleverness. The step has to be taken like a child. The step has to be taken in trust, in foolishness.

Yes, I repeat it: only those who are foolish enough to take the jump will ever be able to find out what the way is. Have you not seen that down through the centuries, this has been happening? When Christ was on the earth, only a few foolish people believed in him, a few foolish people. You may call them apostles now, but they were foolish people – somebody was just a fisherman, another was a woodcutter, somebody was a shoemaker, just those types of people. Not a single rabbi followed him, not a single professor, not a single pundit, not a single respectable man. All were unknown, ordinary people: a fisherman, a woodcutter, a farmer, a prostitute, a drunkard – that type of person followed him, and that too was a very limited number.

And all the rabbis were against him. They were clever people: they knew, they already knew. All the scholars were against him. In fact, all the scholars, all the rabbis, all the learned people, conspired. They arranged it that he should be killed, because he was a danger, and they were afraid. His very presence was creating fear because he was such a living scripture. Who would listen to these dead rabbis who talk about dead scriptures? He was the way. And these rabbis were teaching so many ways to reach God, and here was the man who declared, "I am the way, and I am the truth. Come, follow me. All those who are heavily burdened, come to me and rest in me." Now this was too much!

You can be here like a learned man, standing by the side, looking out of the corner of the eye, not looking directly. Then you will miss.

The fifth question:

Osho,
When you wake up in the morning and hear the birds sing and smell the air, do you never think, "I want just to enjoy that, and I don't feel like giving a lecture"?

I feel it every day! I feel it every day when I listen to the birds in the almond tree. I always enjoy it. I always feel the tremendous beauty of it. That's why I have to lecture every day – because then I have to sing.

My lecture is a song. It is not against the birds that I am singing here, it is in symphony with them. This is my way of singing. And trust me; when birds sing I feel happy, when I sing they feel happy – it is a bargain.

What I am saying to you is not a lecture. *Lecture* is an ugly word. How can I lecture? This is a song, this is a spontaneous out-flow; it is an overflowing. I feel happy, that's why I say so many things to you. In fact, it is not to explain anything to you. I am not explaining; it is simply to convey my joy, my delight in life. That's the way I can dance. These words are my gestures.

Listen to me as you listen to a poet or to a bird. Never listen to me as you listen to a philosopher; it is not a lecture, it is not a sermon. I am not pouring morality into you. I am not giving you any "shoulds," "oughts." I am not giving you any ideals. I am simply conveying that I am tremendously happy. Can't you see it? I am simply conveying that I have arrived; you can also arrive. I am simply making so many gestures so that if one gesture is missed, another may not be missed; if another is missed, I will make a thousand and one gestures. Someday, some gesture may hit you in the right moment. Someday, in some moment, you may be ready and ripe, and suddenly it will happen.

Listening to me is just a way to commune with me. I am speaking, you are listening and a great communion can happen. When the listening is perfect, total, when you have just become ears, suddenly there will be an upsurge of energy, a lightning, a satori. You will have understood. I will not have been trying to explain to you, and you will have understood. I am simply transferring understanding; these are not explanations.

You can miss me only if you are deaf – and many people are deaf. You can miss me only if you are blind – and many people only appear to have eyes, they are blind.

A man visiting an insane asylum found one of the inmates with his ear to a brick wall. "Here, take a listen here," said the inmate, and the visitor obligingly put his ear at the indicated position.

"I can't hear anything," he said, baffled.

"I know," said the inmate. "It has been like that all these years I have been here; I have not heard anything either."

But still he is listening, putting his ear to the wall.

There are two misfortunes in life. There are people who go on listening to walls: lectures, sermons, priests, popes, *shankaracharyas* – people who have not experienced themselves, people who are secondhand, people who are carbon copies. If you listen to them you will listen for years, and you will not be able to find anything. They are walls, there is nothing inside them. This is one misfortune: getting attached to a wall.

There is another misfortune: you may be with a Buddha, a Krishna, a Christ, a Mohammed, but *you* may be a wall. Then he can go on hammering, he can go on speaking, and you don't listen. Jesus says so many times to his disciples, "If you have ears, listen; if you have eyes, see. I am here."

These are not lectures that I am delivering to you; this is my being that I am sharing with you. Become more sensitive, become more loving, become more receptive; become more feminine. Become a womb, and sooner or later you are bound to get pregnant with me.

But there are people who don't really want to listen; they have some investment in not listening. There are people who come to listen, and yet don't want to listen. They cannot miss listening, and they cannot allow it either. When they are not here they feel that they are missing something, they should have been here. When they are here they become stiff, they become afraid, they become scared. If they listen too much, if they go into it too much, maybe they will not be able to return. This is how they go on hanging; they remain in a limbo.

I have heard...

Mulla Nasruddin inserted a classified ad in a local newspaper offering a one hundred rupee reward for the return, with no questions asked, of his wife's pet cat.

"That's a mighty big reward for a cat – and in India!" observed the clerk, accepting the advertisement.

"Not for this one," said the Mulla cheerfully. "I drowned it."

Now there are many people like that: they know they don't want to listen, and yet they come and they try to listen. They know that they have already drowned the cat so there is no possibility of its being found again, but still they go on searching for it. Maybe they are trying to deceive others, but remember, mind: if you try to deceive others, there is every possibility that sooner or later you will be deceived by your own efforts. When others are deceived you will be deceived, by their being deceived.

Be alert. You have to take me in tremendous alertness. Only then... Only then will you be able to see what is transpiring here.

The last question:

Osho,
What are the three most esoteric reasons for your arriving at the lecture at such an exotic number of minutes past eight?

This is from Yatri. He is asking why sometimes I am late. I am amazed myself! The reasons are different. I am amazed because I am amazed at why sometimes I am not late. Time does not exist for me; it is a miracle how I manage.

And he is asking: "What are the three most esoteric reasons for your arriving at the lecture at such an exotic number of minutes past eight?"

First, I am drunk.

Second, I am drunk.
Third, I am drunk.

And the very last question:

Osho,
Can I ask the question before the first, the really, really first question? Since you obviously are not an Einstein, why not give up trying to number the questions from the first to the last?

That's true. I know no mathematics, but one thing I would like to tell you: even Einstein was not better than me. He was sometimes even worse.

Once it happened he was traveling in a bus. To pay the fare, he gave a certain amount of money to the conductor. The conductor deducted the money for the ticket and returned the remaining money.

Einstein counted it – just a few coins, but he thought that he had been cheated. So he said to the conductor, "What do you think? Are you kidding me? You have not returned the right amount of money."

The conductor counted it again – it was just a small amount – he counted it again. He said, "It is absolutely right."

Einstein counted it again. He said, "No!"

The conductor was very angry, and he said, "What is the matter with you? Can't you count? Don't you know figures?"

Einstein has reported this in his memoirs. Even Einstein was not such an Einstein. I am certainly not – I get mixed up: first question, second question, and then I forget, that's true. You should be surprised that I don't start from the last question.

Enough for today.

CHAPTER 9

the song of love

The flute of the infinite is played without ceasing, and its sound is love:
When love renounces all limits, it reaches truth.
How widely the fragrance spreads! It has no end; nothing stands in
its way.
The form of this melody is bright like a million suns: incomparably
sounds the veena, the veena of the notes of truth.

Subtle is the path of love!
Therein there is no asking and no not asking, there one loses one's
self at his feet, there one is immersed in the joy of the seeking:
plunged in the deeps of love as the fish in the water.
The lover is never slow in offering his head for his lord's service.
Kabir declares the secret of this love.

The metaphysician talks without knowing; the mystic knows, but keeps quiet. The master is eloquent silence. The master is a rare combination of the metaphysician and the mystic. The master is a great synthesis between the metaphysician and the mystic. The metaphysician knows how to talk, but he does not know what to talk about. The mystic knows what to talk about, but he does not know how to say it. The mystic is full of experience, but dumb. The metaphysician has no experience, but is very articulate. The metaphysician is of no value, and the mystic is of no use.

You can worship a mystic, but you will never be able to understand him because the communication exists not: he has broken the bridge of language. He is in truth, but he cannot bring the message to you. The metaphysician goes on bringing message after message, but the message is just verbal. If you go deeply into it there is no content in it, it is nonsubstantial.

The master knows as much as can be known, and yet is articulate enough to express, to communicate. Metaphysicians have existed in their thousands, and so have mystics; the master is very rare. Kabir is a great master: he knows, and he knows how to convey it. That's why he declares:

Kabir declares the secret of this love.

His whole being is a declaration. He is not dumb; he sang his whole life, and he sang the songs of truth.

This last song in this series is of tremendous value. Follow me very slowly and try to digest, so that it becomes part of your being because that is the only way to understand it.

The flute of the infinite is played without ceasing, and its sound is love:
When love renounces all limits, it reaches truth.
How widely the fragrance spreads!

The flute of the infinite... In the East we have always symbolized existence as the flute, the hollow bamboo on the lips of God. The song is his. The flute cannot sing, it can only allow the singing, the singer, the song, to flow through it. Existence is a passage; so is man. Man is a flute, the birds are too, and so are the trees and the sun and the moon. The whole of existence is a hollow bamboo – God flowing through it, filtering through it, being expressed in millions of ways.

When I am talking to you, I am not talking to you; I am just a hollow bamboo. And when you are listening to me, you are not listening to me; he is listening through you – you are a hollow bamboo. Be the talker or be the listener; be the dancer or be the audience, we are all hollow bamboos on the lips of the infinite. The song is his and so is silence.

Once you understand this concept of being a hollow bamboo, you are on the path of love. This is the first step.

The flute of the infinite is played without ceasing... And this is the beauty and the contradiction: that the infinite needs a flute of "finity," of the finite. The formless needs form to be expressed through. God needs you as much as you need him. The need is not one-sided; otherwise it would not be so beautiful. If we were only in need of God, then it would be a lopsided state of things. No, there is balance: God is as much in need of us as we are in need of him. The flute needs the singer, but the singer, too, needs the flute. It is true that the flute cannot create the song by itself, but the singer also cannot create the song by himself. The flute is as much a must for him as he is a must for the flute.

This is the concept of interdependence: the whole depends on the parts; the parts depend on the whole. Neither is the part independent nor is the whole independent. In fact, the very idea of independence is neurotic. We are joined together. This gives a tremendous dignity.

On the one hand Kabir says: "Be a hollow bamboo." On the other hand he says: "Remember your dignity; without you God cannot sing the song." Yes, without these tiny birds in the casuarina trees, God cannot sing the song. He depends on them; every morning he needs them. He cannot flower without the roseflowers; every morning he seeks them.

God and his existence are not two separate things, but interdependent, leaning on each other, searching for each other like two lovers. The lover will not be total if the beloved is lost, and the beloved will not be whole if the lover is lost. When they are together, when their togetherness is such that they are melting into each other, only then are both whole.

This has to be understood: the part can never be the whole alone. What to say about the part? Even the whole cannot be the whole alone. He will need the part; without the part the whole will not be so rich. Just think, God without existence. It will be just emptiness, a wasteland. Think of God without trees and without rivers and without oceans; think of God without man and birds and animals; think of God without the sun and the moon and the stars, and it will be just a wasteland, a desert.

The East says that God is as much in need as we are; we depend on each other, we are members of each other, we are together. To know this togetherness is to know what love is. To know this unity, this immense unity, is to know what love is all about.

When you fall in love with a woman or with a man, what do you come to know? What is love? In a very tiny way, you come to feel that you are not separate. In a very, very small way, on a small scale, you start feeling that you are meant for each other, that one is not whole without the other, that the other is a must, that the other is part of your soul and your being, that the other is not outside you. Somehow he is inside you, yet outside; and you are inside him, and yet outside. Lovers penetrate into each other. It is not only a sexual metaphor; the penetration is spiritual, the sexual is only a shadow of it.

Lovers penetrate into each other. Their boundaries are blurred, they become nebulous, their definitions become shaky. When living with a woman or with a man for many years, and suddenly the woman dies or the man dies, the pain that is felt, the suffering, the agony that is felt by the partner who is left behind is not only because somebody has died. It is because now he will never be whole. It is because now a part of his being is destroyed completely, utterly. Now there will exist a black hole in his being, an abyss, emptiness. When a lover dies, something deep inside you dies too. You had become so together; your life was no longer separate, it was overlapping. You were in two bodies, but you had become one soul – that is the meaning of love.

When the same happens with the whole of existence – you start feeling that you are not separate, your boundaries overlap; not only do your boundaries overlap, your centers overlap: your center is the center of the world too, the center of the world is your center too – in that ecstasy of oneness is the fragrance called love.

The flute of the infinite is played without ceasing, and its sound is love. Kabir's original line is: *Murali bajat akhand sadaya.* The word *akhand* is very meaningful. It is translated as "without ceasing": the flute of the infinite is being played without ceasing. But that's not exactly the right sense of the word. *Akhand* is in a way continuous, and yet not. You breathe continuously – otherwise you will die – but sometimes you breathe in and sometimes you breathe out. When you breathe in you don't breathe out; when you breathe out you don't breathe in. And certainly, breathing in is one process, and breathing out is another process. Breathing out will create a gap in the process of breathing in, and breathing in will create a gap in the process of breathing out.

The Eastern concept is that God goes on playing, but that doesn't mean that there are no gaps. *Without ceasing* gives the impression there are no gaps. No, if there were no gaps, music could not be music. Music is not only sounds; music is a combination, an alchemical process of sound and soundlessness. Music is sound *and* the interval, the gap between the two sounds.

Watch, somebody is playing on the flute, watch the notes; somebody is singing a song, watch. I am talking to you, watch – one word is not followed by another word; one word is followed by silence, then another word. Between two words there is an interval; otherwise one word and the other word would not have any definition. They would rush into each other, they would collide. Then there would be no music; there would be only noise, chaos.

Without ceasing means the sound continues, but sometimes it is sound, and sometimes it is soundlessness. Sometimes it is manifestation, and sometimes the whole disappears and there is no manifestation.

In the East we say that when God breathes out, there is existence; when God breathes in, the whole of existence disappears. This is a beautiful idea, of tremendous meaning. Existence is only because God breathes out – then he breathes in, the whole of existence disappears; again he breathes out, there is existence; again he breathes in, existence disappears.

Modern physics has come very close to this. They say that matter seems to be continuous, yet it is not continuous. In between it disappears, but the gaps are so small that you cannot detect them. The movement of the electrons is so subtle that one moment you see the electron at one place, another moment you see it at another place, and you have not even seen how it moved from one place to another; it has not moved, it has not jumped. Now a very absurd idea has arisen: the idea that the electron does not go from one place to another; from one place it simply disappears into nonexistence, and at another place it appears again into existence, pops up again. This is strange – and truth is stranger than fiction. It is!

Modern physics has become more metaphysical than any metaphysics. This is the meaning of *akhand*: even if it disappears, it is there. When it appears it is there, true, when it disappears, then too it is there. When it appears it is there, when it disappears it is there. You can hear it sometimes as manifestation, and sometimes as non-manifestation. Sometimes it takes forms and sometimes it becomes formless – but it is there. If you have the ear to listen to the gaps too, you will see: it is unceasingly there.

Murali bajat akhand sadaya: this flute goes on playing, goes on creating a song, eternally *...and its sound is love.* Existence is made of the stuff called love.

Physics says matter consists of electricity. If you ask Kabir, he will say that matter, existence, consists of warmth, not electricity – the warmth of love. Existence is possible only because of love, because God cares, because he loves. God is not indifferent; God is a lover. It would be better to say, God is love. We can forget the word *God*, but we should not forget the word *love*. *Love* is far more valuable than the word *God*, because love is the very spirit of God. God may be just the body; love is the very soul.

And this whole existence is in love: these trees are moving tremendously in love; these stars, these rivers rushing toward the ocean, are rushing toward a love affair where they can meet and merge. Watch, and you will find everywhere the shadow of love, the thrill, the excitement, the ecstasy of love. Whatsoever the form, if you look deeply you will always find something throbbing at the center which cannot be called anything other than love. *...and its sound is love: When love renounces all limits, it reaches truth.*

When love renounces all limits... There are many limits, and our love is confined in them. That's why even if we love, we are never happy with it. The unhappiness that comes through love is not because of love, but because of the limitations that surround it.

Let it be absolutely clear to you, because many people, finding that love gives misery – yes, it can give, if there are limitations – become antagonistic toward love. They become enemies of love. Then they start escaping from all possibilities of love.

There are still a few monasteries in existence in Europe... One monastery has existed for almost twelve hundred, thirteen hundred years. Once a monk enters the monastery he never comes out of it, it is a commitment for the whole life. And, in the monastery, no woman is ever allowed – for thirteen hundred years not a single woman has entered. The monastery is only for males, for men. And there are monasteries where only women are allowed; no man has ever entered. All possibility of love is dropped.

People escape to the Himalayas; they are escaping from love, not from the world. They are afraid of love, and their fear has some reason behind it. Whenever you are in love, you are in turmoil. Whenever there is love there is difficulty; whenever there is love there is conflict, whenever there is love there is hell. Says Jean-Paul Sartre, "The other is hell." So whenever there is love the other enters your life, and suddenly there is conflict, collision, struggle to dominate each other, to possess each other, to master each other, and the misery arises. Lovers are rarely happy. I am not saying that non-lovers are happy; non-lovers may not be happy, but they are never as unhappy as the lovers.

Lovers are unhappier because love had promised so much in the beginning – great expectation had arisen, great hope was there and then everything is shattered on the rocks. A non-lover had no expectations; he was settled, he was not hoping for heaven. You cannot throw a man into hell if he is not hoping for heaven: you can throw a man into hell only when he hopes for heaven; otherwise there is no possibility.

In the East marriage is not as unhappy as in the West because in the East it is not based on love. When a marriage is not based on love, you don't hope for much out of it; you know the rut, the routine. When the marriage is arranged by the parents and the astrologer, and you have nothing to say about it – in fact you are nobody, you are just a watcher; whatsoever happens, you are watching – and then suddenly a woman that you have not even seen before is thrown with you, there is no expectation, there is no romance, there is no great hope. You were not hankering for the moon; it is an ordinary affair in the day-to-day world: marriage, a social institution with no romance. You start living together.

As people live with their brothers and sisters and with their mothers and fathers, in the East, people live with their wives. You never choose your mother and father. Suddenly one day you find that this is your mother, so what to do? Beautiful, ugly, good, bad – a mother is a mother, so you love the mother. In the same way, people in the East love their wives and their husbands. What can you do? One day you find that she is your wife. But because there is no love affair to precede it, there is not much misery. Heaven was never expected, so you are not thrown into hell. You move on plain ground. The higher you go, the more is the possibility of falling.

When you move on the peaks of the mountains, you can fall into the abyss. When you move on a superhighway there is no fear of falling into an abyss. Marriage moves on plain ground. Marriage is without love, and whatsoever love starts happening after marriage is more brotherly-sisterly than love. It has no romance in it.

When two people find themselves bound together, by and by they become acquainted with each other, and by and by they start liking, just liking each other. By and by, they adjust. It is very mundane; it has no poetry in it.

In the West, marriage is not a bed of roses. The boat is always rocking; it is always on the rocks, it is always in a state of collapse at any moment. Why? If you love, you expect. When you expect, love becomes contaminated, polluted. Then love is not really love; it now has a limitation because of expectation. When you love a person, you start possessing them: you are afraid your woman may move to somebody else. You become so afraid that you cannot even tolerate her looking at somebody. You cannot tolerate the idea that she was laughing with somebody else. That she can laugh without you? It is impossible; it hurts. You start creating a prison for her – a beautiful cage, of course, that you call home, but you create a cage. Certainly, when you start creating a cage, she has to create a cage for you too because nobody can become the jailer unless he becomes a prisoner too. When you possess somebody, you are possessed. When you force somebody to be a slave, you have become a slave in the process itself.

A master is one who has never tried, who has never forced anybody to be a slave. If you try to enslave people you will be enslaved by them. That's a simple process: possess something and the thing will possess you. Become attached to something and you will feel that now you are in a great bondage. Because of the limitations of love, love becomes condemned, and people feel it is because of love that they are suffering. Try to understand what limitations there are.

Kabir says that when love renounces all limits, it reaches truth. The limits have to be understood.

Martin Buber, one of the greatest thinkers of this age, has divided love in two ways. The first he calls I-it. You love your car, you love your house: this is I-it love. You love your child, you love your woman: this is I-thou love. "These are two types of love," Buber says, "I-it and I-thou."

Now, watch carefully. The I-it love affair is very limited because the other is just a thing, and a thing can never give you freedom. And in fact, when you become too attached to something, you also start becoming a thing yourself because your love determines your being.

A person who loves his car cannot be more of a person; loving a car, you show what type of person you are. A person who loves money becomes more and more like the money: just dirty currency notes. He becomes like them. You can see it in the eyes, if a man is too much of a miser, you can see it in the eyes: currency notes, dirty notes, floating. He loses his soul; he is reduced to something that he loves.

Beware! Never love a thing below yourself; otherwise you will be falling. When your love object becomes your goal, you start falling toward it. Whomsoever you love, you start falling toward him. Never love a thing; otherwise your soul will be reduced to a thing. This is the greatest limitation, I-it.

And the problem is more complicated because if you love your car you understand it is a car. But there are people who love their wives also in the same way: I-it. The wife is not thought to be a person.

In the East they call the wife your wealth. Wife – your wealth? That's how it has been thought of down the ages. In the East the relationship between the husband and the wife is an I-it relationship. In many countries, if you kill your wife there will be no problem. It is not a problem for the law to worry about: she was your wife; you are entitled to kill her. If you beat your wife, nobody is going to say anything to you – it's your affair, you can beat your wife. This is how things have existed.

Of course, the wife has retaliated in her own ways. She may not beat the husband, but she can beat him in a thousand and one ways, indirectly. And she does it. Women have become very, very proficient, very clever at beating the husband – in such tricky ways that you cannot even say, "You are beating me." They have found indirect ways, the ways of the weak. The weak also has to protect himself and retaliate. The weak finds his own way; his methodology is different.

For example, a woman may start crying, and she will beat you with her crying. Or a woman may fall ill, and you know why she is having a headache. And she will not cook food for you, and she will not take care of the children – she will lie down on the bed and will say she has a fever. Now she is beating you and the kids and the whole family – it is her way. Or the woman will become cold: whenever you approach her, whenever you take any initiative toward love, she will freeze. She will become simply cold, she will look at you with condemnatory eyes. She will reduce you to an animal. She will think that you are a sex maniac or something. And whenever you make love to her, she will lie down there like a corpse, she will not cooperate. And of course she will be very jealous and very possessive. She will not give you any freedom because you have not given her any freedom. It is the law of nature. If you are having an I-it relationship, then the other will try to have an I-it relationship with you – that's a natural response.

As I see it, out of a hundred people, almost ninety-nine percent of people live in an I-it relationship – even with people. The husband is not a person, the wife is not a person. The husband is a thing to be possessed, so is the wife; the husband is a thing to be used, so is the wife. We have reduced each other to things. That is the ugliness that comes out of love if it has such a limitation – this boundary of the I-it relationship.

Drop this boundary. Move a little higher, move to a little bigger concept. And that concept Buber calls I-thou. Let your woman be a thou, not an it; let your man be a thou, not an it; let your child be a thou. Respect the other. The other is a soul of immense value. The other is God. Call him thou, and not only call him, but behave in such a way that you never think of the other as a thing.

Never try to use anybody; share, but never use. Respect the dignity of the other; never interfere, and then love has a bigger space, less limited. But still, it will be limited.

Buber talks only about two: I-it and I-thou. I would like to talk about two more possibilities. The third possibility, higher than I-thou, is "not I-thou" – when you say, "I am not, only you are." That's where prayer arises, when you say, "I am not, you are. I am totally one with you. I have no separate entity." When you can say that to your lover, the relationship has gone beyond the human. I-it is below human, I-thou is human, no I-thou is superhuman, the state of prayer.

I-it is sexual, I-thou is what is ordinarily called love, no I-thou is prayer. That's why the devotee says to God, "I am not. Not my, but

thy will be done." The devotee surrenders his I; a man in prayer surrenders his I, bows down his head and says, "Only you are. I am just
a part in you, just a part, a mere part, nothing to brag about. There
is no need to make any fuss about me, I am not." This is the third –
you have a still vaster sky available to you.

And the fourth I call "no I, no thou'; that is the state of meditation. When you say, "I am not, you are," a subtle feeling of "I" will
persist because even to call the other thou, I is needed. Without the I,
the thou cannot exist – maybe not in the conscious now, maybe not
so gross, very refined, but there will remain a shadow. Otherwise,
who will say "Thou"? To call God "thou" or your lover "thou," you
have to be there.

The fourth state is "no I, no thou." Now there is even no prayer.
Even that much duality has been dropped. There is silence, meditative silence, *zazen*. One is simply sitting, doing nothing. There is
nothing to say, there is nobody to say it, there is nobody for it to be
said to. The addresser has disappeared, and so has the addressed.
That's why I say Buddhism reaches to the highest: no I, no thou.

Buddhism says there is no God and no soul. That is the meaning
of it. It is not a metaphysical theory, it is a statement of the highest
form of love: there is no God and there is no soul. I am not and you
are not – finished! Then there is no point in uttering a single word.
Now silence can prevail, there is no need even for a dialogue.

With I-it, bodies meet: it is sexual, physical, very gross. With I-
thou, minds meet: it is psychological, not so gross, but not yet so
subtle either. With no I-thou, spirits start meeting, souls start meeting.
But still they are separate. Come closer, come closer... They go on
coming closer, but still a subtle demarcation exists. The devotee is
still there – not very assertive, not very egoistic, very humble, but in
his humbleness also, the I exists. The fourth is where even souls disappear: no bodies, no minds, no souls. You have come home. Only
one exists, without any demarcation.

This is what Kabir says: *When love renounces all limits, it reaches
truth. How widely the fragrance spreads!* And then the fragrance that
you have been carrying for lives together, that you have been carrying like a seed, spreads from your being. Now it has become a
lotus flower, now it is open to the sky, to the wind, to the sun, the
rains. And the fragrance spreads and goes on spreading to the very
corners of existence. Your love affair has spread all over existence.

Now you are in an orgasmic state with existence itself. This is ecstasy. This is the ultimate bliss, benediction.

In this ultimate state of love, this ultimate flowering of your being, love is no longer a relationship; it becomes a state. I-it is a relationship, very much confined by the "it"; I-thou is still a relationship – a little freer, more free: your rope is bigger to roam around – but "thou" is still a limiting concept. Still it is a relationship. Not I-thou – things are melting. You are in the melting pot, but you have not yet disappeared totally, utterly. Certainly the relationship has become very big, but still it is a relationship. In the fourth it is no longer a relationship because for the relationship to exist, two are needed. It is a state of being.

Up to the third, you can say love exists as a dialogue. Beyond the third, the dialogue has disappeared. Now it is not that you love; now you *are* love. Now love is all that is there: the lover has disappeared, the beloved has disappeared, only love remains.

In all our life situations, this trinity has to be remembered: the knower, the known and the knowledge; the lover, the loved and love; the observer, the observed and the observation. This is the trinity. By and by, we have to dissolve. When the knower is no more and the known is no more, then knowledge is freed of all limitations. Then knowledge is immense, as immense as existence itself. And so is love when the lover and the loved have disappeared. *When love renounces all limits, it reaches truth*. It becomes truth itself.

It has no end; nothing stands in its way.
The form of this melody is bright like a million suns: incomparably sounds the veena, the veena of the notes of truth.

One more thing to be pondered over: Kabir again and again says that when love has flowered totally there is a bright light, as if suddenly millions of suns have arisen all around you. And this is not only Kabir saying so: Mohammed says so too, and so does Christ and all the mystics of the world. They have said that when you arrive at the innermost core, suddenly there is an explosion of light. This cannot be just a metaphor – different countries, different languages, different centuries, but all over the world mystics have been agreeing on one thing: that at the last moment there is an explosion of light. Thousands of suns have suddenly arisen. The light is so dazzling one cannot open one's eyes. The light is so bright it takes time to get adjusted to it and to look into it. In fact, when for the first time it happens, the mystic feels as if he has fallen into a dark night – it is so dazzling.

Christian mystics have said that before the light happens, one has to pass through a dark night of the soul. It is almost as if you look at the sun directly; then, within seconds, you will feel as if you are going blind. Suddenly the sun will disappear, the light will disappear; you will become almost blind, you will feel that all around is darkness. If the sun is too much and your eyes cannot absorb it, they will refuse, they will close – hence the darkness. And if thousands of suns are suddenly there, how can you conceive that you will be able to see it?

In the beginning it becomes very dark, frighteningly dark, the mystic feels he has gone blind. But even if it is dark it is very soothing; even if it is dark it is very relaxing; even if it is dark the mystic wouldn't like to open his eyes and see the outside world. The inner darkness is far better than the outer light; relatively, comparatively, it is far better. The mystic relaxes into the inner darkness, and by and by he becomes adjusted, his eyes become capable of seeing this light.

What is this light? Again I would like to remind you: physicists say that matter consists of electricity, and if you go on dividing, then finally the atom is divided into tremendous light, only electrons remain. That's the whole theory of the atomic explosion, of atomic energy. A single atom, when it explodes, becomes such a great light.

When the atom bombs were dropped on Hiroshima and Nagasaki, never before had such light ever been seen – tremendous light and explosion, just for a few seconds, a great light all over. If it is possible by dividing a small atom which cannot be seen with the bare eyes, then one has to think, meditate: maybe when the inner cell of life, the atom of life, the atom of your being, explodes, the same may be happening, because life is the same energy, out and in. Matter and consciousness, it is the same energy.

Physicists say the atom explodes in light, and mystics say the soul explodes in light. They seem to be in deep agreement. In fact, nobody is trying to make a bridge between religion and science. If it is done, it will be of great value. The insights are parallel – they must be, they have to be because it is one existence. Somewhere, all that science has discovered and all that religion has discovered, howsoever their languages are different, somewhere there must be an agreement, because we are seeking and searching the same truth; in different ways maybe, different technologies, different methods, different approaches, different gestalts, but we are searching for the same truth. Somewhere or other, the mystic and the scientist must be in agreement.

The form of this melody is bright like a million suns... One more thing: from the very ancient times in the East, it has been thought that every sound has a particular color. That's why in Indian music the melody is called the raga: *raga* means "the color." Each sound has its own color; it is one of the very ancient doctrines of Eastern music. And now scientists are also coming closer to it: there must be some correspondence between sound and color because sound is nothing but vibrations of electricity, and electricity is color, light. When a ray of light is broken through a prism it becomes seven colors; when those seven colors meet again it becomes white light. There are seven sounds, just as there are seven colors. There is definitely a possibility that the seven colors and seven sounds have something in common.

That's the theory of Indian music, and Kabir is not only a mystic, not only a metaphysician, he is a musician too. He says: *The form of this melody is bright like a million suns.* And when the inner melody, the inner sound, the soundless sound, the *anahat nad*, the *omkar* explodes, Kabir says, its color is absolutely white, because now all notes and all sounds disappear into one. Just as seven colors disappear into one color – white – seven sounds disappear into one sound, the sound of silence.

In a deep silent night, sometimes you hear it, or if you close your ears tightly, suddenly inside there is a sound. If you become deeply meditative and all thinking disappears, then you will hear the deepest sound. When the mind functions not, the prism is dropped. It is through the prism of the mind that one sound becomes seven sounds. It is through the prism of the mind that sound is divided, split. When the prism is removed, the mind is removed, suddenly all sounds become one. And the color of that one sound – what Zen people call "the sound of one hand clapping" – is white.

This seems to be a very factual statement, and I am telling it to you because one day or other you will come across it. If you continue meditating, one day or other you will move to this inner light. And this is a point of great crescendo. The music is tremendous; the melody is tremendous. It is the ultimate, and the light is tremendous. And both are together, as if two aspects of the same energy.

Subtle is the path of love!
Therein there is no asking and no not asking, there one loses oneself at his feet, there one is immersed in the joy of the seeking: plunged in the deeps of love as the fish in the water.
The lover is never slow in offering his head for his lord's service.
Kabir declares the secret of this love.

Kabir's is a declaration of the secret of this love. He says: "This is my path." And the path of love is for many. It is easier to move from the path of love than through any other path because love is so close to your heart.

The only problem that has arisen for the contemporary person, for the contemporary man, is that he no longer beats in his heart. He is hung up in the head. More and more we are trained for the head, and the heart has been neglected, ignored. There is no training for the heart, there is no discipline for the heart; no school, no university bothers about the heart. About feeling we are savages – worse than savages. Our whole culture is of the head, so the head becomes top-heavy and the heart goes on shrinking. It should not be so. This is the greatest calamity that has happened to humanity in the whole history of the mind, of consciousness. We are too much in the head, there is too much investment in the head; the heart is left far behind. In fact, we have bypassed it; we have not even gone through it.

We don't allow feelings. A man of feeling seems to be weak; the man of no-feeling seems to be very strong. We teach people not to be emotional. We teach people not to cry, not to laugh too loudly. We teach people to remain always in control. And if you are in control, then love is not going to happen to you because love happens only when you are in a state of noncontrol.

Love is something bigger than you; you cannot control it. If you want to control, you can remain in hate. Hate can be controlled; hate is smaller than you. Love cannot be controlled; love is bigger than you. If you try to control love, you will miss all possibilities. You will become a loveless being – and that's what a dead person is: a loveless being who exists in the head and who has forgotten his own heart.

Kabir says: *Bhakti ka marag jhina re* – subtle is the path of love.

Yes, it is not gross. The head is very gross. The head is nothing but logic, arithmetic, calculation, cunningness, cleverness – good to exploit people, good to torture people, good to collect money, have a big bank balance, good to become a politician, good to overpower people, good to destroy. The head is very gross.

The heart is very subtle, and absolutely useless as far as the world is concerned. Through the heart is poetry, not calculation. Through the heart is emotion. Through the heart is sensitivity, not cleverness. Through the heart is compassion, not exploitation. The heart is not needed at all in the market; the heart cannot purchase any commodity. And the heart will not make you a great politician or a great general; it will not make you a great warrior, it will not make you a bloody Adolf Hitler or somebody else.

With the heart, by and by you will move away from the path of competition – that cut-throat competition, that violent struggle where everybody is against everybody – this hostile world, this ugly world. You will, by and by, move to the side. You will no longer be on the superhighway of ugliness; you will no longer be a part of this ugly society. You will not play these games of nationalism, fascism, socialism, communism; you will not in any way be concerned with ideologies. You will love and you will enjoy and you will delight. Let the difference be very clear to you.

Just a few days ago a young man said to me, "I am meditating and great love is arising in me for humanity."

I said, "For humanity? How are you going to love humanity? Where will you find humanity? Humanity, you say? Human beings will be enough. Love a human being, not humanity. 'Humanity' is a trick of the head. Humanity? How will you love humanity? Where will you hug humanity? Where will you hold hands with humanity? You will always find a human being wherever you go – nowhere any humanity. Humanity is an ideology, a concept, an abstraction in the head. Life is always particular; the head is always conceptual. You will always find a certain human being, a man, a woman…"

And when I said to the young man, "Love a human being," he was shocked. In fact, he was trying to escape into the "love humanity" to avoid human beings. No, he was not very happy when I said that. I could see in his eyes that he was not very happy – as if I had brought him down when he was flying very high. He was not flying at all; he was simply playing a verbal game.

If you love humanity, you can kill human beings to save humanity. If you love peace, you can go to war. Never love peace and never love democracy and never love communism – all ideologies.

Love concrete human beings, love concrete trees, love concrete rocks, particulars. And only then will you know what love is. Forget great abstractions, they are dangerous. Man has been fighting because of them, destroying each other. A Mohammedan is ready to fight for Islam, and he will kill human beings for the love of Islam. Now this is foolish. The Christian is even ready to kill Christians if it is to save Christianity. What is this Christianity?

Love the concrete, love the immediate. Enjoy this moment, don't prepare for tomorrow. Today is beautiful – delight in it, let it be a celebration.

Subtle is the path of love! Why subtle? – because one has to be sensitive, one has to be more and more in the heart, one has to become capable of feeling and response. Feel, cry, laugh, dance, weep, shout, but do it from the heart. And by and by you will feel a new change, a transformation – energy falling from the head toward the heart. You will start moving in a totally different way. New values will arise because the head has different values.

You fall in love with a beautiful woman, but the head says, "What are you doing? This woman is beautiful but she has no money." The head says, "Better find a girl who has money." The head is calculating, the heart is mad. Hence I say to you, if you want to love, be mad. Only mad people – mad in the sense that they are not calculating, mad in the sense that they risk the outer for the inner, mad in the sense that they can risk tomorrow for today – only mad people can move on the path of love.

Therein there is no asking and no not asking... You have to understand that love can be of four types. One, you simply ask – that is immature love. A child simply asks. He cannot give, in the first place; he does not know how to give. He is a child, he can be forgiven. He asks the mother, he asks the father, he asks everybody; everybody should love him. He is very demanding. But one has to grow out of it; this is very immature. The first kind of love is immature, when you demand: you say, "Give me this, give me that. If you give me, I will know you love me; if you don't give me, then certainly you don't love me." That is the only way the child knows whether you love him or not. If you bring him more toys, more ice cream, more things; then he knows you love him. He can under-stand only one language: of giving him things – give to him.

There is nothing wrong, every child has to pass this phase, but many people remain stuck there. Then they have become grown up, they may have their own children; the man may now be forty, maybe has three children of his own, and still he goes on demanding. A man of forty comes home and he waits for the child to give him a kiss, and he says, "Look, Daddy is here. Now give a kiss." What type of daddy are you? You are still immature, you are still asking. And this type of man will ask for love from the wife, and this type of woman will ask for love from the husband; everybody asking, and nobody ready to give; all children, nobody mature enough to give – hence so much conflict.

The second, higher type of love is when you start giving – when you give, and you don't bother about whether others are giving to you or not. But remember, you can get stuck in the second too. One can get so stuck that one will not allow somebody to give *you* anything. The missionary, the do-gooder, these people, they will not allow. If you allow them to do something good to you, they are ready, but they will not take anything back because that is against their ego. How can they take? They are mature people, they only give, they don't take. They have moved to another extreme. They are more mature than the first, but there is still another maturity. This is again ego: "I can only give."

One man I know is a rich man, a very rich man, and he has been giving all sorts of help to his relatives, friends. He has distrib-uted much of his money. He used to come to me. He said once, "One thing I could never figure out: I have been helping everybody, but nobody ever feels grateful toward me."

And I know he is right – he has been helping, he is really gen-erous, a rare generous man. Just give him a hint and he will give; whatsoever he can give, he will give. He will never say no. And he has given; all his relatives and friends have become rich because of him. And this too I know, that nobody is grateful toward him. And I told him, "You may not like it, but the problem is you always give, you never allow them to give anything to you. You are too egoistic: generous, but you cannot conceive of receiving anything from any-body. That is against your ego."

He pondered over it, he started crying. He said, "Maybe this is true. I have never taken anybody's help in my life. I am a self-made man. I can give, but I cannot receive. Maybe you are right."

I said, "There is no need to receive big things, but small things. Just tell somebody, 'I am feeling ill; come and sit by my side and I will feel happy' – that will do. Small things – but give the other a chance to show his love toward you; otherwise he is always burdened and burdened. And when one is burdened, one can never forgive you."

The third type of love is when a person can take and can give – can easily take, can easily give – and there is no problem. The flow is equal, just like breathing in and breathing out. This is the third type of love, very mature.

And the fourth, the last, is when you don't know what is giving and what is taking because the other is no longer there, you are part of the whole.

There is then ...*no asking and no not asking, there one loses oneself at his feet, there one is immersed in the joy of the seeking: plunged in the deeps of love as the fish in the water. The lover is never slow in offering his head for his lord's service.* Remember, only one offering will do: offer your head. Offer your thinking, thought, your reason; that will do. Just cut off your head and be of the heart. And Kabir says: "This is the secret that I declare to you."

Don't go on offering flowers, they won't help. Offer your head, offer your thinking, your will. And Kabir says: When you are ...*immersed in the joy of the seeking...* A real lover, a real follower on the path of love, is not worried about the goal. The journey is the goal.

"Heaven is all the way to heaven. Has he not said: 'I am the way'?"

In the end he is not bothered about what is going to happen tomorrow. He is not result-oriented; the journey is his goal. It is tremendously beautiful. The *bhaktas*, the devotees, have been singing in the East: "God, we don't seek salvation. We don't want *moksha*, nirvana. This world is beautiful, your game is beautiful; allow us to play. The journey is so tremendously beautiful – who bothers about the goal? The journey is the goal."

The devotee, the lover, loves seeking for itself. He is not in a hurry to find God. He says, "Go on hiding. Let us play the game of hide-and-seek. The seeking is so beautiful." And he is not in a hurry, he is not impatient. He says, "I will wait. Whenever you decide to come, come. You will find me ready; my door will be open. I will be waiting at the door and food will be ready. Come and we will feast. And there is no hurry. You have a thousand and one things to do, do them; take your time. I can wait."

A lover is absolutely patient, and enjoys the very seeking, the very play, the very existence. His goal is not in the future, he is immersed in the moment, in the immediate – that is his meditation. This is possible if you drop your head, if you drop your mind. With just the dropping of the mind, the whole energy moves to the heart, and love arises.

Love is the secret key; it opens the door of the divine. Laugh, love, be alive, dance, sing; become a hollow bamboo, and let his song flow through you.

Murali bajat akhand sadaya: his flute is continuously singing, his song is continuously on. Any moment you decide to become his flute, he will take you in his hands, he will put you to his lips, he will start singing a song. And that song is the song of love, the song of freedom, the song of nirvana.

Enough for today.

CHAPTER 10

please wake up

The first question:

Osho,
You tell us the paths are of will and surrender. The path of will is
certainly not for me, but then surrender also does not seem to be
perfect.
Now, what to do? I am totally confused. Kindly show me my path.

The first thing: if you are really totally confused, out of that confusion will come clarity. But you are not totally confused. Once
confusion is total, it becomes the path; then there is no need
for any other path. We seek paths out of confusion, because we are
confused, but not totally confused, and we think that we can figure
things out. Total confusion means that you are totally helpless; there
is no way to go. You don't know anything about the goal, about
yourself, about the way. You know nothing. You are in a state of
blank. If confusion is total, mind becomes blank. But you are never
totally confused – partially, certainly; totally, never.

Total confusion is one of the ways to reach to godliness. It means
all your knowledge has proved meaningless – and when I say all, I

mean all. Not that you say, "I know a little bit. This much is right, this much is true." Total confusion means you are in a tremendous dark night of the soul. There is no light available and there seems to be no possibility. You are hopeless. There is no hope. The future has disappeared; the past has proved meaningless. The anguish has come to the utter peak. From that very peak, mind disappears because it can continue only if you are partially confused. Mind cannot exist in total confusion.

In fact, mind cannot exist in anything which is total. Total love, mind disappears; total will, mind disappears; total surrender, mind disappears. Totality is against mind; they never exist together. Total confusion: mind disappears. Try to understand this. Confusion can remain only if it is not total. Mind can remain only if you are not totally in anything. Be total in anything whatsoever, and mind cannot cling to you even for a single moment. But you have used the word *totally* just to emphasize; you don't know the meaning of it.

A totally confused person cannot even ask this question. How will he ask? How will he articulate a question? A question arises out of knowledge. A totally confused person will come to me, will look at me with empty eyes, with mad eyes; he cannot formulate a question. The questioner means the mind; the questioner means you are still clinging to certain knowledge. You are still hoping that a path can be found, that somebody can show you the path. You still think yourself capable – that you will be able to find some way to get out of it. Your desperation is not utter; your anguish is not perfect.

If you cannot think that will is your path, and you cannot think that surrender is your path, then I will say: confusion seems to be natural to you, so let that be your path. But be totally confused; don't be halfheartedly in it. Be so totally confused that nothing of knowledge remains in you – no certainty, no security, no scripture, no religion, no belief. And I say it to you because I myself worked on the way of confusion.

Of course, when the total confusion comes closer to you, you will become more and more mad. You will not know what is what. Then courage will be needed, tremendous courage is needed. Sufis call it a technique: the technique of confusion. Confusion uproots everything that you know, leads you into emptiness, darkness. When all knowledge is dropped, how can confusion remain?

Just listen to it: you come to me, you believe in God and I say there is no God. Then there is confusion, not because I have said there is no God, but because you believe that there is God. Now there are two conflicting things in you: a part of you says there is God, another part has become convinced by me that there is no God, hence confusion. Confusion means conflict. Confusion means you have two sorts of knowledge which are diametrically opposite, which are pulling you apart.

For the future, the technique of confusion is going to become more and more important. It was never so important in the past because a Hindu was born a Hindu and he never bothered about Christians and Mohammedans and Parsis and Jainas. From the very beginning he knew that he was right and everybody else was wrong. A Mohammedan was a Mohammedan, and he knew the truth was in the Koran and everything else was just nonsense. The Christian was a Christian, and he knew the way went through Christ and there was no other way; all other ways go to hell.

It was absolute certainty, based in ignorance, and I am not in support of it, but there was no confusion. There was certainty and everybody was happy with his certainty. Certainty is very dangerous; nobody has achieved truth through certainty. But people were more comfortable, it was more convenient. Mediocre, stupid minds felt very good that they knew. The very idea that we know, that we are in the right and everybody else is in the wrong, is a great protection. It leads you nowhere because unless one moves through confusion clarity never comes.

Clarity is not certainty; certainty is not clarity. Certainty is a blind belief. The world has lived in certainty, but now that is no longer possible. That comfort is no longer available. The world has become smaller and smaller and smaller; it is a global village now. The Hindu has to know about the Christian – there is no way to avoid it – the Christian has to know about the Hindu. People can read, people can listen to the radio, can see the TV. People have become more capable of knowledge, and knowledge has exploded from everywhere. Now all this knowledge is creating confusion – who is right?

Mohammedans, Christians, Jews, believe in only one life. There was no confusion before; that was "the truth." Now it is very difficult. Even for an idiotic Christian, it is very difficult to continue to believe in one life because millions of Hindus, millions of Buddhists, Jainas,

Sikhs... Half the world is not a small matter. Half the world says there is rebirth, reincarnation. Now it is impossible not to listen to this other half, and they also have their reasoning; confusion arises.

Confusion means now you have become available to all sorts of knowledge. And when you come to me, you will certainly be more and more confused. One day I speak on the Mohammedans, another day I speak on the Jews, another day on Buddhists, Hindus, Jainas, and I continue... I am making all the secret sources of knowledge available to you. It is natural that you will become confused.

But don't be in a hurry. Confusion is being used here as a technique and it is going to become the most important technique in the coming world. Now there is no way to move back into your tunnels and become a Hindu, and blind to everything else, and become a Jew, blind to everything else; now there is no way. It is impossible for a Christian to deny Buddha, and when Buddha comes in, of course your belief in Jesus starts wavering. Even Buddhists now have to trust that Christ is also somewhere near – he may not be exactly at the center, but somewhere near. He may not be a buddha, but is at least a bodhisattva, a potential buddha, very close.

But then there are troubles, then the whole of Jesus – his attitude, his approach, his philosophy, his way of life – is so contradictory to Buddha's. Buddha sits silently under his tree, unconcerned about the world; Jesus is very much concerned, very much involved with the world. It is not just an accident that the Jews had to kill him, and it is not just an accident that Buddha was not killed by Hindus. He was not doing anything, he was just sitting under his *bodhi* tree, meditating. But Jesus was meddling with the social affairs, the politics, organization, society, church, religion. He was going to destroy the whole structure, he was a revolutionary; he had to be killed.

Now there is Jesus, there is Buddha, there is Krishna. Krishna is another dimension; Buddha is sitting under his tree, Krishna is playing on his flute. You cannot imagine Buddha playing on a flute. Jesus is hanging on the cross, and Krishna is dancing with so many girlfriends. Such diverse dimensions have become available together; now you are confused.

But to me, confusion is more valuable than certainty. Certainty is mediocre, certainty is stupid. Certainty simply means that you don't know. Only a person who is very ignorant can be certain.

Once it happened...

Somebody was talking to Voltaire and he mentioned a name, the name of a very famous theologian, philosopher, and the man who was talking about this theologian said to Voltaire, "He knows everything!"

Voltaire looked surprised and said, "Is he so stupid as to know everything?"

A wise man hesitates; a wise man cannot be so certain. A wise man knows the multiplicity of life. A wise man knows the multidimensional existence. A wise man knows that all that we know is nothing in comparison to that which remains to be known. The unknown is always more than the known. The known is just like a grain of sand. Buddha has said so: "Whatsoever I know," he says, "is just like a grain of sand, and whatsoever I don't know is the whole sand of the earth, of all the Ganges, of all the rivers, of all the seas."

Certainty is not something valuable. It is comfortable, true, and so is stupidity comfortable. An idiot seems to be the most blessed man. Why? – he has no confusion, he has really no mind to be confused. He has such a tiny flicker of intelligence that he cannot afford confusion. The greater the intelligence, the greater you can afford confusion. Hence I say this age is the age of confusion because this age is the age of intelligence.

The old certainty has gone and the old foolishness too – good! And I hope it is gone for good. Confusion has entered, this is the first step toward clarity. If you are really courageous, you will question everything that you know, and you will question absolutely. You should not be soft about it. You should question everything that you know, and through questioning, all that you know is eliminated. And don't be in a hurry to be certain, otherwise you will not be able to question. Your questioning will become dishonest. If your questioning is honest, then it has to go to the very core of your being.

A seeker of truth becomes a fire, a thirst, a great hunger. He puts his whole life at stake. Of course, he has to take the risk of being confused; he *will* be confused. But if you persist, and you don't cling to something just for clarity, just for certainty, just to be comfortable; if you don't cling to something, if your search is authentic, one day you will see that all has disappeared.

First comes confusion; confusion cuts the roots of your knowledge. Once all knowledge has disappeared, confusion also disappears

– because confusion cannot exist without knowledge. You believe in God and somebody says there is no God; there is confusion because you believe, and he says there is no God – conflict. But if you are able to see that maybe there is no God, and your belief was just a belief, and you drop the belief, you say, "Okay, I will now believe only when I know, and I have not known yet... So, good, this man who says there is no God has helped me to get rid of a belief that was only a belief and not my own experience. It was borrowed, so I drop it."

If you drop the belief... I am not saying to start believing that there is no God because then someday again you will be confused. Then you can come to somebody else who is tremendously happy, prayerful: his very vibe says that there is more to life, and he says there is God, and God has happened to him – again you will be confused. Now, you were clinging to the belief that there is no God, and here comes this man...

No, don't cling to any belief. Drop all belief. Remain in that vacuum of no belief, either in God or in no God. No belief – Christian, Hindu, Mohammedan, theistic, atheistic; no belief – then who can confuse you? How can you be confused? Somebody brings some news; you will say, "Thank you. I will ponder over it, I will meditate over it. I don't believe in anything, so there is no question of getting confused." If confusion is used totally, your beliefs will disappear; it will clear the whole ground. And in that state of no belief, confusion becomes impossible. When confusion becomes impossible, clarity arises, and that clarity is not of belief, not of scripture, not of belonging to a church, not of comfort, not of convenience, not produced by anybody. It is your own transparency of awareness, and through that clarity is truth.

You say, "I am totally confused." Sorry, I cannot agree with you. In fact, you are asking me to give you something so that you can drop your confusion and can become certain again. No, I am not your enemy; I will not give you any belief. I am ready to give myself, but I will not give you any belief. I am ready for you to partake of my own experience, I am ready to share my being, but I will not give you any belief. I will not make you comfortable because that will be death. Your home has not yet arrived, and somebody makes you comfortable by the side of the road and gives you a tranquilizer, and you are dreaming, sleeping, and thinking this is your home and everything is beautiful – no, I am not going to do that to you. That's what your priests and popes have been doing up to now. I am going to shake you and shock you out of your tranquility, out of your certainty. I am to create a stir in you. I will come like a cyclone. I am to destroy your mind utterly. Only if you are ready for that destruction will creativity be born to you.

You say, "You tell us the paths are of will and surrender. The path of will is certainly not for me." How do you know? How have you become so certain that the path of will is not for you? Try first, be experimental. One learns through trial and error, there is no other way. Don't be a priori; don't say from the very beginning, "This is not for me, and I am certain," otherwise you will again be confused. Some day you will find somebody who has attained through the path of will, and you will see the flowering and the fragrance of the person, and you will start feeling, "Maybe the path of will is for me too. This man has achieved." Your greed will arise. You will again be confused.

This is how you create the possibility for confusion. Don't say "The path of will is certainly not for me" because you have not tried yet. Try it. If you try the path of will, nothing is going to be wrong. If you succeed, good. If you don't succeed, that too is good. Then you have known at least one thing: that it is not for you. That too is a great achievement: to know, "This door is not for me." Otherwise sometimes one goes on knocking on the wrong door.

Once a man came to me and he said, "Osho, a dream constantly recurs, and it has become nightmarish. I have come to you to help me out of this problem."

I said, "What is your dream?"

He said, "Since my childhood" – now he was almost fifty – "it comes again and again, almost once or twice a month. And it is such that I don't see any way out of it. The dream is simple: I am standing at a door, a very beautifully carved wooden door – it must be of a palace – and I knock, and my whole being says to somehow enter the palace. A great urge… But nobody answers. Then I start pushing the door. I do as much as I can; I start perspiring. The effort becomes hectic, and uncertainty again arises in me that it is not going to open, so again I have failed. Some unconscious desire to enter, and the futility of it… And then I wake up, trembling, perspiring. My breathing is not natural, disturbed. And then I cannot sleep for at least two hours. I think about why this dream came to me?"

I asked the man, "Can you remember, is there a sign on the door?"

He said, "Yes, there is a sign! But I never thought about it. How did you know there is a sign?"

"And what does it say?"

And the man closed his eyes and he started laughing. He said, "This is just incredible. The sign says 'Pull' – and I have been pushing!"

So I said, "Next time the dream comes, follow the sign."

After two, three months he came and he said, "I am waiting and waiting and the dream is not coming."

I said, "It may not come because the purpose is fulfilled. You have become alert, you have become aware of it."

Try the path of will, maybe it is for you, maybe it is not for you. I cannot say offhand that it is for you or that it is not for you, because if I say and you believe me, you will be creating the possibility of confusion someday. Don't believe me, try. What is wrong in it? Be a little more playful, it is a beautiful sport – try the path of will.

Why do you say, "Certainly it is not for me"? How can you be certain? This trick of becoming certain without knowing has to be dropped, completely dropped. Try! If you succeed, good. If you don't succeed, then too you have succeeded because the remaining thing is the path of surrender. If you fail on the path of will, then more hopefully, with more energy, with more totality, you can move on the path of surrender. If you don't try on the path of will, you may move on the path of surrender, but you will always remain suspicious about whether it is your path or not.

So the first thing: never decide without experimentation, be scientific. Everything is a hypothesis – try it. It can be valid only by experience; it may prove invalid only by experience. There is no other way to decide. Let the decision come out of your existential experience.

And then you say, "But surrender also does not seem to be perfect." But how can anything be perfect if you are not perfect? The surrender is going to be your surrender, not mine. The surrender is going to be yours, not Meera's or Mahavira's. The surrender is going to be yours, not Krishna's or Christ's. The surrender, of course, is bound to be of the same quality as you are.

The path of will or the path of surrender, are not like superhighways where anybody can walk and the way remains the same. No, the way changes with the walker. You bring your quality. For example, you see a Picasso painting... You can use the same brush and the same colors and the same canvas, but are you hoping that a Picasso will be born? The painting will be yours. The brush and the canvas may be Picasso's, you can even ask permission to paint in his studio; but then too the painting will be yours, it will not be a Picasso.

Exactly like that, when you move onto a path, the path is not a collective possession. Each individual has to create his own path while walking on it. Your surrender is going to be your surrender: it will be as perfect as you are. Don't expect more, otherwise, from the beginning, you are creating obstacles for your growth. And in fact, the path is perfect only when you have arrived, never before – but then the path is not needed. So everybody has to walk on an imperfect path because everybody is imperfect.

And why ask for perfection? Your demands are too much. You go to the chemist: you don't ask for a perfect medicine; you ask for the latest and the best, not for the perfect because the perfect never exists. Tomorrow a better medicine may come and this medicine will be discarded. Every month medicines are being discarded, new ones are being invented; no medicine is perfect, and cannot be. Perfection means now there is no possibility to grow. Perfection means death. Perfection means now everything is finished, the full point has come.

Life is a process; it is not perfect. Nothing is perfect in life; everything is imperfect. So the most you can ask is, "Which is the more perfect way?" That's all – not *the* perfect way, but the more perfect, comparatively. Maybe the path of will is not so perfect for you as surrender, but if you are making an absolute demand, that it is a hundred percent perfect, then from the very beginning you are too greedy.

Move slowly. Your path is *your* path. The path will change you, and you will change the path – and this is going to be a dynamic process, a dialectical process. You will change the path by your change, and then the path will change you, and you are both going to enrich each other. When Meera walks on the path of surrender, of course it is going to be more perfect than when you walk. When Mahavira walks on the path of will, it is going to be more perfect than when you walk.

One more thing: only when Meera has arrived do we come to know, then the fragrance spreads. When Mahavira has reached, then the rumor spreads around the world that somebody has become enlightened – then people rush. When they come to see, it is a perfect thing. Picasso has done his work – the painting is perfect.

But you don't know that Mahavira had moved just like you, wavering in uncertainty and confusion, going astray, coming back, making a thousand and one mistakes. You don't know *that* Mahavira, that Mahavira who was struggling in darkness, alone. Now Mahavira has arrived and has become a light; now everybody comes to see and pay respects to him. But Mahavira had also moved the same way, with the same limitations. When we know Buddha, Mahavira, Krishna, Zarathustra, they have become perfect souls, *siddhas* – then we know. We have not known their seeking stages.

Remember, you are not a *siddha*; otherwise what is the point in seeking? You have not yet arrived, you are arriving. Choose the best that is possible, don't hanker for the perfect; otherwise you may never move. If you are waiting for the perfect airplane to come and then you will go, you may never go because they are being perfected every day. Don't wait for the perfect train. Whatsoever is available choose the best. Be choosy. Think, meditate about it, find out the pros and cons, but don't wait for the perfect.

And start. In the beginning, great things are not going to happen. But those great things can happen only if you begin. To begin with, anything is okay. Start, move – your feet will falter; your body may not be adjusted. Just like when a small child starts walking, how many times does he fall? How many times does he again try, waver; and then, by and by, become strong of foot? That's how one moves into the eternal, also.

One thing: this movement is not toward some outer goal. This movement is toward some inner goal which is, in essence, already there.

So you ask me, "Now, what to do?" Only one thing, I say. And let me tell you a beautiful story. Listen to it very carefully. It is a story from Jorge Luis Borges, one of the most metaphysical writers of this age: *Episode of the Enemy*...

So many years on the run, expectant, and now the enemy

stood at my door. From the window I saw him working his way up the hill. Laboring along the steep road, he leaned on a staff, a clumsy staff which in his hands was no more than an old man's cane, not a weapon. Although I was waiting for it, his knock was so weak I barely made it out. At the door I fumbled with the key to let the man in. I feared he was going to collapse all at once, but he took a few faltering steps and stumbled, utterly worn out, onto my bed.

I bent over him so that he could hear me: "One believes that the years pass for one," I said to him, "but they pass for everyone else too. Here we meet, at last, face to face, and what happened before has no meaning now." While I spoke, he unbuttoned his overcoat. His right hand was in the pocket of his suit coat; something there was aimed at me, and I knew it was a revolver.

Then he told me, in an unwavering voice, "To get myself into your house I fell back on your pity. Now I have you at my mercy, and I am unforgiving."

I tried to get out some words; I am not a strong man and only words could save me. I managed to utter, "It is true that a long time ago I ill-treated a certain boy, but you are no longer that boy, and I am no longer that callous brute. Besides, revenge is no less vain and ridiculous than forgiving."

"That's just it," he replied. "Because I am no longer that boy, I am about to kill you. This has nothing to do with revenge. This is an act of justice. Your arguments, Borges, are only stratagems of your terror designed to keep me from my mission. There is nothing you can do now."

"There is one thing I can do," I said.

"What is that?" he asked.

"Wake up," I said.

And I did.

The whole life that you are acquainted with is nothing but a dream, a nightmare – true. Both the enemy and the friend are parts of a dream; the surrender and the will, both are parts of the dream; theories, philosophies, dogmas, churches are parts of the dream, the human dream. The only thing that has to be done is to please wake up. And nobody can make you wake unless you decide. It is your decision. There is no need to hanker anymore for outer beliefs to cling to, because all beliefs are false. There is no need to seek a philosophy of life; life is enough. All philosophies are false, including my philosophy. When I say all, I mean all.

Wake up! Please wake up! That's all that can be said.

The second question:

Osho,
I want to become a sannyasin, but there are so many hypocrites here amongst your sannyasins, and that is preventing me. What should I do?

My answer is through a small anecdote...

"Why don't you attend church?" asked the village parson of the local innkeeper.

"I don't go," he replied frankly, "because there are so many hypocrites there."

"Please don't let that stop you," said the parson. "There's always room for one more."

The third question:

Osho,
I have done very many groups, and had many pertinent growth experiences in which I have really felt that I have changed and gained tremendous new insight. But I still make the same mistakes and, despite everything I have done, still repeat the past as if I have no choice. What to do? Can change be permanent? Or is the work we do on ourselves simply illusion, signifying nothing? Can sannyas be permanent change?

First, all efforts to improve yourself are bound to fail because the one who is making the effort is the problem: the ego. The ego is constantly making efforts to improve: have more money, have a bigger house, have a bigger car, have a more beautiful woman, or a husband, have this, have that. That is ego. You understand it.

But then the ego plays another game too: it says, "Become

more peaceful, become more loving, attain to meditation, become a *siddha*, be like a buddha." This again is the same game in another direction. The same ego that was trying to decorate itself with outer things now wants to try and decorate itself with inner things.

So the first thing: if you are trying to improve yourself, you are doomed to fail. Once you understand that the ego is the problem, and it is the ego's greed that wants to improve and become this and that – the very idea of becoming is a projection of the ego – revolution comes. And that revolution is nothing that you have to do; that revolution comes through understanding the ways of the ego. Once you have understood that it was the ego that was after money, after power, prestige, politics and the same ego is now playing inner games of meditation, enlightenment, and all that nonsense – once you recognize it is the same ego, in that very recognition a laughter arises in you. You start feeling the ridiculousness of it.

There is no improvement. I am not saying there is no mutation, but there is no improvement. Mutation is there, utter change is there, but no improvement. Improvement means a modified form: you remain the same with a few more plus things with you – a car, a big house, a woman. You remain the same but now a woman is attached to you, a car is attached to you. You remain the same. Now you have become a meditator, you remain the same; now you have become a sannyasin, but you remain the same, deep down you remain the same. And you go on accumulating things: qualities, characteristics, character, morality, virtue, knowledge. You go on, but deep down it is the same old trip, nothing is new. This way, improvement is not possible.

Improvement is not possible at all. When you understand this greed, this hankering to be somebody else, someone else more important, more significant, greater and greater; once you have understood that this is all ego play, in that moment of understanding there is a sudden mutation, a jump, a quantum leap. You are no longer the old; the new has entered.

And remember, the new is not connected with the old at all. That's why I don't say it is an improvement. The new is so absolutely new, so utterly new, that it has nothing to do with the old. The old man has completely gone. It is a totally new being, discontinuous with the past. With this gap, it cannot be called improvement.

Spirituality is not an achievement. It is not an ambitious trip.

You say, "I have done very many groups and had many perti-nent growth experiences." Those growth experiences were not per-tinent, they were just games of the ego. You felt good. The ego patted you and said, "Good boy, doing so good. You are going to improve. One day it is certain you are going to become a Buddha or a Christ. You are on the way, and going so beautifully," and you felt very good.

Those experiences were not pertinent; your ego used them. They became absolutely dangerous. Anything that the ego uses is immediately poisoned. You started feeling very happy: "So now it is happening." You must have started waiting for satori, *samadhi*: "Now it is not very far away. Any moment..."

Your ego reduced all those experiences to toys. You started playing with them. And you must have started expecting them more and more. You have become virtuous, religious; now these things will be happening more and more. Remember, whenever you start saying, "This thing has been beautiful, I was delighted in it and I would like to have it again," you are making a continuity.

The new can happen only when you are not. Now, you will not leave yourself at all, you will always be sitting there. Even if you go through those same groups again, you will not be enriched because you will be waiting: "Now this is going to happen." And when you wait, nothing happens because in your waiting *you* are there.

Things happen unexpectedly. Things happen when you are not even waiting for them. God is seen sometimes only when you are not looking for him, because when you are looking you are tense. God happens in such mundane and trivial moments that you could not have expected. Whenever you are expecting, you are there; and God cannot be there because *you* are there. When you are not expecting, just swimming in a river, just enjoying the moment, the absolute presence of the trees and the birds and the sunlight, and you are completely lost – and of course nobody waits for God to happen in that moment – suddenly he is there. You are doing nothing but playing with your cat, looking into the cat's eyes, and of course, you are not waiting for something great to happen, and sud-denly those eyes of the cat change, and there is depth and there is God, and suddenly you are overwhelmed.

God is always sudden, unexpected. When you are doing your *puja* and ringing your small bell and doing things like that, God never happens because you are so full of expectation. You are waiting and looking to the side: "Has he come or not?" A knock on the door, maybe just a postman, and you are so excited: "Maybe God has come!" When you are waiting, he never comes because when you are waiting, you are too much. He comes only when you are not.

"I have done very many groups, and had many pertinent growth experiences in which I have really felt that I have changed and gained tremendous new insight." I, I, I... You see? "But I still make the same mistakes, and despite everything I have done, still repeat the past as if I have no choice." I, I, I... You will make the same mistakes because it is the same I. You cannot hope that anything else is going to happen.

The "I" is a mechanism; it goes on doing the same thing, it has become very efficient in doing it. It is like a computer: it creates habits, and then it goes on repeating the same habits. Now please, stop any idea of growth. This is not the way. Forget about growth because growth is in the future. Growth is already a postponement: it is going to happen tomorrow. Forget all about tomorrow, tomorrow never comes. Be here now. This moment is the only moment there is. Enjoy this moment in total absorption. Whatsoever you are doing, do it totally, be lost in it. What it is, I am not saying. If you are lost in it, it becomes worship, it becomes prayer.

Cleaning the floor can become a prayer; just doing ordinary things in your kitchen can become a prayer; digging a hole in the garden can become a prayer. There is no need to go to any temple. Only those who don't know how to bring prayer into their lives go to a temple. There is no need to go to a mosque or a *gurudwara* because God is everywhere. Wherever you are totally absorbed, the door of the temple opens.

"Can change be permanent? Or is the work we do on ourselves simply illusion, signifying nothing?" That which you do is illusory, because you are an illusion. Out of you, only illusions are born. You cannot give birth to truth. You are temporal; out of you the time-less cannot be born. You have to give way; you have to put yourself aside. Only you are standing in your own way, nobody else. God is available – just don't stand in the way.

Are you listening? Don't stand in the way of God, that's all. And then he is in the flower, and in the bird on the wing; then he is in the breeze passing through the trees. When you are not there to distort, you will find him everywhere – because he is everything. It is a miracle how we go on missing him. But you are asking for something permanent. The ego can never be permanent; it is a momentary thing. And out of the ego, whatsoever you gain will be lost.

You are asking: Can't a wave be made permanent? The wave cannot be made permanent. The only way is to freeze it so it becomes ice. But then it is not a wave, it is just a piece of ice. Then it is no longer a wave because it cannot wave. The aliveness has gone; the dynamism has gone. You fall in love with a woman and you want to make the love permanent? Then you are in danger – you are trying to make a wave permanent. You go to court and the court puts a seal on your marriage; now it is a legal thing. Love has disappeared; now it is a contract, and ugly.

Love is the most beautiful thing in the world, and marriage the most ugly because law has entered into love. Why do you go to the court? – because you want to make love permanent. "Who knows? She may fall in love with somebody else tomorrow." Now the court will protect you. "Who knows? He may escape." Now the court will protect. You can drag him to the court; he cannot easily escape. What are you doing when you are marrying a woman or a man? You are asking society to protect you, asking the law, the policeman, to protect you. What kind of love is this in which a policeman is needed to protect you? This will be a sort of prison. Call it whatsoever you would like to call it, but it will be bondage. You will be prisoners of each other. And this is how we destroy everything.

Ego is impermanent. If your love is out of the ego, it is impermanent. The mind is temporary, temporal. Mind, in fact, is time. Nothing can be permanent in the mind. If you want to look at the permanent – permanent is not the right word, eternal is the right word – then look deeper into the wave, and there is the ocean. If you want to look to some eternal, look into love deeply and you will find God there. But you bring the policeman rather than searching for God.

When love is happening, don't hanker for permanence. Think and brood, meditate, contemplate the eternal. Those moments are rare love moments. Windows open easily, melting happens easily. You are dazed with something unknown. Don't bother about marriage right now. Right now go into those moments, waves, and find the ocean – because wherever there is a wave, there is bound to be an ocean behind it. When the love-wave is there, the love-ocean must be behind it. That ocean of love is God.

So please don't seek the permanent; otherwise you will always be frustrated because the one who is seeking permanence is impermanent himself. You have chosen the wrong medium: the mind, the ego. Look into your own being.

"Can sannyas be a permanent change?" Again you go on using a very dirty word, *permanent*. Sannyas is both the wave and the ocean. It depends on you. If you simply see the wave, it is impermanent; if you look deep into it and you can find the ocean, it is eternal. The eternal is not permanent; the eternal is beyond time. *Permanent* means staying longer in time. But what does it matter whether you are a sannyasin for one day or one year or one thousand years – what does it matter? The impermanent is impermanent – one day, one year, one thousand years.

Seek something which is beyond time. Then once it is there, you know it has always been there and it will be there always. The eternal is your innermost nature: *swabhava*. It is your innermost being.

Whatsoever you are seeking should not be out of greed and out of ambition. It should not be a desire to repeat. Forget the past. As it disappears, let it disappear and don't think of the morrow. As it has not come yet why bother? When it comes, we will be here to look into it. And whatsoever has happened yesterday, don't ask for it again today. It may have happened yesterday because you were not waiting for it; today you are waiting for it.

It happens every day in meditation: somebody comes to an inner space and becomes thrilled, and the desire to repeat arises. Then next day it is not there; then he feels very frustrated. Then next day he is even more deeply into his depression because it is not coming. And he comes to me and says, "It was better before; at least I had not known it. But now I know it, it is there, and now I am suffering. Why can't I have it again and again?" You cannot have it again and again because it is the very nature of God to happen unexpectedly. He is a guest who comes without informing you.

The Hindi word for guest is *atithi*. It means "one who comes without giving you any date beforehand." *Tithi* means date, *atithi* means one who comes without informing you at all. God is a guest – when he comes, feel thankful; when he does not come, feel thankful. It must be in your favor that he is not needed today, that you need a gap; that you need a plateau so that things that have happened yesterday become settled.

A highly irascible employer was much given to uttering tirades of abuse to his long-suffering staff. One young girl stood it for so long, but when her virtue was questioned she had had enough, and walked tight-lipped straight out of the office.

The following morning, she marched into the tyrannical boss's office and thrust a piece of paper under his nose. "This is from my family doctor," she said firmly, "and it certifies that I am pure and untouched."

He glanced at it and thrust it back at her. "This is no good," he snarled. "It is dated yesterday."

Yes, yesterday is yesterday, gone is gone. Who knows? You may have changed. But all character is of yesterday; all virtue is of yesterday. When you call somebody a saint, what do you mean? You say, "His yesterdays were very saintly," but they are dated yesterday. He may have committed a sin last night. You call somebody a sinner, but that is not right; those are all yesterdays. Yes, he may have committed sins, but last night he may have prayed, he may have meditated, and he may have had a glimpse.

So don't call anybody a saint because a saint belongs to the past; and don't call anybody a sinner because a sinner is of the past. Life and being are always free of the past.

Being is of the present. And when you want something to be repeated, you simply desire for the past to be repeated. What is the point? You have known it. Don't you want to know something higher, something greater? Remain available. That is one of my fundamental teachings: don't desire, remain available. Wait on God and let him do things.

The fourth question:

Osho,
Are we not here to help and serve others in the world?

My answer is an anecdote...

I have heard about a little boy whose mother was lecturing him about selfishness. "You know, darling," she pointed out, "we are in this world to help others."

The little boy considered this for several seconds, then he asked with a great deal of seriousness, "Well then, what are the others here for?"

Please first look at yourself. Don't try to become a do-gooder. These are dangerous people. In the name of doing good, they simply try to interfere with other people's lives. Who are you to help others? You have not even helped yourself yet. Physician, first heal thyself.

It happens many times around me: you listen to me, your mind becomes more and more informed, you start gathering knowledge, and then suddenly the desire arises to help others. What you really want is just to pour your rubbish into their heads. You want to initiate people now. You want to help people to become spiritual. Please, unless you have known what I am saying, don't try to convey it to others because it will be a distorted form. And lies are better than half truths; at least somebody can come to know that this is a lie and will drop it. A half truth is very dangerous: he will never be able to detect that it is a lie because that half truth will prevent him. He will never be able to drop it, he will become cluttered with it.

For four years the little old lady had owned the parrot, and for four long years she had fruitlessly tried to get it to talk. She had tried everything: repeating little phrases endlessly, buying bells, mirrors and the very best food. At last she was at her wits' end. In desperation she turned to the parrot and screamed, "For God's sake, why won't you talk?"

The parrot regarded her with a beady eye. "To tell you the truth," it said suddenly, "I have always felt that it was not a good thing to go around repeating things one hears."

At least be that wise!

The last question:

Osho,
How, just in the presence of a master, can the inner transformation happen? How is it possible?

It is like infection – spiritual infection, healthy infection. Just as illness can be caught, so wellness can also be caught. Just as illness has its own vibration, a certain wavelength, so has wellness a certain vibration, its own wavelength. When you are near to a spiritual person, you start vibrating in a new way. His very presence plays on the guitar of your soul. His very presence starts creating sweetness in you.

Presence is not "just" or mere, as you say. Presence is very vital. The very environment of a spiritual person is dangerous – it can transfigure you completely.

It is like a fellow said on a crowded bus, "I am so full of penicillin, if I should sneeze here in this crowd, I am sure I would cure somebody."

If you are not really in search of being cured, avoid spiritual people, and avoid masters. Their presence is dangerous because it can become a taste in you, and a taste is the beginning of a transformation.

Enough for today.

About Osho

Osho defies categorization. His thousands of talks cover everything from the individual quest for meaning to the most urgent social and political issues facing society today. Osho's books are not written but are transcribed from audio and video recordings of his extemporaneous talks to international audiences. As he puts it, "So remember: whatever I am saying is not just for you... I am talking also for the future generations."

Osho has been described by *The Sunday Times* in London as one of the "1000 Makers of the 20th Century" and by American author Tom Robbins as "the most dangerous man since Jesus Christ." *Sunday Mid-Day* (India) has selected Osho as one of ten people – along with Gandhi, Nehru and Buddha – who have changed the destiny of India.

About his own work Osho has said that he is helping to create the conditions for the birth of a new kind of human being. He often characterizes this new human being as "Zorba the Buddha" – capable both of enjoying the earthy pleasures of a Zorba the Greek and the silent serenity of a Gautama the Buddha.

Running like a thread through all aspects of Osho's talks and meditations is a vision that encompasses both the timeless wisdom of all ages past and the highest potential of today's (and tomorrow's) science and technology.

Osho is known for his revolutionary contribution to the science of inner transformation, with an approach to meditation that acknowledges the accelerated pace of contemporary life. His unique OSHO Active Meditations™ are designed to first release the accumulated stresses of body and mind, so that it is then easier to take an experience of stillness and thought-free relaxation into daily life.

Two autobiographical works by the author are available:
Autobiography of a Spiritually Incorrect Mystic,
St Martins Press, New York (book and eBook)
Glimpses of a Golden Childhood,
OSHO Media International, Pune, India (book and eBook)

OSHO International Meditation Resort

Location
Located 100 miles southeast of Mumbai in the thriving modern city of Pune, India, the OSHO International Meditation Resort is a holiday destination with a difference. The Meditation Resort is spread over 28 acres of spectacular gardens in a beautiful tree-lined residential area.

Uniqueness
Each year the Meditation Resort welcomes thousands of people from more than 100 countries. The unique campus provides an opportunity for a direct personal experience of a new way of living – with more awareness, relaxation, celebration and creativity. A great variety of around-the-clock and around-the-year program options are available. Doing nothing and just relaxing is one of them!

All programs are based on the OSHO vision of "Zorba the Buddha" – a qualitatively new kind of human being who is able *both* to participate creatively in everyday life *and* to relax into silence and meditation.

OSHO Meditations
A full daily schedule of meditations for every type of person includes methods that are active and passive, traditional and revolutionary, and in particular the OSHO Active Meditations™. The meditations take place in what must be the world's largest meditation hall, the OSHO Auditorium.

OSHO Multiversity
Individual sessions, courses and workshops cover everything from creative arts to holistic health, personal transformation, relationship and life transition, work-as-meditation, esoteric sciences, and the "Zen" approach to sports and recreation. The secret of the OSHO Multiversity's success lies in the fact that all its programs are combined with meditation, supporting the understanding that as human beings we are far more than the sum of our parts.

OSHO Basho Spa
The luxurious Basho Spa provides for leisurely open-air swimming surrounded by trees and tropical green. The uniquely styled, spacious Jacuzzi, the saunas, gym, tennis courts...all these are enhanced by their stunningly beautiful setting.

Cuisine
A variety of different eating areas serve delicious Western, Asian and Indian vegetarian food – most of it organically grown especially for the Meditation Resort. Breads and cakes are baked in the resort's own bakery.

Night life
There are many evening events to choose from – dancing being at the top of the list! Other activities include full-moon meditations beneath the stars, variety shows, music performances and meditations for daily life.

Or you can just enjoy meeting people at the Plaza Café, or walking in the nighttime serenity of the gardens of this fairytale environment.

Facilities
You can buy all your basic necessities and toiletries in the Galleria. The Multimedia Gallery sells a large range of OSHO media products. There is also a bank, a travel agency and a Cyber Café on-campus. For those who enjoy shopping, Pune provides all the options, ranging from traditional and ethnic Indian products to all of the global brand-name stores.

Accommodation
You can choose to stay in the elegant rooms of the OSHO Guesthouse, or for longer stays opt for one of the OSHO Living-In program packages. Additionally there is a plentiful variety of nearby hotels and serviced apartments.

www.osho.com/meditationresort
www.osho.com/guesthouse
www.osho.com/livingin

For More Information

www.**OSHO**.com

a comprehensive multi-language website including a magazine,
OSHO Books, OSHO Talks in audio and video formats, the OSHO
Library text archive in English and Hindi and extensive information
about OSHO Meditations. You will also find the program schedule
of the OSHO Multiversity and information about the OSHO
International Meditation Resort.

http://OSHO.com/AllAboutOSHO
http://OSHO.com/Resort
http://OSHO.com/Shop
http://www.youtube.com/OSHO
http://www.Twitter.com/OSHO
http://www.facebook.com/pages/OSHO.International

To contact OSHO International Foundation:
www.osho.com/oshointernational,
oshointernational@oshointernational.com